SELIMUS

broadview editions
series editor: Martin R. Boyne

SELIMUS

Robert Greene

edited by Mathew R. Martin

broadview editions

BROADVIEW PRESS – www.broadviewpress.com
Peterborough, Ontario, Canada

Founded in 1985, Broadview Press remains a wholly independent publishing house. Broadview's focus is on academic publishing; our titles are accessible to university and college students as well as scholars and general readers. With over 800 titles in print, Broadview has become a leading international publisher in the humanities, with world-wide distribution. Broadview is committed to environmentally responsible publishing and fair business practices.

Library and Archives Canada Cataloguing in Publication

Title: Selimus / Robert Greene ; edited by Mathew R. Martin.
Names: Greene, Robert, 1558-1592, author. | Martin, Mathew R., 1970- editor.
Series: Broadview editions.
Description: Series statement: Broadview editions | Includes bibliographical references.
Identifiers: Canadiana (print) 2022019372X | Canadiana (ebook) 20220193789 | ISBN 9781554815081 (softcover) | ISBN 9781770488441 (PDF) | ISBN 9781460407912 (EPUB)
Subjects: LCGFT: Drama.
Classification: LCC PR2544 .S4 2022 | DDC 822/.3—dc23

Broadview Editions
The Broadview Editions series is an effort to represent the ever-evolving canon of texts in the disciplines of literary studies, history, philosophy, and political theory. A distinguishing feature of the series is the inclusion of primary source documents contemporaneous with the work.

Advisory editor for this volume: Juliet Sutcliffe

Broadview Press handles its own distribution in North America:
PO Box 1243, Peterborough, Ontario K9J 7H5, Canada
555 Riverwalk Parkway, Tonawanda, NY 14150, USA
Tel: (705) 743-8990; Fax: (705) 743-8353
email: customerservice@broadviewpress.com

For all territories outside of North America, distribution is handled by Eurospan Group.

Broadview Press acknowledges the financial support of the Government of Canada for our publishing activities.

Canada

Typesetting: George Kirkpatrick

PRINTED IN CANADA

Petal

Contents

Acknowledgements

My many thanks to Olivia King for reading the entire manuscript of this edition. I would also like to thank the fine editorial staff at Broadview Press, who once again have been a delight to work with, and the librarians at the many libraries from which I procured the digital images of the extant quartos of the play. My thanks to Brock's Humanities Research Institute for a research grant to defray some of the costs of digital reproduction.

Introduction

Robert Greene (1558–92) was a shady character. Born in Norwich in 1558, the year of Elizabeth Tudor's ascension to the throne, Greene held two MAs, one from Cambridge (1583) and one from Oxford (1588) (Jordan 1), earning him a place among the group of Elizabethan writers dubbed the "University Wits." The group included Greene, Thomas Lodge (c. 1558–1625), John Lyly (c. 1553–1606), Christopher Marlowe (1564–93), Thomas Nashe (1567–c. 1601), and George Peele (1556–96). The moniker's coiner, the nineteenth-century critic George Saintsbury, also nominated Thomas Kyd (1558–94), another important Elizabethan playwright, for membership (Saintsbury 60–64). Greene settled in London and lived a precarious and prodigal life as a celebrated writer of prose fiction and drama. He kept dangerous company, wrote about it in popular pamphlets about the Elizabethan underworld, and died in poverty "of a surfeit of pickled herring and Rhenish wine" (qtd. in Jordan 216), according to his contemporary Gabriel Harvey (1545–1630), on 3 September 1592, but not before denouncing his profligate ways and atheistic ideas in a prose pamphlet, *A Groatsworth of Wit*, published shortly after his death (Jordan 1) and included in this edition as Appendix A. Death was no obstacle to his literary ambitions: Greene returned as a ghost to haunt the literary world in a number of pamphlets published later (Fallon 194–95). As Kirk Melnikoff and Edward Gieskes emphasize in their recent assessment of Greene's career as a writer, however, Greene was a professional writer: he "was neither a helpless client of predatory printers nor an alternately desperate and sloppy hack selling whatever he could write as fast as he could write it, but rather a shrewd and engaged participant in a rapidly developing market" (13), the Elizabethan market for popular print literature.

Greene was at the height of his fame in London in the late 1580s and early 1590s, roughly the same time that Marlowe was gaining notoriety for his provocative plays. Among his more influential works are to be counted the prose romance *Pandosto: The Triumph of Time* (1588), which the "upstart crow" (Appendix A, p. 184)—Greene's own accusatory epithet for the actor-turned-playwright he felt had been plagiarizing his and other writers' material—William Shakespeare (1564–1616) would later rework into his late romance *The Winter's Tale* (1623), and the play *Friar Bacon and Friar Bungay* (1589), which some critics have suggested influenced Marlowe's *Doctor Faustus* (1589–91). Greene's works also clearly register the impact of the works of some of his now more famous contemporaries, such as Lyly and Philip Sidney (1554–86). Greene's plays *Alphonsus King of Aragon* (1587) and *Selimus* (1591) have heroes and plots that are obviously imitations of the hero and plot of Marlowe's popular first plays for the London professional stage, *1* and *2 Tamburlaine the Great*, which were first performed between 1587 and 1588 and in two parts dramatized the spectacular rise of Central Asian conqueror Temur the Lame (c. 1320–1405). Marlowe's *Tamburlaine* plays sparked a host of imitations of their geographically global plot, their hyperbolic style, and, most of all, their larger-than-life titular character, creating a dramatic fashion that would last for at least a decade. The extensive connections between *Selimus* and the *Tamburlaine* plays are examined later in the introduction and throughout the notes to the play, and cumulatively they register Greene's sensitivity to Elizabethan dramatic fashion, his sophistication as a playwright, and his intellectual independence. *Selimus* thus constitutes a major document in the early reception and transmission of one of the defining moments of early modern English drama. Greene was a known associate of Marlowe, and in the prefatory material to several of his pamphlets Greene alludes to Marlowe and his reputation for radical thought and daring, innovative drama. As well as the three mentioned above, Greene wrote (at least) three other plays: *James IV* (1590), *Orlando Furioso* (1591), and, with Thomas Lodge, *A Looking Glass for London and England* (1589). Greene has also been suggested as the author of *Locrine* (1591) and *George a Green* (1591) (Freebury-Jones 378). The details of the plots of these Greene plays will not be divulged in this introduction, but, the reader should be aware, the details of *Selimus* will be discussed.

Selim I and Ottoman History

Selim I, nicknamed "the Stern" by his contemporaries (Finkel 114), was born in 1470 and reigned as Ottoman emperor from 1512 until his death in 1520. The Ottoman Empire began humbly enough in 1299 with the imperial dream of the prince of one of multiple Turcomen emirates, Osman: lodging in the house of a holy man, Osman dreamed that "he saw that a moon arose from the holy man's breast and came to sink in his own breast. A tree sprouted from his navel and its shade compassed the world" (Finkel 2). In 1453 Selim's grandfather Mehmed II (r. 1444–46, 1451–81) had plucked the "Golden Apple," the capital of the Byzantine Empire, Constantinople, from that tree and renamed it Istanbul, and by the time Selim took the emperorship from his father, Bayezid II (r. 1481–1512), on 25 April 1512 (Shaw 79), the shade of the Ottoman imperial tree had expanded to truly formidable proportions, covering territory in Asia, Eastern Europe, and Africa. During his reign Selim advanced the empire's boundaries, and his son, Suleiman the Magnificent (r. 1520–66), extended them even farther. Selim's most recent biographer, Alan Mikhail, comments that "[s]urpassing all of his predecessors, Selim achieved a conquest far more significant than even Constantinople—the near tripling of the empire's territories through wars in the Middle East, North Africa, and the Caucasus. When he died in 1520, the empire was stronger than it had ever been, a behemoth, far more powerful than any other state on Earth" (11). Selim's ascension to the emperorship was unlikely when he was born to Bayezid II's Christian concubine Gülbahar Hatun on 10 October 1470 in Amasya (Mikhail 15). He was the fourth of Bayezid's ten sons, and the youngest and least favoured of the three sons who would emerge as contenders for Bayezid's imperial seat: Ahmed (named Acomat in Greene's play), Korkud, and Selim (Mikhail 27). As Mikhail observes, the most obvious sign of his lack of favour was the fact that when he was 17, in 1487, he was appointed governor of Trabzon, a strong commercial city at the far eastern edge of the Ottoman Empire with a primarily Christian population and a history of independence. Trabzon had been subdued and brought into the empire through conquest only in 1461 (Mikhail 63–68). Not only would governing Trabzon in itself prove to be a challenge, but its distance from the imperial capital, Istanbul, placed Selim at an initial disadvantage in comparison to his brothers in any potential succession scenario, in which success often depended upon being able to occupy the imperial city before the other competitors. Ahmed, in contrast, had been appointed governor of Amasya, relatively close to Istanbul, and Korkud was not much farther away as governor of Saruhan and Teke (Mikhail 79).

With his mother's substantial support, however, Selim rose to the test and by 1511 was ready to mount a challenge to his father's rule. This is where Greene's play begins. With the empire troubled by internal rebellion, his requests for new governorships for himself and his son Suleiman consistently rebuffed by Bayezid, and the receipt of information that his father intended to abdicate in favour of Ahmed, Selim began his march to Istanbul (Mikhail 211–23). After a series of failed negotiations, father and son confronted each other on the battlefield in July 1511 at Çorlu, a town midway between Istanbul and Edirne, the empire's former capital, where Bayezid had established his court. Selim's forces lost the battle, and Selim was forced to flee (Mikhail 227). Selim kept up the pressure, however, aided by the fact that Ahmed and Korkud had turned their forces against one another in Anatolia and in the process were destroying the empire. According to Mikhail, "Amid the disorder their father had allowed Ahmed and Korkud to create, Selim stood out as the leader the empire needed, a captain who could navigate the Ottoman ship of state through these storms…. Eventually, Selim's military backers presented Bayezid with an ultimatum: rein in your mutinous son [Ahmed] or give up your throne" (233). Bayezid ultimately was forced to take the latter option. In March 1512 he appointed Selim as the commander of the Janissaries, the elite troops of the Ottoman army, with a mandate to quell his brother Ahmed's rebellion, and Selim leveraged that position into the emperorship by then compelling Bayezid to hand the emperorship over to him on 25 April 1512 (238). A year later Selim I had defeated Ahmed's forces. In 1514 his armies took the Safavid Persian capital of Tabriz (264). On 28 August 1516 he entered Aleppo in triumph, having shredded the forces of the Egyptian Mamluk empire three days previously (290); he took Damascus and Jerusalem in the following months (296). Cairo, the Mamluk capital, would fall in January of the next year (303). Having extended the empire's territories in the Middle East and Africa, Selim in his final years turned his sights on the Mediterranean and Europe, planning a conquest of the small but strategically key island of Rhodes, plans that his son Suleiman would realize in 1522 with the conquest of Rhodes and the expulsion of the Knights of St. John from the island (330).

Mikhail observes that one of Selim's epithets was "God's shadow on earth" (12), arguing that Selim "made the Ottoman Empire" a "transformative global power" (10). Selim's military victories before his death in 1520 established the Ottoman Empire as a significant geopolitical player in the early modern world, locked in a balance-of-power politics with Spain and engaging in alliances with lesser European powers such as France and England. The failure of the siege of Malta in 1565 and the defeat in 1571 at the battle of Lepanto, a naval battle that pitted a combined Spanish, Venetian, and papal navy against the formidable Ottoman fleet, may have halted the Ottoman's westward expansion temporarily (Riley-Smith 289–90), but according to modern historians the Ottoman Empire continued to pose a real threat to Europe well into the seventeenth century (Goffman 161). The main action of *Selimus*, however, merely adumbrates this imperial grandeur, dramatizing instead an empire torn apart by civil strife as the three sons of a weak emperor compete for their father's position. Elizabethan theatre-goers would have been familiar with this general scenario from other plays. In the Ottoman context, however, struggles for succession were especially bloody: Selim's grandfather, Mehmed II had decreed that upon an emperor's death his sons would have to battle it out with each other to determine who would succeed him (Finkel 38–39, 71). Neither seniority nor election by the deceased emperor was determinative. Moreover, the victor in the struggle usually attempted to eliminate any remaining potential contenders, as Acomat and Selimus do in the play. "[U]ncle, I resign my right to thee, / And all my title" (13.32–33), declares Prince Mahomet, the son of Bajazet's dead first son Alemshae, as he parleys with Acomat on the walls of besieged Natolia; "Wilt thou?," replies Acomat, "Then know assuredly from me, / I'll seal the resignation with thy blood" (34–35). And he does, later in the scene commanding Mahomet to be tossed off the city walls onto his soldiers' waiting spears and shortly thereafter ordering the strangulation of Mahomet's sister Zonora. Ironically, of course, Acomat is merely doing Selimus's dirty work, and at the conclusion of the play, having already strangled Corcut and having defeated Acomat on the battlefield of Yenisehir, Selimus commands Acomat's strangulation. "Now he is dead" (31.30), he crows, "Who doth remain to trouble Selimus? / Now am I king alone and none but I" (31–32).

Like the historical Selim, Greene's Selimus has no intention of resting on his laurels: "We'll have a fling at the Egyptian crown / And join it unto ours or lose our own" (75–76), he announces immediately before all the play's remaining characters exit the stage to conclude the play. If the play ends with this forward-looking gesture, however, it begins two years earlier, in 1511, with Bajazet's retrospective account in the opening scene of the troubles that have beset his reign (1.3–111), troubles that in subsequent scenes quickly culminate in Selimus's first rebellion. The rebellion fails, as it did historically, but it inspires his brother Acomat to mount his own rebellion in order to protect his claims to the emperorship. Corcut, a scholar, opts out of the armed competition, merely asserting in a letter to Bajazet his right to the crown after Bajazet's death, but Acomat's rebellion alone is more than the beleaguered Bajazet can handle by himself. He recalls Selimus from exile and places him at the head of the Janissaries, with the mandate to quash Acomat's rebellion. Once placed at the head of the Janissaries, Selimus promptly betrays (and later murders) his father, forcing him to abdicate. From this point, scene 18, on, the play foregrounds Selimus's ruthless efforts to consolidate his newly acquired sovereignty and ensure that "Now am I king alone and none but I." As the commentary notes to the play indicate, Greene's dramatization of this short but crucial period of Ottoman history is broadly faithful to his primary historical source, Peter Ashton's *A Short Treatise upon the Turks' Chronicles* (1546), one of numerous accounts of Ottoman history available to the Elizabethan reader. Indeed, even the play's characterization of Bajazet's three sons follows Ashton's summary of their different personalities closely. This framework of Ottoman history, however, is shaped by its Elizabethan context, some of the more salient features of which are explored in the rest of the introduction.

Selimus, Atheism, and Machiavellianism

As the reader will discover, Selimus is an atheist, unlike his brother Corcut, who begins the play as a pious Muslim and ends it as a pious Christian. Selimus's other brother, Acomat, might be said to be an atheist too. Nothing, at least, would give anyone reason to believe that Acomat has any real religious or philosophical convictions, and he does not articulate any. Selimus, in contrast, does. He is an atheist, and in scene 2 of the play, as we shall see, he provides a reasonable if not entirely pleasant defence of his atheism. To modern Western readers living in societies in which the freedom of religious belief is a constitutional right, Selimus's profession of atheism might seem unremarkable. In the context of early modern culture, however, it must have been nothing short of explosive. To gain a sense of this explosiveness, we can begin by looking at one of the classic texts in the history of the development of ideas of religious toleration, Thomas More's early-sixteenth-century fiction about an ideal society, *Utopia* (1516). Utopia, located somewhere or nowhere ("utopia" means "nowhere" in Greek), is in some ways More's (1478–1535) description of everything that his society was not but that he wanted it to be. Among the many unusual features of *Utopia*, such as the use of golden chains to shackle slaves and criminals (67), the Elizabethan reader might most forcefully have been struck by a fundamental element of the Utopian constitution: religious toleration. Having observed the stupidity of religious warfare, the commonwealth's founder Utopos "left the choice of creed an open question, to be decided by the individual according to his own ideas" (101).

Many of Greene's contemporaries would have been terrified by the prospect. According to the Bishop of London, Edward Sandys, in 1571, "This liberty, that men may openly profess diversity of religion, must needs be dangerous.... One god, one king, one faith, one profession, is fit for one monarchy and commonwealth. Division weakeneth; concord strengtheneth.... Let conformity and unity in religion be provided for; and it shall be as a wall of defence unto this realm" (qtd. in Walsham 39–40). For Sandys and the Elizabethans, visible expressions of religious difference detracted from the power of the sovereign, threatened the stability of the commonwealth, and therefore could not be countenanced. When compared to Elizabethan hysteria about religious toleration, More's Utopian position seems presciently liberal. It extends only so far, however: Utopos "strictly and solemnly forbade his people to believe anything so incompatible with human dignity as the doctrine that the soul dies with the body, and the universe functions aimlessly, without any controlling providence" (More 101). Atheism, even in Utopia, is illegal. Here Utopia and Elizabethan England converge: atheism was, according to Adam Hill in *The Cry of England* (1595), "the sin of all sins" (qtd. in Hunter 137), and the popular Puritan theologian William Perkins (1558–1602) declared that atheists should be executed (Hunter 138). Indeed, it was anathema even to one of the founding theorists of our modern conception of religious toleration, John Locke (1632–1704). Although in his *Letter Concerning Toleration* (1689) Locke could passionately declare that "the care therefore of every man's soul belongs unto himself and is to be left unto himself" (35), he emphatically excludes atheism from his general principle: "Those are not at all to be tolerated who deny the being of a God" (58). Why? "Promises, covenants, and oaths, which are the bonds of human society, can have no hold upon an atheist. The taking away of God, though but even in thought, dissolves all" (58). In short, the atheist is a fundamentally lawless being.

By Locke's time, the end of the seventeenth century, the atheist was not a purely imaginary being. The works of Thomas Hobbes (1588–1679) and Baruch Spinoza (1632–77), two thinkers whose philosophies were considered atheistic by their contemporaries, had entered mainstream European philosophical discourse.[1] Following French intellectual historian Lucien Febvre (1878–1956), however, it has often been asserted that in the early modern period "the philosophical tools for coherent atheism had not yet been forged" (Ryrie 727) in Greene's time. This assertion is arguable. Aristotle, the philosophical mainstay of the medieval and early modern university curriculum, offered philosophical arguments for at least two major atheistic arguments, the eternity of the world and the mortality of the soul. As Nicholas Davidson observes, "many Renaissance writers argued that Aristotle and his followers had believed in the eternity of the world and the natural mortality of the soul: beliefs directly at odds with Orthodox Christian doctrine, which insists that the world was created by God and that the soul survives the death of the body" (133). Moreover, Epicurean atomistic materialism, introduced to the Renaissance through Lucretius' newly rediscovered *De rerum natura* (first century BCE), presented an atomistic materialism in which the universe was entirely the sum of the effects of the collisions produced by atoms swerving in a void.[2] In his introduction to *Lucretius and the Early Modern* (2015), David Norbrook writes that Lucretius' poem "offers a passionate frontal assault on the idea that our world shows signs of divine design; outlines a history of this world from creation to a powerfully imagined destruction, as part of an infinite universe; and narrates a radically materialist vision of the development of human society and a horrific vision of social disintegration" (5–6). Pliny (d. 79 CE), Lucian (fl. second century CE), Cicero (106–43 BCE), and Diogenes Laertius (fl. third century CE) were other classical sources to which interested Elizabethan readers could turn in search of philosophical tools for atheistic thought (George Buckley 4–12). As Stephen Greenblatt puts it, however, although atheism in the period was thinkable, it "was almost always thinkable as the thought of another" (*Shakespearean Negotiations* 22). Outside of

---

1 For intellectual histories of atheism, see Allen; Berman; George Buckley; Michael Buckley; Hunter; Popkin; Wooton and Hunter. For a more general account of early modern unbelief, see Thomas.

2 For an exposition of Epicurean philosophy, see Long. For a readable account of the Renaissance rediscovery of Lucretius, see Greenblatt, *The Swerve*. The essays in *Lucretius and the Early Modern*, edited by David Norbrook and colleagues, provide a comprehensive survey of the state of recent scholarship on the circulation and impact of Lucretius' poem in the early modern period.

treatises written to refute them, coherent expressions of philosophical atheism are few, which renders Selimus's extended atheistic speech in scene 2 of *Selimus* all the more remarkable. As do many villains in early modern English drama, Selimus shows himself throughout the play to be a "practical atheist" (Sheppard 411), someone who demonstrates their atheism through their actions. In his speech in scene 2, though, Selimus shows himself also to be a "speculative atheist" (Sheppard 411), someone who has coherent rational arguments for their atheism. Greene's Selimus, then, fully embodies the ultimate early modern European Other, the archetypal early modern criminal mind: unconcerned about whether or which god or gods might have created the universe, Selimus in his opening oration in scene 2 declares the fate of the soul after death to be "just nothing, for, as I suppose, / In Death's void kingdom reigns eternal night" (2.131–32). Selimus's god, if he has one, is "Dame Nature" (123), and his atheism leads him to "have a snatch at all" (137), in the course of which he does not hesitate to break the promises, oaths, and covenants he has made to his father, his brothers, and others. To gauge Selimus's, and Greene's, daring here, we can place Selimus's extended and defiant declamation of atheism in contrast to two notable Marlovian blasphemers' brushes with the law, Doctor Faustus's desperate and slightly pathetic last-minute question, "Why wert thou not a creature wanting soul?" (*Doctor Faustus* 5.2.170), and Tamburlaine's equivocal injunction to his troops after burning the Qur'an to "Seek out another godhead to adore, / The God that sits in heaven, if any God" (*2 Tamburlaine* 5.2.136–37). Radical though they may be in other ways, Faustus and Tamburlaine touch atheism only with the ten-foot pole of conditionals. Selimus employs the indicative to embrace atheism full on, so full on that when in 1603 Sir Walter Ralegh (1552–1618) was accused of atheism during his trial for committing treason with Spain, his accusers adduced Selimus's scene 2 oration as evidence, attributing the lines to Ralegh (Jacquot 1–9).

In the figure of Selimus, Greene created a powerful new dramatic character type that would be reincarnated in later English Renaissance drama in such figures as D'Amville in Cyril Tourneur's *The Atheist's Tragedy* (1611) and Giovanni in John Ford's *'Tis Pity She's a Whore* (1633). Notably, both D'Amville and Giovanni (and one might include *King Lear*'s Edmund in this crew) are tragic villains. That is, unlike their prototype, they come to a tragic end. D'Amville accidentally "strikes out his own brains" (5.2.241 s.d.) with the axe with which he intended to execute his enemy Charlemont. As he is dying, he renounces his atheism: "Nature is a fool. There is a power / Above her that hath overthrown the pride / Of all my projects" (5.2.257–59). Charlemont then concludes the play by declaring, much like Ferneze at the end of Marlowe's *The Jew of Malta*, "Thus by the work of Heaven the men that thought / To follow our dead bodies without tears / Are dead themselves" (299–301). Giovanni remains an impenitent atheist as he meets his end, having ripped out his sister's heart, having been fatally wounded by a counter-revenger, and bleeding to death at a birthday party. Though urged by one of the guests, the Cardinal, to "Strive yet to cry to Heaven" (5.6.104), Giovanni turns his attention elsewhere: "Death, thou art a guest long look'd for; I embrace / Thee and thy wounds" (105–06). Nonetheless, immediately after Giovanni's death, another character supplies the moral gloss on his demise: "Strange miracle of justice!" (109). Having let loose their monstrous atheists to strut and fret their time upon the stage, Tourneur's and Ford's plays conclude by reining them in, killing them, and converting them into hortatory moral exempla. By doing so, they conform to the precedent set by such earlier moralizing writers as Thomas Beard (d. 1632), who in his *Theatre of God's Judgements* (1597) offers the reader accounts of the lurid ends of a long list of notorious atheists from ancient and modern history, culminating in Christopher Marlowe, whose grisly death (he stabbed himself in the head in a street fight, according to Beard) "was not only a manifest sign of God's judgement but also a horrible and fearful terror to all that beheld him" (277). Five years earlier and a year before Marlowe's death, Greene himself in *A Groatsworth of Wit* would adopt the pose of the penitent atheist and convert his own death into a hortatory moral exemplum addressed to Marlowe: "Wonder not—for with thee will I first begin—thou famous gracer of tragedians, that Greene, who hath said with thee, like the fool in his heart, 'There is no God,' should now give glory unto His greatness, for penetrating is His power, His hand lies heavy upon me" (Appendix A, p. 182). *Selimus*, in stark contrast, concludes with the atheist's triumph over his foes; as the curtain drops (figuratively), the Conclusion attempts to seduce the witnesses of his triumphs with the promise that "If this first part, gentles, do like you well, / The second part shall greater murders tell" (31.6–7). No *Selimus the Sequel* survives, but the Conclusion's promise constitutes not a renunciation of atheism but an aggressive attempt to spread it. In his pamphlet *Perimedes the Blacksmith* (1588), Greene recounts that "lately, two gentlemen poets ... had it in derision for that I could not make my verses jet upon the stage in tragical buskins, every word filling the mouth like the faburden of Bow Bell, daring God out of heaven with that atheist Tamburlaine" (sig. A3r). The two gentlemen poets were clearly mistaken.

Early modern writers often superimposed onto the bogeyman atheist another cultural stereotype, the figure of the Machiavellian. Fearing the cultural transmission to England of all things Italian, Roger Ascham in *The Schoolmaster* (1570) fulminated against the "Englishmen Italianated" (sig. J4r) who "count as fables the holy mysteries of Christian religion [and] make Christ and His Gospel only serve civil policy" (sig. J4r). Instead of the Gospel, according to Ascham, these Italian Englishmen zealously adhere to the works of the early-sixteenth-century Florentine political theorist Niccolò Machiavelli (1469–1527), such as the notorious *The Prince*, which was available to Elizabethans in the original and in French and Latin translations, although not in English translation until 1640 (Scott 150). They are "Epicures in living and *atheoi* in doctrine" (sig. J4v), he concludes. French writer Innocent Gentillet (1535–88) sustained Ascham's linkage of classical Epicurean philosophy, atheism, and Machiavellianism in his popular *Anti-Machiavel* (1576; English trans. 1602). "This atheist Machiavelli," Gentillet declares,

> teacheth the prince to be a true contemner of God and of religion and only to make a show and fair countenance outwardly before the world to be esteemed religious and devout, although he be not. For divine punishment, for such hypocrisy and dissimulation, Machiavelli fears not because he believes not there is a God but thinks that the course of the sun, of the moon, of the stars, the distinction of the spring time, summer, autumn, and winter, the politic government of men, the production that the earth makes of fruits, plants, living creatures, that all this comes by encounter and adventure, following the doctrine of Epicurus (the doctor of atheists and master of ignorance), who esteems that all things are done and come to pass by Fortune and the meeting and encountering of atoms. (Appendix B1, p. 191)

If classical Epicurean philosophy had become synonymous with the unbridled pursuit of pleasure which was supposed to be the doctrine's logical outcome, so too in the Elizabethan mind were atheism and Machiavellianism linked. Only because the

Machiavellian does not believe in God, and hence in rewards and punishment after death, can they pursue the treacherous power politics and strategies of deception, including using religion as a tool of "civil policy," that will allow them to maintain and augment their real-world power. The treatment of religion as a political device was an especially dominant characteristic of the Machiavel in the Elizabethan imagination, and dramatists such as Marlowe and Greene foregrounded it in their Machiavellian creations. "I am Machevill" (7), announces the prologue to Marlowe's *The Jew of Malta*, and "I count religion but a childish toy, / And hold there is no sin but ignorance" (14–15). "My policy hath framed religion" (2.64), the Duke of Guise vaunts in Marlowe's final play, *The Massacre at Paris*. "Religion: *O Diabole!*" (65), he scoffs, "Fie, I am ashamed, however that I seem, / To think a word of such a simple sound / Of so great matter should be made the ground" (66–68). Selimus rounds out the chorus. When kings, and with them politics, began to disrupt the mythic pre-historic world of the Golden Age, Selimus argues,

> Then they established laws and holy rites
> To maintain peace and govern bloody fights.
> Then some sage man, above the vulgar wise,
> Knowing that laws could not in quiet dwell
> Unless they were observed, did first devise
> The names of gods, religion, heaven, and hell,
> And 'gan of pains and feigned rewards to tell:
> Pains for those men which did neglect the law;
> Rewards for those that lived in quiet awe.
> Whereas indeed they were mere fictions—
> And if they were not, Selim thinks they were,
> And these religious observations
> Only bugbears to keep the world in fear
> And make men quietly a yoke to bear,
> So that religion, of itself a bauble,
> Was only found to make us peaceable. (2.94–109)

Combining classical and contemporary sources, Selimus's condensed exposition of the political function of religion is a forceful and defiant fusion of the atheist and Machiavellian positions. Although Machiavelli remains unmentioned in the play (even Elizabethan playwrights could occasionally avoid anachronism), Selimus is one of the most remarkable, and articulate, Machiavellian figures in Elizabethan drama.

Selimus and the "Turk Play"

Elizabethans had their attention directed towards the East and the Ottoman Empire for a number of reasons. As detailed earlier in the introduction, the Ottoman Empire demonstrated its geopolitical significance in such military events as the siege of Malta (1565) and the battle of Lepanto (1571), prompting Elizabeth to seek closer military, diplomatic, and commercial ties with the Ottomans, partly as a way to counterbalance the threat of Spanish hegemony in Europe (Matar 123–24). William Harborne's (c. 1542–1617) embassy to the Porte in 1578 culminated in an exchange of letters between Murad III and Elizabeth in 1579–80, in which each granted trading privileges to the other's subjects, and in the chartering of the Levant Trading Company in 1581 (Vitkus, *Turning Turk* 39). Knowledge of the Ottoman Empire was increasingly available to the Elizabethan reader through a variety of printed sources, including Greene's major historical sources for *Selimus*: Thomas Newton's *A Notable History of the Saracens* (1575), a translation of Augustino Celio Curione's *Saracenicae Historiae libri III* (1567), Peter Ashton's *A Short Treatise upon the Turks' Chronicles* (1546), and a translation of Paolo Giovio's *Commentarii della cose de Turchi* (1531) (Vitkus, *Three Turk Plays* 18). The Ottoman empire was a major early modern English concern.

Considerable recent scholarly work has been done studying the ways in which early modern English professional drama registered the Ottoman Empire's presence in the Elizabethan field of cultural vision. Rejecting the applicability of a rigid Orientalist paradigm to an era in which the English were the subordinate partners in their relations with the Ottomans, scholars such as Richmond Barbour, Jonathan Burton, Matthew Dimmock, Linda McJannet, and Daniel Vitkus argue that "English cultural production had to work to compensate for this anxious marginality felt in relation to the Mediterranean cultural center" (Vitkus, *Turning Turk* 39), generating on stage the dramatic character of the Turk, "a figure of both war and commerce, vitally interwoven with domestic and global concerns in the complex fabric of English culture" (Burton 34). In the pre-Orientalist context of early modern England's relationship to the Ottoman Empire, which Burton calls "trafficking" (15), the drama can be seen to be registering the fluid power dynamics of that relationship and the anxieties that it caused in the various, often stereotypical, and often contradictory representations of the Turk it offered to its audiences.

Even when absent, the Turk often looms in the geopolitical background of early modern English plays as the apocalyptic threat against which individual and collective racial, national, and religious identities can and must be defined. One might take as a late Elizabethan example Shakespeare's history play *Henry V* (1599), the third play in Shakespeare's second trilogy about medieval English history. Having devastated and conquered France motivated by his own imperial ambitions for the French crown (and a desire to distract his own nobles from waging civil war), at the end of the play the victorious English Henry V seeks to mend the divisions he has created by marrying the French princess Katherine. As he woos her in act 5, scene 2 of the play, Henry's undeniable charm has the potential to distract the audience from the fact that his goal is to appropriate Katherine's reproductive sexuality as the site and vehicle for the construction and perpetuation of his own unified empire. "Thou must therefore needs prove a good soldier-breeder," Henry tells her, "Shall not thou and I, between Saint Denis and Saint George, compound a boy, half French, half English, that shall go to Constantinople and take the Turk by the beard?" (192–95). Responding to the menacing pressure of the Turkish empire, in Henry's imagination the royal couple will fuse in their progeny the national and religious identities whose divisiveness has forestalled European imperial designs. Indeed, under this pressure even England's own internal divisions may be healed: "[T]ake me by the hand," Henry pleads, "and say 'Harry of England, I am thine,' which word thou shalt no sooner bless mine ear withal but I will tell thee aloud, 'England is thine, Ireland is thine, France is thine, and'"—of course—"'Henry Plantagenet is thine'" (219–23).

It is not, however, Shakespeare's but Marlowe's drama, especially the *Tamburlaine* plays, that is accorded the central position in the development of the dramatic figure of the Turk. Mark Hutchings, for example, contends that the *Tamburlaine* plays' "new aesthetic (and its suitability for staging tyrannous sultans) led directly and indirectly to the rapid growth of the Turkish genre in the London repertories" (6). As Hutchings's comment suggests, Elizabethan drama often developed the figure of the Turk into such stereotypes as the bragging Turk (Marlowe's Bajazeth), the sensual Turk (Greene's Acomat), and the cruel Turk (Greene's Selimus), and critics have tended to focus on these stereotypes as expressions of both English fear and English admiration and envy (Bartels 5). Nonetheless, according to Dimmock, in *Selimus* at least Elizabethan drama shows itself to be capable of pressing beyond these stereotypes. Noting that "*Selimus* is the earliest play extant to be based entirely within the bounds of the Ottoman empire and to be primarily concerned with Ottoman dynastic history" (170), Dimmock argues that the play's focus on the internally divisive situation of three sons contending for their father's imperial throne generates significant differences among the various Turkish characters: if Selimus is, in Vitkus's words, "a monster and a caricature" (*Three Turk Plays* 19), this monstrosity serves as a foil for the piety of the play's third brother, Corcut, and the nobility of the captain of the Janissaries, Mustapha. In Greene's play, the "Turk" is not a monolith; rather, "the representation of the 'turke' in *Selimus* is defined by diversity" (Dimmock 177). *Selimus*, then, anticipates later shifts in the Turk-play genre. The figure of the Turk was inflected by the Ottoman Empire's association with Islam, the religion of the empire's ruling stratum if not the religion of the majority of its population, and Burton argues that in early modern English drama "Islam functions as a discursive site upon which contesting versions of Englishness, Christianity, masculinity, femininity, and nobility are elaborated and profferred" (28). "The result," he contends, "is a representative practice, particularly in English drama, which accommodates the solicitous, peaceful Turk and the bloody miscreant Turk, the convert and the temptress, the saint and the tyrant" (28). If, though, between 1580 and 1600 plays featuring Turks tend to be romances that frequently stereotype the Turk as a bloody and cruel tyrant, then, according to Burton, "as English commercial and diplomatic concerns grow increasingly involved with Muslim peoples, tragedy and tragicomedy largely supersede the heroic romance by focusing on the dangers of captivity, conversion and/or the moral collapse of Christians in Muslim lands" (33–34). On the early modern English stage, then, the various figures of the Turk do not cohere into a stable identity, a unified Other, but rather, in their heterogeneity and fissures, reflect the heterogeneous and contradictory desires and fantasies of the English imaginations that produced them.

Selimus and Marlowe's *Tamburlaine* Plays

Much of the criticism of Greene's work in general and *Selimus* in particular has been comparative. If their canonicity has endowed the likes of Marlowe and Shakespeare with the sculpted solidity of things, Greene's expansive literary corpus—prose, poetry, and plays—has benefitted from a more fluid, intertextual approach stressing networks of connections among different works, genres, and modes of literary and cultural production and consumption. As is explained in the "Note on the Text," Greene's authorship of *Selimus* has not been established with complete certainty, and Greene, or "Greene," problematizes the traditional function of the author as the anchor of literary interpretation. The essays in the most recent essay collection devoted to Greene's work, Melnikoff and Gieskes's *Writing Robert Greene* (2008), amply illustrate this: "This volume collectively ... traces the various ways in which Greene as a professional producer engaged with a broad social space of fellow writers, audiences, patrons, and employers" (15). One of the major lines of criticism in this comparative context has been the relationship between Greene's works and the better-known and more frequently read works of his more illustrious contemporaries. The relationship has often been conceptualized in the somewhat reductive terms of either source or imitation. As mentioned earlier, for example, Greene's magician play *Friar Bacon and Friar Bungay* can be construed as a kind of source for Marlowe's arguably later *Doctor Faustus*. Similarly, the resonances between the blinding of Aga in *Selimus* and the blinding of Gloucester in *King Lear* have led some critics to conclude that "[i]t is indeed hard to resist the conclusion that Shakespeare had the text of *Selimus* directly before him in 1605" (Ronan 362). As Jenny Sager notes, however, the relationship between Greene and Shakespeare was a two-way street. Comparing the moment Bajazet sees the mutilated Aga in *Selimus* to the moment Marcus sees the raped and mutilated Lavinia in Shakespeare's earlier tragedy, *Titus Andronicus*, Sager observes that "[i]n both *Selimus* and *Titus Andronicus*, the reactions of the onstage spectator move in a spiral. The spectator is firstly awestruck, their reaction is one of empathy and they are entirely engaged in the spectacle. Then they contemplate what they are seeing, their reaction becomes cognitive and they are distanced from the spectacle. Finally, realising that the spectacle defies explanation—they have never seen anything like it—they are awestruck once more and the whole sequence starts again" (42–43). Shakespeare's and Greene's plays collaborate in the creation of what Sager calls a "theatre of 'attractions'" whose "strength ... lies not in its use of narrative or diegesis but in its use of display, exhibition and spectacle. Each of Greene's plays is organised around a specific spectacle of attraction, which functions as a distilled unit of impression, which carries profound thematic implications for the work as a whole but which also retains its significance outside of that particular representational context" (9). "Greene's drama is a critique of spectacle that is, ironically enough, one long series of spectacles" (36), she later adds.

The relationship between Greene's plays and Marlowe's drama is equally complicated. *Alphonsus King of Aragon* and *Selimus*, for example, have been dismissed as second-rate imitations of the bloody action, hyperbolic style, and larger-than-life protagonist of Marlowe's *Tamburlaine* plays. Other critics have complicated the straightforward linearity of the relationship, however, by considering imitation as a form of reply by one work to another, a form of literary and dramatic dialogue. This more nuanced approach is especially prominent in *Selimus* criticism. Undeniably, *Selimus*'s major literary relationship is to the *Tamburlaine* plays, but, as critics like Irving Ribner and Peter Berek have argued, that relationship is not necessarily derivative or passive. "*Alphonsus* and *Selimus* are not only imitations of *Tamburlaine*; in terms of doctrine, they are also answers to *Tamburlaine*" (165), Ribner writes. Ribner interprets that answer as the answer of orthodox Christianity to the unbridled tyranny of Marlowe's protagonist (170), an interpretation with which Berek broadly agrees but presents in less favourable (and more gender-coded) terms in his influential essay "Tamburlaine's Weak Sons: Imitation as Interpretation before 1593." Berek ultimately concludes that *Selimus*, along with nine other plays he identifies as imitations of *Tamburlaine*, is one of *Tamburlaine*'s "weak sons" (59). "At a time when Henslowe's diary reveals the continuous popularity of *Tamburlaine*," he argues, "these plays invite their audiences to condemn characters for bursting the restraints of conventional beliefs and codes of conduct" (58). According to Berek, "all the early imitations of *Tamburlaine* suggest that Marlowe's audience, and therefore his imitators, wanted to be entertained by his splendid rhetoric and glamorous stage effects without having to yield to the discomfort of unconventional ideas. Caging their father, *Tamburlaine*'s weak sons help build edifices which both display and restrict his heirs" (59).

Berek's verdict implicitly connects Greene's play to Tamburlaine's "effeminate brat" (2.4.1.160) Calyphas, whom Tamburlaine executes in *2 Tamburlaine* 4.1 for refusing to fight in battle. In *2 Tamburlaine*, Calyphas is Tamburlaine's weak son, and the relationship that Marlowe's play constructs between the overbearing father and his weak son is precisely the relationship that Greene's play revises in the relationship between Bajazet and Selimus. Central to the father–son relationship in both plays, however, is the son's relationship to the mother or the maternal. In psychoanalytic terms, what is at stake in both plays is the relation between the law of the father and the maternal that it must repress in order to establish itself. Calyphas's refusal to join his brothers on the battlefield confirms the suspicions Tamburlaine voiced to their mother Zenocrate earlier in the play: his sons' "looks are amorous, / Not martial as the sons of Tamburlaine" (2.1.3.21–22), a suspicion Zenocrate herself reinforces in her reply that "My gracious lord, they have their mother's looks" (2.1.3.35). Although they are associated with sex and the maternal, Tamburlaine's other two sons, Amyras and Celebinus, attempt to identify with their father through their hyperbolically violent language and martial activity. In contrast, Calyphas identifies with his mother: "While my brothers follow arms, my lord, / Let me accompany my gracious mother" (2.1.3.65–66). In 4.1, he refuses to be dragged by his brothers onto the battlefield, preferring instead to stay in his tent, play cards, and dream of "Who shall kiss the fairest of the Turks' concubines first, when my father hath conquered them" (62–63). This enrages Tamburlaine: "How may my heart, thus fired with mine eyes, / Wounded with shame and discontent" (91–92), he declaims as he hauls Calyphas in front of his victorious army, "Shroud any thought may hold my striving hands / From martial justice on thy wretched soul?" (93–94). As he prepares to kill his "effeminate brat" (160), he angrily apostrophizes Jove: "Here, Jove, receive his fainting soul again, / A form not meet to give that subject essence / Whose matter is the flesh of Tamburlaine" (109–11). He then declares war on Jove "for sending to my issue such a soul" (120): "Now shall ye feel the strength of Tamburlaine" (133). Tamburlaine's words are doubly significant. First, they reveal that Tamburlaine's attempt to eliminate the effeminacy of his son is also an attempt to eliminate the maternal. Tamburlaine accords Zenocrate no share in Calyphas's flesh; rather, his son's flesh is wholly his, the father's, and as father he has the absolute right of life and death over it. Second, they indicate that Tamburlaine is not positioning himself as just a father but as *the* father, as what Freud called the Primal Father of the primal horde (*Totem and Taboo* 182–83). Tamburlaine claims not to be like Jove in his exercise of power but to be greater than Jove, not to be following the law of the Father but to be its lynchpin, its ontological foundation. Hence, at the end of *2 Tamburlaine*, after demonstrating his strength against both Jove and Mahomet, Tamburlaine veers between a mystical monotheism and atheism. He advises his soldiers that

Mahomet remains in hell;
He cannot hear the voice of Tamburlaine.
Seek out another godhead to adore,
The god that sits in heaven, if any God,
For He is God alone, and none but he. (2.5.2.134–38)

As we have seen, *Selimus* is much more resolutely atheist in its ideas than the *Tamburlaine* plays, and the play heralds not the further imposition of the law of the Father but, rather, the triumphal return of the repressed maternal. Greene's Bajazet in no way possesses Tamburlainian stature. He is a lachrymose, worried old man who would like nothing better than to be rid of the emperorship. "[T]hough on all the world we make extent, / From the South Pole unto the Northern Bears, / And stretch our reign from east to western shore" (1.13–15), he sighs in the play's opening scene, "Yet doubt and care are with us evermore" (16). "He knows not what it is to be a king / That thinks a sceptre is a pleasant thing" (31–32), he later adds with just a hint of petulance. He has tried to be like his father, Mehmed II, the conqueror of the Golden Apple, Constantinople—and failed: "The Christian armies, oftentimes defeated / By my victorious father's valiance, / Have all my captains famously confronted / And cracked in two our uncontrollèd lance" (65–68), he laments in the middle of his litany of the military defeats and other setbacks that he has recently suffered. Indeed, he does not even live up to his forefather and namesake Bajazet I, whose tragic fate at Tamburlaine's hands is at the centre of *1 Tamburlaine*:

For Fortune never showed herself so cross
To any prince as to poor Bajazet.
That woeful emperor first of my name,
Whom the Tartarians locked in cage
To be a spectacle to all the world,
Was ten times happier than I am,
For Tamburlaine, the scourge of nations,
Was he that pulled him from his kingdom so,
But mine own sons expel me from the throne.
Ah, where shall I begin to make my moan,
Or what shall I first reckon in my plaint? (19.2–12)

Bajazet, then, is emphatically not the Primal Father. He persistently fails in his identificatory efforts, and his sons, like the sons in Freud's myth of the primal horde, seek to take advantage of that failure. Yet even as he confronts his rebellious sons, he persists. "Is this thy duty, son, unto thy father— / So impiously to level at his life?" (5.1–2), he demands of Selimus as they face off across the battlefield at Çorlu, "Can thy soul, wallowing in ambitious mire, / Seek for to reave that breast with bloody knife / From whence thou hadst thy being, Selimus?" (3–5). "[T]hou, like to a crafty polypus, / Doest turn thy hungry jaws upon thyself, / For what am I, Selimus, but thyself?" (19–21), he later adds. Like Tamburlaine in this one respect, Bajazet seeks to establish the law of the Father, the pious duty of a son to his father, through the complete repression of the maternal: it is from his breast, Bajazet asserts, that Selimus had his being. But Selimus is not Calyphas: if Bajazet is a Tamburlainian "weak father," then Selimus must be considered a Tamburlainian "strong son." "Art thou a father?" Selimus scornfully replies, "Nay, false Bajazet, / Disclaim the title which thou doest not merit" (63–64).

Failed father though he may be, then, Bajazet attempts to subdue the maternal to the patrilineal symbolic order. Appropriating the maternal to his own masculine body, Bajazet seeks to confine power exclusively to the realm of fathers and sons governed by the law of the Father. Selimus's ultimately successful rebellion wildly liberates the displaced maternal from this subordination. All of Bajazet's sons are to a greater or lesser degree linked to the effeminate and maternal. Corcut, the eldest, is a scholar, and, as one of Bajazet's advisers snidely remarks, "he that never handled but his pen, / Will be unskilful at the warlike lance" (10.94–95). And indeed, Corcut does not pursue the emperorship through the warlike lance. Instead, having heard of Selimus's first, failed rebellion, he requests that Bajazet honour the promise he made to him when as a child he substituted for Bajazet as emperor while Bajazet warred against his, Bajazet's, brother Cem in their competition for their dead father's throne. Bajazet then had promised Corcut the emperorship, and Corcut now asks Bajazet to honour that promise when he dies. In quiet contradiction of the effeminacy connoted by his preference for the pen over the lance, he asks Bajazet to uphold the patrilineal symbolic order. Acomat, Bajazet's favourite, is more clearly linked to the feminine. He "leads his life still in lascivious pomp" (10.88) and "never saw his foeman's face / But always slept upon a lady's lap" (91–92). The Janissaries consider him as unfit as Corcut to be emperor. Acomat disagrees and, when Bajazet turns down his request that Bajazet abdicate in his favour, declares his intention to demonstrate that "I can use my sword / And like a lion seize upon my prey" (11.28–29). He then mounts his own rebellion, relegating his effeminacy to the past as he adopts a hyperbolically martial persona that is explicitly modelled on Tamburlaine. Into these murky waters steps Selimus. The Janissaries favour him: "the rule and power over us / Is only fit for valiant Selimus" (10.100–101), who, Bajazet concedes, "hath won my people's heart" (1.90) and "is a friend to chivalry" (93). Unlike his brothers, Selimus is a man, and, in the face of Corcut's request and Acomat's rebellion, he is the man for the moment. In spite of his rebellion earlier in the play, he is asked by Bajazet to take the head of his army of Janissaries and quell Acomat's rebellion, an opportunity that he parlays into forcing Bajazet into abdicating and assuming the emperorship himself. In no way, however, does Selimus's success mitigate his ties to either the maternal or atheism. "Now, Selimus, consider who thou art" (1), Selimus ponders to open his speech in scene 2. Identity and identification will be Selimus's themes. He begins by considering the conventional implications of his identity as Bajazet's son:

> Some man will say I am too impious
> Thus to lay siege against my father's life
> And that I ought to follow virtuous
> And godly sons. (43–46)

He quickly ironizes this commonplace, however:

> Is he my father? Why, I am his son.
> I owe no more to him than he to me.
> If he proceed as he hath now begun
> And pass from me the Turkish seigniory
> To Acomat, then Selimus is free,
> And if he injure me that am his son,
> Faith, all the love 'twixt him and me is done. (62–68)

The irony then gives way to bald atheism as Selimus seeks to defend his seemingly impious rejection of the ostensibly natural ties that bind father and son. "[R]eligion," he declares

> Was only found to make us peaceable.
> Hence in especial come the foolish names
> Of father, mother, brother, and such like,

> For who so well his cogitation frames
> Shall find they serve but only for to strike
> Into our minds a certain kind of love,
> For these names too are but a policy
> To keep the quiet of society. (108–16)

This rejection of the signifiers of the patrilineal symbolic order culminates simultaneously in a rejection of the ontological lynchpin of that order, God, and in an embrace of its maternal substitute, Nature.

> Why should we seek to make that soul a slave
> To which Dame Nature so large freedom gave?
> Amongst us men there is some difference
> Of actions, termed by us "good" or "ill,"
> As he that doth his father recompense
> Differs from him that doth his father kill.
> And yet I think—think others what they will—
> That parricides, when death hath given them rest,
> Shall have as good a part as the rest—
> And that's just nothing, for, as I suppose,
> In Death's void kingdom reigns eternal night,
> Secure of evil and secure of foes,
> Where nothing doth the wicked man affright,
> No more than him that dies in doing right.
> Then since in death nothing shall to us fall,
> Here while I live, I'll have a snatch at all,
> And that can never, never be attained
> Unless old Bajazet do die the death. (122–39)

Unlike Corcut's religious erudition, Selimus's philosophical atheism leads to action. Unlike Acomat's later unmasking as he changes the livery of Venus for that of Mars, Selimus's unmasking embraces the feminine and the maternal. His violence is anchored in Dame Nature's freedom from the patrilineal symbolic order. Although more Tamburlainian than either of his two brothers, the strong Selimus is emphatically a mama's boy, and his success returns the repressed maternal in triumph over a world of metaphysically hollow patriarchal law upheld by materially weak fathers. Powerfully, and ironically, then, Greene's "effeminate brat" forcefully dramatizes the weakness of its "father"'s logocentric (if not theological) masculinity.

Early Modern English Theatre and the Queen's Men

The 1570s mark a turning point in the history of early modern English drama. There was no lack of theatre in London or the provinces before this point. Medieval and early-sixteenth-century English drama came in many forms: extended dramatizations of biblical narratives, known as mystery plays, performed over several days in multiple outdoor locations on religious holidays; shorter plays on religious themes and subjects, like saints' plays, miracle plays, and morality plays; secular but often no less didactic dramas designed for performance in such locations as banqueting halls, where they might serve as interludes between other forms of festivity; civic and court pageantry, staged to celebrate the inauguration of a new mayor or to entertain the monarch during such festive seasons as Christmas; educational drama, performed by schoolboys of all ages. Not all of this drama was amateur. Travelling actors performed interludes and other fare in expectation of some recompense for their acting, whether that be food and lodging or cash (preferably both). Professional actors seem occasionally to have been hired in the production of mystery plays and other forms of largely amateur drama, too (Harris 136). Nor was this drama necessarily inexpensive to produce. Organized and mounted by the guilds of a municipal corporation, for example, mystery plays were large affairs that involved considerable expense. Court entertainments spared no cost, their lavishness being a reflection of royal grandeur. On the whole, though, English drama before the 1570s was occasional or irregular. Plays or pageants were performed to celebrate a special occasion or during a special season, or at irregular intervals in shifting venues (the performances of a travelling troupe, for example).[1]

In the 1570s that changed, at least in the vicinity of London. In 1567 the Red Lion playhouse was constructed, and in 1576 James Burbage (c. 1531–97), who managed a company of adult actors known as the Earl of Leicester's Men, built another one in Shoreditch, then a suburb north of London (Gurr, *Playgoing* 13). Aptly named the Theatre, this playhouse was followed a year later

---

1 Glynne Wickham's *The Medieval Theatre* is an excellent introduction to English theatre before 1576. Siobhan Keenan's *Travelling Players in Shakespeare's England* provides a comprehensive overview of Elizabethan travelling troupes and the various venues in which they performed.

by the Curtain (13). More freestanding, open-air playhouses were built over the next forty years in the suburbs to the north and the south of London proper. These playhouses offered adult acting companies a permanent performance venue, where they could mount a regular performance schedule (six days a week) and generate stable revenue by attracting a large and regular audience. During this time companies of boy actors were also performing in hall theatres in London, but the London adult acting companies did not acquire the regular use of a hall theatre until 1608, when Shakespeare's company made a hall theatre in the liberties of Blackfriars one of their regular performance venues.[1] All acting companies were required to have an aristocratic patron to avoid legal prosecution for vagrancy. Technically, the aristocrats were the actors' employers. Many aristocrats supported acting companies during this period, but the major adult acting companies in the 1580s and 1590s were the Queen's Men, formed in 1583, and the Lord Chamberlain's Men and the Lord Admiral's Men, both formed in 1594. Although acting companies were primarily commercial ventures, the legal fiction was that their regular, commercial performances were merely rehearsals for the court performances that they would give for the Queen's entertainment during festive seasons such as Christmas.

The open-air playhouses were large, wooden, polygonal structures that could seat between two and three thousand spectators, who sat in the three tiers of galleries or stood in the yard area surrounding the stage. The price of admission was a penny to stand in the yard, another penny to sit in the first level of galleries, and an additional penny to ascend to the upper galleries (Gurr, *The Shakespearean Stage* 122). The galleries were thatched, and performances typically began mid-afternoon, ensuring that there was still sunlight by the end of the play. The raised stage projected into the yard area from one of the inner walls and was roughly 30 feet by 40 feet at the Globe, Shakespeare's theatre; Marlowe's main stage, the Rose, was "a hexagon of less than thirty-five feet wide with a depth of less than half that" (Gurr, *Shakespeare's Opposites* 132). At the back of the stage was a house-front façade with two side doors for entrances and exits, a central discovery space, and an upper balcony area that could also be used as an acting area.

---

1 For a history of amphitheatre and hall theatres from Marlowe's day to the closing of the theatres in 1642, see Andrew Gurr's *The Shakespearean Stage 1574–1642*. Liberties were former monastic districts that retained their pre-Reformation municipal privileges.

The dressing room area was behind the façade (Gurr, *The Shakespearean Stage* 122). The acting area, then, had three distinct vertical levels: the upper balcony, the middle main stage, and the area below the stage. Elizabethan playwrights used the obvious dramatic symbolism of these different levels to great effect (Gurr, *The Shakespearean Stage* 182). The main stage also contained three different horizontal areas: if the main action of the play took place in the central area of the stage, a withdrawal to the back of the stage could suggest a retreat into privacy or secrecy and the advance toward the front of the stage could be used by an actor to engage the audience, either through an aside or through direct address. The different sides of the stage, each perhaps centred on one of the stage façade's doors, could also be used as distinct acting areas. With its various levels and acting areas the amphitheatre stage could be a very complex space. By modern standards the amphitheatre stage might seem rather bare, however. There were no background scene paintings or special lighting effects: the façade remained largely the same throughout the play, the performances took place in natural light, and consequently in the drama written for this stage the scene is set and detailed mainly through the references and descriptions in the actors' lines (Gurr, *The Shakespearean Stage* 187–200). Nonetheless, these early modern stages appealed to the eyes as well as the ears of their customers with the actors' colourful (and expensive) costumes and such stage props as the large brazen head that is at the focus of Friar Bacon's magical labours in Greene's *Friar Bacon and Friar Bungay* and the elaborate apparatus by which the rebellious Absalom is hanged by the hair in George Peele's *David and Bathsheba*. The large and socially heterogeneous crowds attending a performance in an Elizabethan amphitheatre were visually as well as aurally entertained: they were spectators as well as audience members.

The open-air amphitheatres were not the only performance venues for the adult acting companies, and the acting company to which *Selimus* belonged, the Queen's Men, was primarily a touring company, especially after 1590 (McMillin 68). The Queen's Men was formed in 1583, its actors culled from the other acting troupes existing at the time. Although by 1594, when the Lord Chamberlain's Men and the Lord Admiral's Men were formed and granted a virtual duopoly on playing in London, the Queen's Men had lost their dominance of London theatre, the latter continued to perform successfully and profitably in the provinces until 1603. Indeed, in their landmark study of the company, *The Queen's Men and Their Plays*, Scott McMillin and Sally-Beth

MacLean contend that the Queen's Men were a company created to tour, to spread Protestant and nationalist culture throughout the country, and to strengthen the bonds of Elizabethan society as a centralized imaginary community (33). They were, in fact, "the best known and most widely travelled professional company in the kingdom" (67). The company had multiple touring circuits: "East Anglia; the south-east through Canterbury to the Cinque Ports and their coastal affiliates; the south-west via the coast through Southampton and Dorset or along one of several inland roads to Bristol; the Midlands centring on Coventry at the hub of a network of roads running in all directions; the West Midlands along the hilly terrain of the Welsh borders; the north-east via the Great North Road or another important road through Leicester; and the mountainous north-west most commonly reached across Coventry or from the north-east through the Yorkshire hills in Airedale" (39). McMillin and MacLean contend that it is almost certain that as soon as they were formed the Queen's Men were divided into two groups to cover all the tour routes (north and south). They toured during the summer months and stopped in London in the winter. They received higher than average payments on tour, and in London they rented various performance venues, as if London were another tour stop (44). In 1594, the number of actors trudging the roads would have been, according to McMillin and MacLean, fourteen, eleven men and three boys, who routinely played the female roles (100). On tour, the company would have played in a variety of different performance venues, including indoor venues such as town halls, halls in the great houses of aristocrats, and outdoor venues such as fields and inn yards. *Selimus* shows the influence of its Queen's Men provenance not merely in the fact that with a suitable doubling scheme all its roles can be played by fourteen actors (McMillin 58) but also in its dramaturgical similarities to other plays known or suspected to have been in the Queen's Men's repertory. These dramaturgical similarities are most salient in the clowning of Bullithrumble, which connects him to the clowning in other Queen's Men's plays such as *The Famous Victories of Henry V*, Greene's own *Friar Bacon and Friar Bungay*, and *Locrine* (Walsh 69), and in Selimus's feigned performance of the penitent prodigal son role in scene 18 of the play, which bears a striking resemblance to Prince Henry's performance of the same role in *Famous Victories*. Readers interested in learning more about the Queen's Men and exploring the Queen's Men's repertory can visit Queen's Men Editions on the University of Victoria's website.

Robert Greene: A Brief Chronology of His Life and Times

1301	Osman I is the first Ottoman Emperor.
1389	The battle of Kosovo, in which Ottoman Emperor Murad I defeats Christian forces but is assassinated after the battle.
1396	The battle of Nicopolis, in which Murad's son Bayezid I crushes a Crusader army led by Sigismund, King of Hungary.
1402	Temur the Lame defeats Bayezid I at the battle of Ankara, Anatolia, and allegedly parades him through his camp in a cage.
1444	Ottoman Emperor Murad II defeats Ladislaus King of Hungary at the battle of Varna.
1453	Ottoman Emperor Mehmed II takes Constantinople.
1470	Selimus is born, one of at least eight sons of Bayezid (later Bayezid II).
1476	William Caxton establishes a printing press in Westminster.
1481	Bayezid II becomes Ottoman Emperor.
1511	Selimus rebels; the rebellion fails.
1512	Selimus forces his father to abdicate and becomes Selim I.
1517	Selim I conquers Egypt. University of Wittenberg professor Martin Luther (1483–1546) attacks the sale of indulgences in his "Disputation of Martin Luther on the Power and Efficacy of Indulgences," sparking the Protestant Reformation.
1520	Ottoman forces take Belgrade. Selim I dies.
1522	Ottoman Emperor Suleiman the Magnificent takes Rhodes, ousting the Knights of St. John.
1529	Suleiman unsuccessfully besieges Vienna.
1534	The Act of Supremacy establishes Henry VIII as the head of the English church, legally entrenching the Protestant Reformation in England.

1535	Francis I of France concludes a military treaty with the Ottoman empire.
1547–53	Reign of Protestant Edward VI.
1553–58	Reign of Catholic Queen Mary, married to Philip II of Spain.
1554	John Lyly, "University Wit," playwright, and writer of prose fiction, is born in Kent.
1556	George Peele, "University Wit," and author of *David and Bathsheba* and other plays, is born in London.
1558	Robert Greene is born in Norwich.
	Protestant Elizabeth Tudor, daughter of Anne Boleyn and Henry VIII, takes the throne of England.
	Thomas Lodge, Greene's collaborator and fellow "University Wit," is born in London.
	Thomas Kyd, author of *The Spanish Tragedy*, is born in London.
1564	Christopher Marlowe is born in Canterbury.
	William Shakespeare is born in Stratford-upon-Avon.
1565	The Ottomans unsuccessfully besiege Malta.
	The Low Countries rebel against their Spanish overlords. War between the Dutch and the Spanish ends only when the Spanish recognize Dutch independence in 1648 in the Peace of Westphalia.
1567	Thomas Nashe is born in Lowestoft.
1570	Publication of the first modern atlas, Abraham Ortelius's *Theatrum Orbis Terrarum*.
1571	The battle of Lepanto, at which the combined naval forces of Spain, Venice, and the papacy defeat the Ottoman fleet.
1572	The Act for the Punishment of Vagabonds criminalizes actors without aristocratic patrons.
	Between 24 and 27 August, thousands of French Protestants are massacred in Paris and other urban centres in France.
1573	Ben Jonson is born in London.
1576	James Burbage builds the Theatre, a free-standing, open-air playhouse, in Shoreditch, then north of London.
1576–84	The Children of Her Majesty's Chapel perform regularly at a hall theatre in Blackfriars, London.

1578	William Harbourne undertakes a diplomatic mission to the court of Ottoman Emperor Murad III's court, resulting in an exchange of letters between Murad and Queen Elizabeth and the granting of trade capitulations in 1580.
	Lyly's *Euphues, or the Anatomy of Wit* is published, and its style is widely imitated, giving rise to "Euphuism," an ornate style based on the multiplication of elaborate comparisons.
1581	War in the Low Countries hardens into religious warfare between the Protestant northern United Provinces and the Catholic southern Spanish Netherlands.
1580–92	Greene lives as a professional writer in London, composing pamphlets for the popular press and plays for the professional stage.
1583	Greene receives his MA from Cambridge.
	The Queen's Men, an elite acting troupe patronized by Queen Elizabeth I, is formed.
1585–88	Queen Elizabeth's favourite, Robert Dudley, Earl of Leicester (1532–88), backed by an English army, is the United Provinces' governor-general.
1587	The imprisoned Mary, Queen of Scots is executed by Elizabeth I's command.
	First performance of Marlowe's *Tamburlaine the Great* Part One.
1588	The English repulse a massive Spanish naval invasion (the Spanish Armada).
	First performance of Marlowe's *Tamburlaine the Great* Part Two.
	Greene receives his MA from Oxford.
1589	Sir Francis Drake and Sir John Norris lead an English naval expedition against the Spanish along the Iberian coast. The expedition fails.
1590	The first three books of Spenser's *The Faerie Queene* are published.
1592	Greene dies. *Greene's Groatsworth of Wit* is published posthumously.
1593	Marlowe dies, stabbed in the eye by Ingram Frizer at an inn in Deptford on 30 May. On 12 May Marlowe's former roommate, the playwright Thomas Kyd, is arrested and interrogated for his possible connections to the circulation in London

of threatening anti-immigrant libels. Kyd implicates Marlowe in the writing or copying of part of a heretical treatise found in Kyd's quarters. On 18 May Marlowe is summoned to meet the Privy Council; after obeying the summons on 20 May, Marlowe is released but required to remain available should the Privy Council have further need of him. The connection between these events and Marlowe's death on 30 May is unclear.

1594	Thomas Kyd dies.
	The Lord Chamberlain's Men and the Lord Admiral's Men are formed.
	Publication of *The First Part of the Tragical Reign of Selimus*.
1596	English naval and army forces under the Earl of Nottingham and the Earl of Essex sack the Spanish city of Cadiz.
	George Peele dies.
	Publication of books four through six of *The Faerie Queene*.
1596–97	Spain attempts to mount further naval invasions of England.
1597	Under the leadership of the Earl of Essex, the Earl of Suffolk, and Sir Walter Ralegh, an English naval expedition attacking the Spanish in the Azores fails.
1598	Edict of Nantes, which provided a degree of religious toleration for French Protestants under Henry IV.
1599	The Globe is built on the southern banks of the Thames from the timbers of the Theatre.
	The Earl of Essex sails for Ireland with an army under orders from the Queen to crush the Irish rebellion. He fails and returns later in the year.
1601	The Earl of Essex rebels. The rebellion fails, and he is executed.
	Thomas Nashe dies.
1603	Elizabeth I dies; James VI of Scotland takes the English throne as James I of England.
1604	James I establishes peace with Spain.
1606	John Lyly dies.
1616	William Shakespeare dies.

1618–48	The Thirty Years' War, ended by the Peace of Westphalia, devastates Europe.
1625	James I dies; his son, Charles I, becomes king. Thomas Lodge dies.
1637	Ben Jonson dies.
1642–51	Civil war breaks out in England between parliamentarians and royalists.
1642	Parliament closes the theatres.
1649	Charles I is executed.
1649–60	Interregnum, during which England is ruled by parliament and the army, with Oliver Cromwell and, briefly, his son Richard acting as Protector from 1653 to 1659.
1660	Charles I's son becomes Charles II when he returns to England at parliament's request to take the throne. The theatres reopen.

A Note on the Text

Selimus was first printed in 1594 and subsequently reissued in 1638. Since then, the play has received six modern editions. *Selimus* was reprinted in 1883 in volume 14 of *The Life and Complete Works in Prose and Verse of Robert Greene*, edited by Alexander Grosart, who in 1898 published a single-volume edition of the play in the Temple Drama series. In 1909, a Malone Society Reprint of the play was published, prepared by W. Bang under the general editorship of W.W. Greg. A.F. Hopkinson published an edition "for private circulation" in 1916. In 1994 Nadia Raid completed an old-spelling edition of the play for her dissertation, and the play was included in *Three Turk Plays from Early Modern England* (2000), edited by Daniel Vitkus.

The First Part of the Tragical Reign of Selimus, Sometime Emperor of the Turks, and Grandfather to Him that Now Reigneth was written and first performed sometime between 1588, the date of the first performances of Marlowe's *Tamburlaine* plays, and 1592, the year of Greene's death. The play was not entered in the Stationers' Register. The title page of the 1594 quarto of the play does not give an author, stating only that the play was "playd by the Queenes Maiesties Players" and "Printed by Thomas Creede." The quarto collates A4 (-A1) B-I4 K4 (-K4). In 1638, John Crooke and Richard Serger reissued the play with a new title page that called the play *The Tragedy of Selimus Emperor of the Turks* and attributed it to "T.G.," which led Gerard Langbaine to attribute the play to a later playwright, Thomas Goffe (1591–1629), author of *The Raging Turk, or Bajazet the Second* (1631). In 1594, however, Goffe would have been three years old, and "T.G." may simply be a misprint of "R.G." (Grosart 2 vi). The verso of the new title page is blank rather than reprinting the prologue found on A2v of the 1594 quarto, but otherwise the 1594 quarto and the 1638 reissue are identical (Greg and Bang v). The 1594 quarto and its 1638 reissue consequently constitute the copy-text of this edition. Grosart, the play's first modern editor, attributes the play to Greene in part on the strength of passages from *Selimus* reproduced in Robert Allott's Elizabethan verse anthology *England's Parnassus* (1600) (Grosart 2: x–xii). Greg adds four more passages to the two Grosart found in Allott yet does not consider this evidence to be "conclusive" (vi) proof of Greene's authorship of the play. Though it may not be conclusive, however, the evidence provided by Allott's anthology, combined with the internal evidence Grosart adduces in addition (Grosart 2 xii–xxi), strongly supports the case for Greene's authorship. According to Raid, "the most reasonable conclusion [about the play's authorship] is either that Greene wrote the first version [of the play] which was later slightly updated, perhaps by someone in the Queen's Men, or that someone influenced by Greene and Marlowe wrote it or revised an old play" (38). Most recently, on the basis of computer-assisted linguistic and stylistic analysis, in separate articles Donna Murphy and Darren Freebury-Jones have suggested that Greene co-authored the play with Thomas Lodge, with whom Greene also collaborated on *A Looking Glass for London and England* (1589) (Freebury-Jones 394–95).

The 1594 quarto poses no significant textual challenges, and emendation has been kept to a necessary minimum. Twelve copies of the 1594 quarto and four copies of the 1638 reissue are extant and held in the following libraries: the British Library (1594 and 1638); the National Library of Scotland (1594 and 1638); the Bodleian Library (1594 and 1638); the Victoria and Albert Museum (1594, three copies); the Boston Public Library (1594); the Folger Shakespeare Library (1594); the Harvard University Houghton Library (1594); the Huntington Library (1594 and 1638); the University of Illinois (1594); and the Yale University Beinecke Rare Book and Manuscript Library (1594). In the preparation of the text for this edition, fifteen of the sixteen copies were collated, and the results of the collation are recorded in the textual notes. Unfortunately, the Bodleian Library copy of the 1594 quarto was unavailable at the time of collation.

How to Read a Collation Note

In this edition the notes to the text are of two types: commentary notes and collation notes. The commentary notes explain the meaning of words and provide literary, historical, and dramatic information to aid the reader in the understanding of the play. The collation notes are of two types: the first type indicates variations of wording among the different copies of the play's first printed edition (abbreviated "Q," for quarto, the roughly paperback size of most early modern English printed plays); the second type indicates the changes (emendations) that modern editors have made to the wording of Q. Of the first type there are only two, the first one at 5.50. The line in this edition reads as follows: "And thou thoughtst scorn Selim should speak with thee!" The note to this line is "wit Q BPL F HU 1 UI VAM 2 BD 2." What the note indicates to the reader is that in the quarto copies held in the Boston Public Library (BPL), the Folger (F), the Huntington Library (HU 1), the University of Illinois (UI), the Victoria and Albert Museum (VAM 2) and the Bodleian Library (BD 2), the line concludes with "wit," not "with thee," which is how the line concludes in the other copies of the play. It is fairly obvious from inspection that "wit" is the product of insufficient ink on the typeface of the font that made up the entire two-word phrase, "with thee." Either the ink on the typeface ran out as the play was being printed, or the typeface was insufficiently inked when the printing initially began but the printer caught the problem as the play was being printed, stopped the press to re-ink the typeface properly, and then continued the printing (this is called a "stop-press correction"). This correction, which might seem trivial to the modern reader, is worth recording because the (erroneous) reading produced by "wit" cannot be dismissed as sheer nonsense, even if the meaning it creates is odd. The other collation note of this type occurs at 16.33 and is the product of the same out-of-ink scenario. An example of a collation note of the second type, indicating a modern editorial emendation, is the note to "monster-guarded" in line 31.42. Having vanquished all his foes, Selimus boasts, "thou hast trod / The monster-guarded paths that lead to crowns" (31.41–42). Actually, all the early modern copies of Q read "monster-garden," and "monster-garden" does make sense, although not as much sense as "monster-guarded." Editors since Grosart in 1898 have decided that "garden" is a typographical error and have emended to "guarded." Nonetheless, it is important to let the modern reader know that "guarded" is a modern editorial choice, not the original. The collation note alerting the reader to this modern editorial intervention reads as follows: "Ed. (Grosart 2); monster-garden Q." "Ed" indicates that the word is an editorial intervention. "(Grosart 2)" states which editor in which edition first made the intervention, in this case Grosart in his second, 1898 single-volume, edition of the play. "monster-garden Q" tells the reader that the original reading in Q is "monster-garden." In a number of places in the original, words seem to have been omitted, and modern editors have supplied their best guesses to fill the gaps. In the collation notes to these emendations, the reader will find the phrase "not in Q." *Selimus* is a brilliant play, and the modern reader, general or scholarly, is understandably far more interested in the play's characters, action, and meaning than in modern editorial theories about early modern textual instability, but it is hoped that the collation notes create an awareness of the process that led to the play text that we hold in our hands (or view on our laptop screens), an awareness that only adds to our appreciation of the play.

THE
Firſt parc of the Tra=

gicall raigne of Selimus, fometime Empe-
rour of the Turkes, and grandfather to Lim
that now raigneth.

Wherein is fhowne how hee moſt vnnaturally
raifed warres againſt his owne father *Baiazet*, and pre-
uailing therein in the end caufed him to
be poyfoned:

Alfo with the murthering of his two brethren,
Corcut, and *Acomat*.

As it was play'd by the Queenes Maiefties
Players.

LONDON

Printed by Thomas Creede, dwelling in Thames
ftreete at the figne of the Kathren wheele,
neare the olde Swanne.

1 5 9 4.

THE FIRST PART OF THE TRAGICAL REIGN OF SELIMUS, SOMETIME EMPEROR OF THE TURKS

List of characters, in order of appearance:[1]

Prologue.

Bajazet, Emperor of the Turks.

Mustaffa, Bajazet's advisor and son-in-law, and captain of the Janissaries.

Cherseoli, Governor of Greece, and Bajazet's advisor and son-in-law.

Janissaries, elite Turkish soldiers.

Messengers.

Selimus, Bajazet's youngest son.

Sinam, Selimus's advisor.

Ottrante, Tartar lord and Selimus's advisor.

Occhiali, Selimus's advisor and messenger.

Soldiers.

Acomat, Bajazet's second-eldest surviving son.

Vizier, Acomat's advisor.

Regan, Acomat's advisor and messenger.

Cali, Turkish lord and Bajazet's advisor.

Hali, Turkish lord, Cali's brother, and Bajazet's advisor.

Mahomet, prince of Natolia and son of Alemshae, Bajazet's deceased first son.

Belierbey of Natolia, Mahomet's advisor.

Zonara, Mahomet's sister.

Aga, Turkish lord and Bajazet's advisor.

Abraham, Bajazet's apothecary.

Bullithrumble, a shepherd.

Corcut, Bajazet's eldest surviving son.

Corcut's page.

Solyma, Mustaffa's wife and Bajazet's daughter.

Aladin, Acomat's son.

Amurath, Acomat's son.

Tonombey, son of the Sultan of Egypt.

Queen of Amasia, Acomat's wife.

Conclusion.

---

1 The List of characters is not in Q. See the Note on the Text, p. 44, for information on understanding references to the different editions of the play.

[Prologue]

...e.

...o feignèd[2] toy nor forgèd tragedy,
Genius,[3] ... here present unto your view,
But a most lamentable history,[4]
Which this last age[5] acknowledgeth for true.
Here shall you see the wicked son[6] pursue   5
His wretched father[7] with remorseless spite
And, daunted once, his force again renew,
Poison his father, kill his friends in fight.
You shall behold him character[8] in blood
The image of an implacable king   10
And, like a sea or high resurging flood,
All obstant lets[9] down with his fury fling,
Which, if with patience of you shall be heard,
We have the greatest part of our reward.

Exit.[10]

---

1 Although the point from which a character entered the stage would obviously depend upon the nature of the venue in which the play was being performed, the early modern London open-air amphitheatres that
constitute one probable major performance venue for *Selimus* had up
to six possible entry points onto the main stage: at the back of the stage,
the tiring house's façade had two side doors and a central door or set
of doors, behind which was a recessed "discovery space" ("the place
behind the stage" [*Alphonsus King of Aragon* sig. F1v]); characters could
also ascend and descend from the "heavens" above the stage via stage
machinery, enter from below the stage via a trapdoor, and even move
onto the raised main stage, which thrust out into the audience, from the
standing-room yard area surrounding the stage (Ichikawa 7).
2 False, invented, fictional.
3 Gentlemen and gentlewomen, audience.
4 The history play, in contrast to "forgèd tragedy," was the hallmark
of the Queen's Men's repertoire, to which the play's 1594 title page
attributes *Selimus* (Walsh 32).
5 This present day.
6 Selimus.
7 Bajazet.
8 Write.
9 All obstacles.
10 Characters could exit the stage at any of the six entrance points list-
ed in the note to the Prologue's entrance. Typically, modern editors consider a scene to have concluded when all the characters have

[Handwritten annotation: Suddenly, Tober was reminded of the training she had done just that morning. Enemies around her, nameless, faceless. All her life, the enemy had been faceless -- and she had never questioned it.]

[Scene 1[1]
Bajazet's court in Adrianople[2]]

Enter Bajazet[3] Emperor of Turkey, Mustaffa,[4] Cherseoli,[5] and the Janissaries.[6]

Bajazet. Leave me, my lords, until I call you forth,
For I am heavy[7] and disconsolate.

Exeunt all but Bajazet.

So, Bajazet, now thou remainst alone,
Unrip the thoughts that harbour in thy breast
And eat thee up, for arbiter[8] here's none   5
That may descry[9] the cause of thy unrest—
Unless these walls thy secret thoughts declare,

---

exited the stage. "Exit" is a Latin verb meaning "[He, she or it] ex-its." "Exeunt" is the Latin plural: "[They] exit." In the 1594 quarto of *Selimus*, the English third-person plural "Exit" instead of the Latin "Exeunt" is often used to indicate the exit of multiple characters.

1   The scene divisions in the play are editorial insertions, following Greg's Malone Society Reprint (1909) edition.

2   Following its main source, Peter Ashton's *A Short Treatise upon the Turks' Chronicles* (1546), the play's first scene is set in Bajazet's court in Adrianople (modern Edirne), which was the capital city of the Ottoman Empire from 1369 until 1453, when Mehmed II conquered Constantinople (Byzantium) and moved the empire's capital there (Imber 25–26), renaming it Istanbul. Edirne is in the East Thrace region of modern Turkey, bordering on Greece and Bulgaria. Bayezid II moved his court from Istanbul to Edirne in 1509 after an earthquake severely damaged Istanbul (Finkel 100). The year is 1511, sometime in June, immediately after Bajazet's forces have quelled a Persian-inspired internal revolt in south-western Anatolia (Finkel 100; Shaw 79).

3   Bayezid II (r. 1481–1512), emperor of the Ottoman Empire.

4   Captain of the Janissaries and Bajazet's son-in-law. Ashton identi-fies him only by his title, Aga ("Captain") (sig. E6r).

5   Ashton identifies Cherseoli as Belierbey (Governor) of Greece and Bajazet's son-in-law (sig. E6r).

6   Elite Ottoman troops drawn from the extensive Christian pop-ulation of the Ottoman Empire (Uyar and Erickson 18–20). Ash-ton writes that "The emperor hath always about him his guard of 12,000 Janissars, most strong and puissant footmen, the which be also of those which have forsaken Christ" (sig. Q2v).

7   Distressed, grieved, sorrowful (*OED*, adj. 1, 25a).

8   Judge.

9   Discern.

And princes' walls, they say, unfaithful are.
Why, that's the profit of great regiment:[1]
That all of us are subject unto[2] fears,   10
And this vain show and glorious intent[3]
Privy suspicion on each scruple rears.[4]
Ay,[5] though on all the world we make extent,[6]
From the South Pole unto the Northern Bears,[7]
And stretch our reign from east to western shore,   15
Yet doubt and care are with us evermore.
Look how the earth, clad in her summer's pride,
Embroidereth her mantle gorgeously
With fragrant herbs and flowers gaily dyed,
Spreading abroad her spangled tapestry,   20
Yet under all a loathsome snake doth hide.
Such is our life: under crowns cares do lie,
And fear the sceptre still attends[8] upon.
Oh, who can take delight in kingly throne?
Public disorders joined with private cark,[9]   25
Care of our friends and of our children dear,
Do toss our lives as waves a silly bark.[10]
Though we be fearless, 'tis not without fear,
For hidden mischief lurketh in the dark
And storms may fall, be the day ne'er so clear.   30
He knows not what it is to be a king
That thinks a sceptre is a pleasant thing.[11]

---

1 Rule, sovereignty, authority.
2 Subjected to; the subjects of.
3 Design, effort, endeavour (*OED*, n., 1b, 3).
4 I.e., the grandeur of authority rests on the shaky foundation of private suspicions.
5 Ed. (Grosart 2); I Q.
6 I.e., extend our authority.
7 Ursa Major, "the Greater Bear," and Ursa Minor, "the Lesser Bear," two constellations in the northern hemisphere. According to Robert Record in *The Castle of Knowledge* (1556), "The most northerly constellation is the Lesser Bear, called Ursa Minor.... This is the chief mark whereby mariners govern their course in sailing by night.... Nigh unto it is the Greater Bear, called Ursa Major" (263).
8 Waits.
9 Trouble, distress, anxiety (*OED*, n., 3).
10 Fragile or flimsy (*OED*, adj., 3c) boat.
11 In his anthology *England's Parnassus* (1600), Robert Allott reproduces lines 31 and 32 under the heading "Kings" and attributes them to "R. Greene" (sig. L7r) (Grosart 2 x).

Twice fifteen times hath fair Latona's son[1]
Walked about the world with his great light[2]
Since I began—would I had ne'er begun!— 35
To sway this sceptre. Many a careful[3] night,
When Cynthia[4] in haste to bed did run,
Have I with watching vexed my agèd sprite.
Since when, what dangers I have overpassed
Would make a heart of adamant[5] aghast. 40
The Persian Sophy, mighty Isma'il,[6]
Took the Levant[7] clean[8] away from me,
And Caraguis Bashaw, sent his force to quell,
Was killed himself the while his men did flee.
Poor Hali Bashaw, having once sped[9] well 45
And gained of him a bloody victory,
Was at the last slain fighting in the field,
Charactering honour in his battered shield.[10]

---

1 Phoebus Apollo, god of the sun in classical myth.
2 I.e., thirty years have passed.
3 Full of care.
4 Goddess of the moon in classical myth.
5 "[A] hard, strong rock or mineral, not otherwise identified, to which various other (often contradictory) properties were attributed. In later use chiefly a poetical or rhetorical name for an embodiment of surpassing hardness" (*OED*, n., 1a).
6 The first Safavid Shah of Persia (r. 1501–24) (Imber 37).
7 "The eastern part of the Mediterranean, with its islands and countries adjoining" (*OED*, n.1, 1). Between 1505 and 1507, Isma'il conquered parts of Eastern Anatolia north of Syria (Imber 37). The conflict between Safavid Persia and the Ottoman Empire was exacerbated by sharp religious differences: the Ottomans were "orthodox" Sunni Muslims, claiming religious authority from the broad Islamic tradition transmitted through the preceding Umayyad and Abbasid dynasties, while the Safavids were Shiites, who asserted a superior authority based on the lineage of the Twelve Imams who descended directly from the Prophet Muhammad (Finkel 94). According to Ashton, Isma'il, "expounding after a new and strange sort the Mahometans' law, had brought in also a new religion, and by this means got and obtained the kingdom of Persia" (sig. G3r).
8 Completely.
9 Fared, done.
10 In Ashton's history, Isma'il's expanding forces are confronted by Bajazet's captain "cleped [called] Goragnes Bashaw, whom at that time they overcame and beside the city Lucia sticked him up upon a stake. After Goragnes was thus slain, Hali Bashaw, who was an eunuch, pursued the Persians forthwith with a mighty (*continued*)

Ramirchan[1] the Tartarian[2] Emperor,
Gathering to him a number numberless   50
Of big-boned Tartars, in a hapless[3] hour
Encountered me, and there my chiefest bliss,[4]
Good Alemshae[5]—ah, this remembrance sour!—
Was slain, the more t'augment my sad distress.
In losing[6] Alemshae, poor I lost more   55
Than[7] ever I had gained theretofore.
Well may thy soul rest in her latest[8] grave,
Sweet Alemshae, the comfort of my days.
That thou might'st live, how often did I crave?
How often did I bootless[9] prayers raise   60
To that high power that life first to thee gave?

---

power, and when he had now (fighting himself like no eunuch but like a strong and valiant champion) in a manner utterly murdered and destroyed the Persian's host, being at the point to have had the victory, he was slain" (sig. G3v).

1 Historically, Mengli I Giray, Khan of the Crimean Tartars between 1478 and 1515, whose daughter, Hafsa Hatun, Selimus married in 1511 (Clot 26).

2 In early modern geography, Tartary was roughly the equivalent of modern Central Asia. In his landmark early modern atlas, first published in 1570, Abraham Ortelius describes the region of Tartaria as "that huge tract and portion of the mainland ... that is between the east sea (or, as he calleth it, *Mare Mangicum*, the sea of *Mangi* or of *Sin*, a country all the world over and vulgarly known by the name of *China*) and the south countries, *Sin* or *China*, that part of *India* which is beyond *Ganges*, the country of the *Saci*, the river *Iaxartes*, (now they call it *Chesel*), the *Caspian* sea, *Mar delle Zabacche* (*Meotis palus*, it was called of the ancient writers) and westward up as high almost as the Muscovites. For all these countries well near the Tartars did possess, and in these places they were seated, so that it comprehendeth that country which the old historiographers called *Sarmatia* of *Asia*, both the *Scythians* and *Seria*, the country where the *Seres* dwelt, which now I take to be named Cataio" (*Theatrum Orbis Terrarum* fol. 105).

3 Unlucky.

4 Ed.; blesse Q.

5 Historically, Alemshae was the fourth of the five sons who participated in the struggle to take Bajazet's place as Ottoman emperor. He died in 1512 (Shaw 79). The other four were Acomat (historically, Ahmet), Corcut, Selimus, and Sehinsah (d. 1511) (Shaw 78–79).

6 Ed. (Grosart 2); leesing Q.

7 Ed. (Grosart 2); Then Q.

8 Last, final.

9 Futile, useless.

Trusty wast thou to me at all assays,[1]
And, dearest child, thy father oft hath cried,
That thou hadst lived, so he himself had died.[2]
The Christian armies, oftentimes defeated   65
By my victorious father's[3] valiance,
Have all my captains famously confronted
And cracked in two our uncontrollèd[4] lance.
My strongest garrisons they have supplanted[5]
And overwhelmèd me in sad mischance,   70
And my decrease so long wrought[6] their increase,
Till I was forced conclude a friendly peace.[7]
Now all these are but foreign damages
Taken in war, whose die[8] uncertain is,
But I shall have more home-born outrages   75
Unless my divination[9] aims amiss.
I have three sons all of unequal ages,
And all in diverse studies set their bliss:
Corcut, my eldest, a philosopher,
Acomat pompous, Selim[10] a warrior.   80
Corcut in fair Magnesia[11] leads his life
In learning arts and Mahound's dreaded laws;[12]

---

1 Trials, tests.
2 I.e., your father often has cried, "Would that you had lived and I had died."
3 Bajazet's father was Mehmed II (r. 1451–81). In 1453, he captured Constantinople, the capital city of the Byzantine Empire, and throughout his reign he expanded the Ottoman Empire's European territories (Imber 25–33).
4 Untamed, undefeated.
5 Taken over, dispossessed, overturned (*OED*, v.1, 2b).
6 Brought about.
7 Like his predecessors, Bayezid II made frequent but inconclusive incursions into such Eastern European territories as Serbia, Hungary, and Poland, with whom he most recently concluded a peace agreement in 1499. Equally inconclusive were Bayezid's naval wars against the Ottoman's major commercial rival, Venice, with whom he signed a peace agreement in 1503 (Shaw 73–76).
8 Singular of "dice."
9 Prediction, prognostication, fortune-telling.
10 Ed. (Grosart 2); Selmi Q. "Selim" becomes Selimus I in 1512 and reigns until his death in 1520.
11 Founded by Greek colonists, the city was located on the western, Aegean coast of Anatolia.
12 The prophet Mahomet's dreaded laws, i.e., the laws of Islam.

Acomat loves to court it with his wife
And in a pleasant quiet joys to pause;
But Selim[1] follows wars in dismal strife   85
And snatcheth at my crown with greedy claws.[2]
But he shall miss of that he aimeth at,
For I reserve it for my Acomat.
For Acomat? Alas, it cannot be.
Stern Selimus hath won my people's heart;   90
The Janissaries love him more than[3] me
And for his cause will suffer any smart.[4]
They see he is a friend to chivalry,[5]
And sooner will they from my faith[6] depart
And by strong hand, Bajazet, pull thee down   95
Than[7] let their Selim[8] hop without the crown.
Ah, if the soldiers overrule thy state
And nothing must be done without their will,
If every base and upstart runagate[9]
Shall cross a prince and overthwart[10] him still,   100
If Corcut, Selimus, and Acomat
With crowns and kingdoms shall their hungers fill,
Poor Bajazet, what then remains to thee
But the bare title of thy dignity?
Ay,[11] and unless thou do dissemble[12] all   105

---

1 Ed. (Grosart 2); Selmi Q.
2 The play's characterization of Bajazet's three sons follows Ashton
closely. "Selimus," writes Ashton, "was always accompted and tak-
en with the Janissars to be valiant and liberal and out of measure
desirous of war and enemy to peace, for the which qualities all the
soldiers loved him better than either Acomat, who, being Sanjack
[governor] of Amasia and Cappadocia, delighted more in ease and
pleasure than in battle and manly prowess, or Corcut, who, being
in Magnesia near unto the seaside of Rhodes, bestowed his time
and endeavour in the study of philosophy and knowledge of Mahometans' law and divinity" (sig. G5r).
3 Ed. (Grosart 2); then Q.
4 Hurt, pain.
5 Knights or horsemen equipped for battle (OED, n., 1).
6 I.e., faith or loyalty to me.
7 Ed. (Grosart 2); Then Q.
8 Ed. (Grosart 2); Selmi Q.
9 Rogue, vagabond, scoundrel.
10 Thwart, oppose, hinder (OED, v., 1a).
11 Ed. (Grosart 2); I Q.
12 Conceal, disguise.

And wink at Selimus' aspiring thought,
The bashaws[1] cruelly shall work thy fall,
And then thy empire is but dearly bought.
Ah, that our sons, thus to ambition thrall,[2]
Should set the law of Nature[3] all at naught!   110
But what must be cannot choose but be done.
Come, bashaws, enter. Bajazet hath done.

[*Mustaffa, Cherseoli, and the Janissaries enter*] *again.*

Cherseoli. Dread Emperor, long may you happy live,
Loved of your subjects and feared of your foes.
We wonder much what doth Your Highness grieve   115
That you will not unto your lords disclose.
Perhaps you fear lest we your loyal peers
Would prove disloyal to Your Majesty
And be rebellious in your dying years.
But, mighty prince, the heavens can testify   120
How dearly we esteem your safety.
    Mustaffa. Perhaps you think Mustaffa will revolt
And leave Your Grace and cleave to Selimus,
But sooner shall th'Almighty's thunderbolt
Strike me down to the cave tenebrious,[4]   125
The lowest land[5] and damned spirits' holt,[6]
Than[7] true Mustaffa prove so treacherous.
Your Majesty, then, needs not much to fear,
Since you are loved of subject, prince, and peer.

---

1 Lords, nobles, Ottoman governing elite.
2 Captive.
3 The law of Nature purportedly dictates that sons should reverence
   and obey their fathers. In his *French Academy* (1586), the French
   Christian humanist Pierre de La Primaudaye (1546–1629) asserts
   that "Nature, saith Plutarch, and the law which preserveth Nature,
   have given the first place of reverence and honour, after God, unto
   the father and mother, and men cannot do any service more acceptable to God than graciously and lovingly to pay to their parents that
   begot them and to them that brought them up the usury of new and
   old graces which they have lent them, as, contrawise, there is no
   sign of an Atheist more certain than for a man to set light by and to
   offend his parents" (537).
4 Dark. "The cave tenebrious" is hell.
5 Grosart 2 emends to "bank."
6 Woods, wooded hill (*OED*, n.1, 2a, 3).
7 Ed. (Grosart 2); Then Q.

First shall the sun rise from the Occident 130
And loose[1] his steeds benighted in the East,
First shall the sea become the continent,
Ere we forsake our sovereign's behest.[2]
We fought not for you 'gainst Persian's tent,
Breaking our lances on his sturdy crest, 135
We fought not for you 'gainst the Christian host,[3]
To become traitors after all our cost.
    Bajazet. Hear me, Mustaffa and Cherseoli:
I am a father of a headstrong brood,
Which, if I look not closely to myself, 140
Will seek to ruinate their father's state[4]
Even as the vipers in great Nero's fen
Eat[5] up the belly that first nourished them.[6]
You see the harvest of my life is past,
And agèd winter hath besprent[7] my head 145

---

1   Grosart 2 emends to "leave."
2   Command, injunction, bidding (*OED*, n.).
3   Army.
4   Position as Emperor (*OED*, n., 15a, b).
5   Grosart 2 emends to "Ate."
6   Paulo Giovio uses this image in his poetic eulogy on Bayezid II's reign. Ashton's translation does not contain the poem, but Richard Knolles in *The General History of the Turks* (1603) provides both the original and his own translation: "The cruel viper so brings forth her foul untimely brood, / Which eat and gnaw her belly out, their first and poisoned food" (497). According to Pliny, at birth vipers, unlike other snakes, "eat through the sides of their dam, and kill her" (*Natural History* 10.62). Nero's fen, according to Edward Sugden, is "[a] marsh near the city of Artaxata in Armenia, on the Araxes. The city was destroyed by Corbulo in 58 CE and rebuilt under the name of Neronia by Tiridates, to whom Nero had given the kingdom of Armenia" (*Topographical Dictionary* 362). Sugden notes that in these lines "[t]here is doubtless a reference to Nero's murder of his mother Agrippina" (362). The Roman Emperor Nero (r. 54–68 CE) murdered Agrippina in 59 CE in order to eliminate her as a political rival. Suetonius records that "being terrified with her threats and violent shrewdness, he determined to kill and dispatch her" and that "he ran in all haste to view the dead body of his mother when she was killed" and "handled every part and member of it, found fault with some, commended others, and, being thirsty in the meantime, took a draught of drink" (*Twelve Caesars* 196). "It is impossible," Greene declares in *The Card of Fancy* (1587), "for a man to sleep by the viper and not be envenomed" (Grosart 4.65).
7   Besprinkled.

With a hoar-frost of silver-coloured hairs,
The harbingers[1] of honourable eld;[2]
These branch-like veins, which once did guide[3] my arms
To toss the spear in battailous[4] array,
Now, withered up, have lost their former strength.　　　　150
My sons, whom now ambition 'gins to prick,
May take occasion of my weakened age
And rise in rebel arms against my state.
But stay, here comes a messenger to us.

Sound within.[5] Enters a Messenger.

　　Messenger. Health and good hap to Bajazet,　　　　155
The great commander of all Asia.
Selim[6] the Sultan of great Trebisond[7]
Sends me unto Your Grace to signify
His alliance[8] with the King of Tartary.
　　Bajazet. Said I not, lords, as much to you before,　　　160
That mine own sons would seek my overthrow?
And see, here comes a luckless messenger
To prove that true which my mind did foretell.
Does Selim make so small account of us
That he dare marry without our consent—　　　　165
And to that devil, too, of Tartary?
And could he then, unkind, so soon forget

1　Ed. (Grosart 2); harvingers Q.
2　Age.
3　Grosart 2 emends to "gird."
4　Ready for battle, warlike (*OED*, adj.).
5　According to Dessen and Thomson's *A Dictionary of Stage Directions in English Drama, 1580–1642*, the stage direction "sound" "occurs in over 450 stage directions typically as a verb to signal *sound* produced *within* (1) mostly for military signals, (2) sometimes for *music*" (208). "Within" indicates "the location of a *sound* or the presence of a figure *within* the tiring house and therefore offstage out of sight of the playgoer" (253).
6　Ed. (Grosart 2); Selmi Q.
7　Located on the southern coast of the Black Sea, the Byzantine city of Trabzon was captured by Mehmed II in 1461 (Imber 28). Its surrounding region then became a province of the Ottoman Empire. Previous to the action of the play, Bayezid had appointed Selimus the governor of the province.
8　Selimus cemented his alliance with the Crimean Tartars by marrying the Khan's daughter, Hafsa Hatun, in 1511 (Clot 26).

The injuries that Ramir did to me,
Thus to consort himself with him 'gainst me?
    Cherseoli. Your Majesty misconstrues[1] Selimus. 170
It cannot be that he in whose high thoughts
A map of many valours is enshrined
Should seek his father's ruin and decay.
Selimus is a prince of forward[2] hope,
Whose only name[3] affrights your enemies. 175
It cannot be he should prove false to you.
    Bajazet. Can it not be? Oh yes, Cherseoli,
For Selimus' hands do itch to have the crown,
And he will have it or else pull me down.
Is he a prince? Ah no, he is a sea 180
Into which run naught but ambitious reaches,[4]
Seditious complots, murder, fraud, and hate.
Could he not let his father know his mind,
But match himself when I least thought on it?
    Mustaffa. Perhaps my Lord Selimus loved the dame 185
And feared to certify[5] you of his love
Because her father was your enemy.
    Bajazet. In love, Mustaffa? Selimus in love?
If he be, lording, 'tis not lady's love
But love of rule and kingly sovereignty, 190
For wherefore[6] should he fear t'ask my consent?
Trusty Mustaffa, if he had feared me,
He never would have loved mine enemy.
But this his marriage with the Tartar's daughter
Is but the prologue to his cruelty, 195
And quickly shall we have the tragedy,
Which, though he act with meditated bravery,[7]
The world will never give him plaudity.[8]
What, yet more news?

---

1 Ed. (Grosart 2); misconsters Q.
2 Precocious, advanced, extreme (*OED*, adj., 7, 9).
3 I.e., name alone.
4 Schemes (*OED*, n.1, 15b).
5 Inform, notify.
6 Why.
7 Boldness, daring, defiance (*OED*, n., 1).
8 Applause.

Sound within. Enters another Messenger.

Messenger. Dread Emperor, Selimus is at hand.   200
Two hundred thousand strong Tartarians
Armed at all points does he lead with him,
Besides his followers from Trebisond.
    Bajazet. I thought so much of wicked Selimus.
Oh, forlorn hopes and hapless Bajazet!   205
Is duty then exiled from his breast,
Which Nature hath inscribed with golden pen
Deep in the hearts of honourable men?
Ah, Selim, Selim, wert thou not my son
But some strange, unacquainted foreigner   210
Whom I should honour as I honoured thee,
Yet would it grieve me even unto the death
If he should deal as thou hast dealt with me,
And thou, my son, to whom I freely gave
The mighty empire of great Trebisond,   215
Art too unnatural to requite me thus.
Good Alemshae, hadst thou lived till this day,
Thou wouldst have blushed at thy brother's mind.
Come, sweet Mustaffa, come, Cherseoli,
And with some good advice recomfort me.   220

Exeunt all.

[Scene 2
Selimus's camp in the environs of Adrianople]

Enter Selimus, Sinam Bashaw, Ottrante, Occhiali, and the soldiers.

Selimus. Now, Selimus, consider who thou art.
Long hast thou marched in disguised attire,
But now unmask thyself and play thy part,
And manifest the heat of thy desire.[1]
Nourish the coals of thine ambitious fire,   5

---

1 Entering the scene in shepherd's clothing, Tamburlaine begins Marlowe's *1 Tamburlaine* with a similar change of costume: "Lie here, ye
   weeds that I disdain to wear; / This complete armour and this cur-
   tle-axe / Are adjuncts more beseeming Tamburlaine" (1.2.41–43).

And think that then thy empire is most sure
When men for fear thy tyranny[1] endure.[2]
Think that to thee there is no worse reproach
Than[3] filial duty in so high a place.
Thou oughtst to set barrels of blood abroach[4]   10
And seek with sword whole kingdoms to displace.
Let Mahound's laws be locked up in their case,
And meaner men and of a baser spirit
In virtuous actions seek for glorious merit.
I count it sacrilege for to be holy   15
Or reverence this threadbare name of "good."[5]

---

1   Rooted in the political thought of Plato and Aristotle, Renaissance
    political theorists distinguished legitimate kings from tyrants on le-
    gal and psychological grounds. A tyrant was one who acquired sov-
    ereign power illegitimately or used it to abrogate the law in pursuit
    of his own personal pleasures and interests; governed by passion
    rather than reason, the tyrant was cruel, sexually excessive, and ef-
    feminate (Bushnell 36). In *Vindiciae contra Tyrannos: A Defence of
    Liberty against Tyrants* (1579; English translation 1648), Hugh Lan-
    quet writes that "the prince which applies himself to nothing but his
    peculiar profits and pleasures, or to those ends which most readily
    conduce thereunto, which contemns and perverts all laws, which
    useth his subjects more cruelly than the barbarest enemy would do,
    he may truly and really be called a tyrant, and that those which in
    this manner govern their kingdoms, be they never so large an ex-
    tent, are more properly unjust pillagers and freebooters than lawful
    governors" (234). La Primaudaye echoes Lanquet's definition in his
    French Academy (579). English Renaissance dramatists were heavily
    influenced by first-century CE Roman philosopher and dramatist
    Seneca's dramatization of the tyrant figure in his tragedies.
2   The "atheist" (246) Machiavellians hold that a prince "must cause
    himself to be feared rather than loved" (248), according to Inno-
    cent Gentillet's *Anti-Machiavel* (1576; English trans. 1602). In *The
    Prince*, Niccolò Machiavelli (1469–1527) explains that "Men worry
    less about doing an injury to one who makes himself loved than to
    one who makes himself feared. The bond of love is one which men,
    wretched creatures that they are, break when it is to their advantage
    to do so; but fear is strengthened by a dread of punishment which is
    always effective" (96–97).
3   Ed. (Grosart 2); Then Q.
4   Spilling out, flowing (*OED*, v.).
5   Machiavelli states that "a man who wants to act virtuously in every
    way necessarily comes to grief among so many who are not virtuous.
    Therefore if a prince wants to maintain his rule he must learn how
    not to be virtuous, and to make use of this or not according to need"
    (*The Prince* 91).

Leave to old men and babes that kind of folly;
Count it of equal value with the mud.
Make thou a passage for thy gushing flood
By slaughter, treason, or what else thou can,   20
And scorn religion: it disgraces man.[1]
My father Bajazet is weak and old
And hath not much above two years to live;
The Turkish crown of pearl and Ophir[2] gold[3]
He means to his dear Acomat to give.   25
But ere[4] his ship can to her haven drive,
I'll send abroad my tempests in such sort
That she shall sink before she get the port.
Alas, alas, His Highness' agèd head
Is not sufficient to support a crown.   30
Then, Selimus, take thou it in his stead,
And if at this thy boldness he dare frown
Or but resist thy will, then pull him down,
For since he hath so short a time t'enjoy it,
I'll make it shorter, or I will destroy him.[5]   35
Nor pass[6] I what our holy votaries[7]
Shall here object against my forward[8] mind.
I reck[9] not of their foolish ceremonies
But mean to take my fortune as I find.
Wisdom commands to follow tide and wind   40
And catch the front of swift Occasion[10]

---

1 Guise in Marlowe's *Massacre at Paris* (c. 1593) echoes this sentiment
  when he exclaims, "Religion: *O Diabole!* / Fie, I am ashamed, however that I seem, / To think a word of such a simple sound / Of so
  great matter should be made the ground" (2.66–69).
2 "A place of uncertain location ... famous for gold which was mined
  there" (*Oxford Dictionary of the Bible* 273).
3 In *1 Tamburlaine*, Theridamas praises the pleasures brought by
  wearing "a crown enchased with pearl and gold" (2.5.60).
4 Before.
5 Grosart 2 emends to "it."
6 Care.
7 Devout or religious people; monk, nun, or priest (*OED*, n., 1, 2, 3).
8 Bold, ambitious.
9 Ed. (Grosart 2); wreake Q. Reckon, care about, consider.
10 In Renaissance iconography Occasion, or opportunity, has hair only
  at the front of her head and therefore may be seized only as she approaches, not as she departs. Thus, in Geffrey Whitney's *A Choice of
  Emblems* (1586) an interlocutor asks Occasion why she is "behind all
  bald" (11), to which she replies "That none should hold, that let me
  slip before" (12).

Before she be too quickly overgone.
Some man will say I am too impious
Thus to lay siege against my father's life
And that I ought to follow virtuous   45
And godly sons; that virtue is a glass[1]
Wherein I may my errant life behold
And frame myself by it in ancient mould.[2]
Good sir, your wisdom's overflowing wit
Digs deep with learning's wonder-working spade.   50
Perhaps you think that now, forsooth,[3] you sit
With some grave wizard in a prattling shade.
Avaunt,[4] such glasses! Let them view in me
The perfect picture of right tyranny.[5]
I like a lion's look not worth a leek[6]   55
When every dog deprives him of his prey.
These honest terms are far enough to seek
When angry Fortune menaceth decay.
My resolution treads a nearer way:
Give me the heart conspiring with the hand   60
In such a cause my father to withstand.
Is he my father? Why, I am his son.
I owe no more to him than[7] he to me.
If he proceed as he hath now begun
And pass from me the Turkish seigniory   65
To Acomat, then Selimus is free,
And if he injure me that am his son,
Faith,[8] all the love 'twixt him and me is done.

---

1 Mirror.
2 Pattern.
3 Truly (*OED*, adv.).
4 Go away, depart.
5 The play here echoes the mirror metaphor with which Marlowe introduces *1 Tamburlaine* (first performed 1587): "View but his [Tamburlaine's] picture in this tragic glass / And then applaud his fortunes as you please" (Prologue 7–8), the Prologue tells the audience.
6 "A culinary herb, *Allium Porrum* (family Liliaceae), allied to the onion, but differing from it in having the bulbous part cylindrical and the leaves flat and broad" (*OED*, n., 1). The leek was used proverbially as something possessing little value (*OED*, n., 3). The fickle lover Pharicles in Greene's Euphuistic prose romance *Mamillia* (1583) "fried at every fire and changed his look at every leek" (Grosart 2.77).
7 Ed. (Grosart 2); then Q.
8 A mild oath.

But for[1] I see the schoolmen[2] are prepared
To plant 'gainst me their bookish ordinance,[3]   70
I mean to stand on a sententious[4] guard
And without any far-fetched circumstance
Quickly unfold mine own opinion
To arm my heart with irreligion.
When first this circled round,[5] this building fair,   75
Some god took out of the confusèd mass
(What god I do not know nor greatly care),
Then every man of his own dition[6] was,
And everyone his life in peace did pass.
War was not then, and riches were not known,   80
And no man said, "this, or this, is mine own."
The ploughman with a furrow did not mark
How far his great possessions did reach.
The earth knew not the share,[7] nor seas the bark.[8]
The soldiers entered not the battered breach,   85
Nor trumpets the tantara[9] loud did teach.
There needed them no judge nor yet no law,
Nor any king of whom to stand in awe.[10]
But after Ninus,[11] warlike Belus' son,

---

1 Because.
2 University men, academics, scholars.
3 Regulations, laws; metaphorically, ordnance, cannons.
4 Learned, aphoristic, moralizing, wise (*OED*, adj., 1, 2, 3).
5 Globe.
6 Rule, command, judgement (*OED*, n., 1).
7 Ploughshare.
8 Boat, ship.
9 Battle alarms, bugle, drum or trumpet calls (*OED*).
10 Lines 75 to 88 offer a condensed version of the classical myth of the
   Golden Age, in which "There was no fear of punishment, there was
   no threatening law / In brazen tables nailed, to keep the folk in awe. /
   There was no man would crouch or creep to judge with cap in hand,
   / They lived safe without a judge in every realm and land. / The lofty
   pine tree was not hewn from mountains where it stood, / In seeking
   strange and foreign lands, to rove upon the flood. / Men knew none
   other countries yet, than where themselves did keep: / There was no
   town enclosed yet with walls and ditches deep. / No horn nor trumpet was in use, no sword nor helmet worn, / The world was such that
   soldiers' help might easily be forborne. / The fertile earth as yet was
   free, untouched of spade or plough, / And yet it yielded of itself of
   everything enough" (Ovid, *Metamorphoses* 1.105–16).
11 The first king of the ancient Assyrian empire, who, according to
   Diodorus Siculus, conquered Babylonia and therein (*continued*)

The earth with unknown armour did warray,[1]   90
Then first the sacred name of king begun,
And things that were as common as the day
Did then to set possessors first obey.
Then they established laws and holy rites
To maintain peace and govern bloody fights.   95
Then some sage man, above the vulgar wise,
Knowing that laws could not in quiet dwell
Unless they were observed, did first devise
The names of gods, religion, heaven, and hell,
And 'gan of pains and feigned rewards to tell: 100
Pains for those men which did neglect the law;
Rewards for those that lived in quiet awe.
Whereas indeed they were mere fictions—
And if they were not, Selim thinks they were,
And these religious[2] observations   105
Only bugbears to keep the world in fear
And make men quietly a yoke to bear,
So that religion, of itself a bauble,[3]
Was only found to make us peaceable.[4]

---

founded a great city named after himself, Ninus (or Nineveh) (*Library of History* II.1–4). According to Diodorus, Belus, the name of Ninus' father, was also the Babylonian name for Zeus (*Library of History* II.8). In the Renaissance Ninus is often presented as an archetypal tyrant figure.

1 "To make war upon, ravage by war" (*OED*, v., 1a). Grosart 2 emends to "array."

2 Ed. (Grosart 2); religions Q.

3 Trinket. At the beginning of Marlowe's *The Jew of Malta*, Machevill tells the audience that "I count religion but a childish toy" (Prologue 14).

4 In *The Discourses*, Machiavelli offers Rome as a specific example of the ideas Selimus expresses in lines 96–109. Romulus, Rome's founding figure, established Rome by military force (like Ninus). His successor, Numa Pompilius, "finding a very savage people, and wishing to reduce them to civil obedience by the arts of peace, had recourse to religion as the most necessary and assured support of any civil society" (146). Machiavelli then concludes that "[i]t is therefore the duty of princes and heads of republics to uphold the foundations of the religion of their countries, for then it is easy to keep their people religious, and consequently well conducted and united" (150). La Primaudaye makes the same point even more forcefully: "Religion surely is the foundation of all commonwealths, of the execution of laws, of the obedience of subjects towards their magistrates, of their fear towards princes, of mutual love among themselves, and of justice towards others" (576).

Hence in especial come the foolish names   110
Of father, mother, brother, and such like,
For who so well his cogitation frames
Shall find they serve but only for to strike
Into our minds a certain kind of love,
For these names too are but a policy[1]   115
To keep the quiet of society.
Indeed, I must confess they are not bad
Because they keep the baser sort in fear,
But we whose mind in heavenly thoughts is clad,
Whose body doth a glorious spirit bear   120
That hath no bounds but flieth everywhere,
Why should we seek to make that soul a slave
To which Dame Nature so large freedom gave?[2]
Amongst us men there is some difference
Of actions, termed by us "good" or "ill,"   125
As he that doth his father recompense
Differs from him that doth his father kill.
And yet I think—think others[3] what they will—
That parricides, when death hath given them rest,
Shall have as good a part as[4] the rest—   130
And that's just nothing, for, as I suppose,
In Death's void kingdom reigns eternal night,
Secure of evil and secure of foes,
Where nothing doth the wicked man affright,
No more than[5] him that dies in doing right.[6]   135

---

1 "Policy," writes La Primaudaye, "signifieth the regiment of a city or
   commonwealth and that which the Grecians call political government [and] the Latins call the government of a commonwealth or of
   a civil society" (577).
2 "Nature, that framed us of four elements, / Warring within our
   breasts for regiment, / Doth teach us all to have aspiring minds"
   (1.2.7.18–20), Tamburlaine declaims, and "Our souls" (21) are "always moving as the restless spheres" (25) and "never rest / Until we
   reach the ripest fruit of all, / That perfect bliss and sole felicity, / The
   sweet fruition of an earthly crown" (26–29).
3 Ed. (Grosart 2); other Q.
4 Grosart 2 emends to "as have."
5 Ed. (Grosart 2); then Q.
6 John William Cunliffe suggests that the atheistic ideas expressed
   in lines 128 to 135 evince the influence of Seneca's tragedy *Troades* ("The Trojan Women"), specifically the Chorus with which the
   second act concludes (*The Influence of Seneca on Elizabethan Tragedy* 64). In Jasper Heywood's 1559 translation, the (*continued*)

Then since in death nothing shall to us fall,
Here while I live, I'll have a snatch at all,[1]
And that can never, never be attained
Unless old Bajazet do die the death.
For long enough the greybeard now hath reigned   140
And lived at ease while others lived uneath,[2]
And now it's time he should resign his breath.
'Twere good for him if he were pressèd out;
'Twould bring him rest and rid him of his gout.
Resolved to do it, cast to compass[3] it   145
Without delay or long procrastination.
It argueth an unmanured[4] wit,
When all is ready for so strong invasion,
To draw out time; an unlooked-for mutation[5]
May soon prevent us if we do delay;   150
Quick speed is good where wisdom leads the way.[6]
Occhiali?
    Occhiali. My lord.
    Selimus. Lo, fly, boy, to my father Bajazet
And tell him Selim his obedient son   155
Desires to speak with him and kiss his hands.

Chorus declaims, "Lay down your hope, that wait here aught to win;
/ And who dreads aught, cast off thy careful cark. / Wilt thou it wot,
what state thou shalt be in / When dead? Thou art as thou hadst
never been" (69). The Chorus then adds, "Death hurts the corpse
and spareth not the sprite. / And, as for all the dens of Taenar deep,
/ With Cerberus' kingdom dark that knows no light, / And straitest
gates that he there sits to keep, / They fancies are, that follow folk by
sleep. / Such rumors vain, but feignèd lies they are, / And fables, like
the dreams in heavy care" (69).

1 According to Gentillet, "there is no wickedness in the world so
strange and detestable but they [Machiavellians] will enterprise,
invent, and put it into execution, if they can" because "they are
atheists, contemners of God, neither believing there is a God which
seeth what they do nor that ought to punish them" (249).

2 Not easily, with difficulty (*OED*, adv.).

3 Accomplish.

4 Uncultivated, unfertilized (*OED*, adj.).

5 Change (in circumstances).

6 Lines 145–51 paraphrase Ashton's summary of one of Selimus's
"common sayings": "[H]e is not worthy to be called wise that will
not shortly dispatch that thing which he has once decreed to do, for
because that, through delaying long of and lingering, the good occasion ofttimes is lost and a let, perchance contrary to your intent and
purpose, may hap in the meantime to rise" (sig. N2v).

Tell him I long to see his gracious face
And that I come with all my chivalry
To chase the Christians from his seigniory.
In any wise, say I must speak with him. 160

Exit Occhiali.

Now, Sinam, if I speed—
    Sinam.   What then, my lord?
    Selimus. What then? Why, Sinam, thou art nothing worth!
I will endeavour to persuade him, man,
To give the empire over unto me.
Perhaps I shall attain it at his hands; 165
If I cannot, this right hand is resolved
To end the period[1] with a fatal stab.
    Sinam. My gracious lord, give Sinam leave to speak.
If you resolve to work your father's death,
You venture life. Think you the Janissaries 170
Will suffer you to kill him in their sight
And let you pass free without punishment?
    Selimus. If I resolve? As sure as heaven is heaven,
I mean to see him dead or myself king.
As for the bashaws, they are all my friends 175
And, I am sure, would pawn their dearest blood
That Selim might be Emperor of Turks.
    Sinam. Yet Acomat and Corcut both survive
To be revengèd for their father's death.
    Selimus. Sinam, if they or twenty such as they 180
Had twenty several[2] armies in the field,
If Selimus were once your emperor,
I'd dart abroad the thunderbolts of war
And mow their heartless squadrons to the ground.[3]

---

1 Sentence (*OED*, n., 16a).
2 Separate, distinct (*OED*, adj., 1).
3 In his *French Academy*, La Primaudaye opens his chapter on the educa-
    tion of a prince with a discussion of differing types of royal succession
    and describes commonwealths in which "either he is preferred that is
    fittest to govern or he that is most warlike and in greatest favour with
    the soldiers, as, in Turkey, Selim the first of that name, being the third
    and youngest son of Bajazet the Second, usurped the empire by the aid
    of the Janissaries upon his father, whom he caused to be poisoned, and
    slew Acomat and Corcut his two elder brothers, with all his nephews
    and others of Ottoman's race, saying that nothing was pleasanter than
    to rule when all fear of kindred was taken away" (642).

Sinam. Oh yet, my lord, after Your Highness' death 185
There is a hell and a revenging God.
   Selimus. Tush, Sinam, these are school conditions[1]
To fear the Devil or his cursèd dam.[2]
Thinkst thou I care for apparitions,
Of Sisyphus and of his backward stone,[3] 190
And poor Ixion's lamentable moan?[4]
Now,[5] I think the cave of damnèd ghosts
Is but a tale to terrify young babes,
Like devils' faces scored[6] on painted posts
Or feignèd circles in our astrolabes.[7] 195
Why, there's no difference when we are dead,

---

1 Rules, morals (*OED*, n., 5, 11). In "Of the Education of a Prince
  in Good Manners and Conditions," La Primaudaye writes that the
  tutor of a prince "must persuade him that whatsoever is taught in
  the law of God belongeth to none so much as to the prince and that
  as he is to reign by him so likewise it belongeth to his office to reign
  according to His will, that he may enjoy prosperity in this world and
  eternal felicity in the blessed life to come" (*French Academy* 646).
  The tutor should persuade his charge that "dignity, greatness and
  majesty are not to be sought after by the help of Fortune or by human means but by wisdom, integrity of life and manners, and by
  virtuous and noble deeds. Plato saith, not without cause, that a commonwealth will never be happy until princes play the philosophers
  or philosophers take the rudder of the empire in hand" (646).
2 Mother (*OED*, n.2, 3). The Devil and his dam were a proverbial
  combination (Tilley D225).
3 Having incurred the anger of Jove, Sisyphus was condemned forever
  to roll a boulder up a hill in Hades; as Sisyphus reached the top of
  the hill, the boulder would always escape Sisyphus's grasp and roll
  back down, forcing Sisyphus endlessly to repeat the task (Grimal
  422).
4 For having attempted to rape Juno, Jove chained Ixion "to a burning
  wheel which rotated continuously" (Grimal 240). In Greene's *Orlando Furioso* (1594), Orlando threatens his page with "the torments
  that Ixion feels" and "the rolling stone" (sig. F1r) if he does not find
  Orlando's beloved, Angelica.
5 Grosart 2 emends to "No no."
6 Drawn, etched, carved.
7 "Any of various portable instruments formerly used for making
  astronomical measurements, esp. the altitudes of celestial objects,
  typically taking the form of a graduated metal disc with rotating
  parts and a sighting arm" (*OED*, n.). In his *Exercises* (1597), Thomas
  Blundeville defines the astrolabe as "the instrument of the stars, by
  help whereof the manifold motions and appearances of the heavens
  and of the stars therein contained are known" (sig. Pp1v).

And death once come, then all alike are sped.[1]
Or if there were, as I can scarce believe,
A heaven of joy and hell of endless pain,
Yet, by my soul, it never should me grieve, 200
So I might on the Turkish Empire reign,
To enter hell and leave[2] fair heaven's gain.
An empire, Sinam, is so sweet a thing,
As I could be a devil to be a king.[3]
But go we, lords, and solace[4] in our camp 205
Till the return of young Occhiali,
And if his answer be to thy desire,
Selim, thy mind in kingly thoughts attire.

Exeunt all.

[Scene 3
Bajazet's court in Adrianople]

Enter Bajazet, Mustaffa, Cherseoli, Occhiali, and the Janissaries.

Bajazet. Even as the great Egyptian crocodile,
Wanting[5] his prey, with artificial tears[6]
And feignèd plaints his subtle tongue doth file[7]
T'entrap the silly[8] wand'ring traveller
And move him to advance his footing near, 5
That,[9] when he is in danger of his claws,
He may devour him with his famished jaws,
So playeth crafty Selimus with me.

---

1 Finished, dispatched, terminated (*OED*, v., 8, 9).
2 Ed. (Grosart 2); leane on Q.
3 "A god is not so glorious as a king," declares Theridamas in Marlowe's *1 Tamburlaine*, "I think the pleasure they enjoy in heaven /
   Cannot compare with kingly joys in earth" (2.5.57–59).
4 Relax, entertain ourselves (*OED*, v., 3).
5 Lacking.
6 Crocodile tears were proverbial (Tilley C831). In *Mamillia*, Greene
   describes lovers who, to seduce a woman, "fall with the crocodile
   to their feigned tears, seeking with dissembled sighs and sobs ... to
   move her to take pity of their plaint, whom after with greedy grips
   they bring to utter ruin and decay" (Grosart 2.261).
7 Smoothe.
8 Defenceless, weak, innocent, ignorant, foolish (*OED*, adj., 2b, 3b,
   5a, 6a).
9 So that.

His haughty thoughts still wait on diadems,
And not a step but treads to majesty.   10
The phoenix[1] gazeth on the sun's bright beams;
The echinaeis[2] swims against the streams.[3]
Naught but the Turkish sceptre can him please,
And there, I know, lieth his chief disease.[4]
He sends his messenger to crave access   15
And says he longs to kiss my agèd hands,
But, howsoever he in show profess,
His meaning with his words but weakly stands,
And sooner will the Syrtis' boiling sands[5]
Become a quiet road[6] for fleeting ships   20
Than[7] Selimus' heart agree with Selim's lips.
Too well I know the crocodile's feigned tears
Are but[8] nets wherein to catch his prey,
Which who so moved with foolish pity hears
Will be the author of his own decay.[9]   25
Then hie thee, Bajazet, from hence away:
A fawning monster is false Selimus,
Whose fairest words are most pernicious.
Young man, would Selim come and speak with us?
What is his message to us, canst thou tell?   30
    Occhiali. He craves, my lord, another seigniory,

---

1 See p. 133, note 3.
2 According to Pliny, the fish echinaeis is "a foot long and five fingers
  thick" and "oftentimes it stayeth a ship" by leeching onto it (*Natural
  History* 9.25).
3 "In vain it is, to strive against the stream," Medea advises Iphigenia in Greene's *Alphonsus King of Aragon* (1599), "Fates must be followed, and the gods' decree / Must needs take place in every kind of
  cause" (sig. E4v). If his comparison of Selimus to the phoenix star-
  ing at the sun suggests the degree of Selimus's boldness, Bajazet's
  comparison of Selimus to the echinaeis measures the extent of Selimus's defiance. In *England's Parnassus*, Allott reproduces lines 11
  and 12 under the heading "Phoenix" and attributes them to "R.
  Greene" (sig. Kk5v) (Gilbert 4).
4 Disquiet, annoyance, discomfort (*OED*, n., 1a).
5 The Syrtis are "two great gulfs on the north coast of Africa, south of
  Sicily, much feared by sailors on account of treacherous sand banks"
  (*Oxford Dictionary of the Bible* 347).
6 Sheltered anchorage near a shore, roadstead (*OED*, n., 3a).
7 Ed. (Grosart 2); Then Q.
8 Grosart 2 emends to "but the."
9 See p. 71, note 6.

Nearer to you and to the Christians,
That he may make them know that Selimus
Is born to be a scourge[1] unto them all.
    Bajazet. He's born to be a scourge to me and mine.   35
He never would have come with such an host
Unless he meant my state to undermine.
What though in word he bravely seem to boast
The foraging of all the Christian coast?
Yet we have cause to fear when burning brands[2]   40
Are vainly given into a madman's hands.
Well, I must seem to wink at his desire,
Although I see it plainer than[3] the light.
My lenity[4] adds fuel to his fire,
Which now begins to break in flashing bright.   45
Then, Bajazet, chastise his stubborn sprite,
Lest these small sparkles grow to such a flame
As shall consume thee and thy house's name.
Alas, I spare when all my store[5] is gone
And thrust my sickle where the corn[6] is reaped.   50
In vain I send for the physician
When on the patient is his grave-dust heaped.
In vain, now all his veins, in venom steeped,
Break out in blisters that will poison us,
We seek to give him an antidotus.   55
He that will stop the brook must then begin
When summer's heat hath dried up his spring
And when his pittering streams are low and thin,
For let the winter aid unto him bring,
He grows to be of watery floods the king,   60
And though you dam him up with lofty ranks,[7]
Yet will he quickly overflow his banks.[8]
Messenger, go and tell young Selimus

---

1 Whip, punishment.
2 Torches.
3 Ed. (Grosart 2); then Q.
4 Mildness, gentleness, mercifulness (*OED*, n.).
5 Stock.
6 Grain.
7 Positions, titles, honours.
8 In *England's Parnassus*, Allott reproduces lines 56 to 62 under the heading of "Delay" and attributes them to "R. Greene" (sig. E4r) (Grosart 2 x).

We give to him all great Samandria,[1]
Bordering on Belgrade of Hungaria,   65
Where he may plague those Christian runagates,[2]
And salve the wounds that they have given our states.
Cherseoli,[3] go and provide a gift,
A royal present for my Selimus,
And tell him, messenger, another time   70
He shall have talk enough with Bajazet.

                                        Exeunt Cherseoli and Occhiali.

And now, what counsel gives Mustaffa to us?
I fear this hasty reckoning will undo us.
    Mustaffa. Make haste, my lord, from Adrianople's[4] walls,
And let us fly to fair Byzantium,[5]   75
Lest if your son before you take the town,
He may with little labour win the crown.
    Bajazet. Then do so, good Mustaffa. Call our guard
And gather all our warlike Janissaries:
Our chiefest aid is swift celerity.[6]   80
Then let our wingèd coursers[7] tread the wind
And leave rebellious Selimus behind.

                                                    Exeunt all.

                            [Scene 4
           Selimus's camp in the environs of Adrianople]

Enter Selimus, Sinam, Occhiali, Ottrante, and their soldiers.

    Selimus. And is his answer so, Occhiali?
Is Selim such a corsive[8] to his heart
That he cannot endure the sight of him?
Forsooth, he gives thee all Samandria,

---

1 Semendra, a city and region in Serbia (Finkel 100; Shaw xiv–xv).
2 Ed. (Grosart 2); runnages Q.
3 Ed. (Grosart 2); *Cherseo* Q, set as a speech heading.
4 Ed. (Grosart 2); *Andrinople* Q. Andrinople is Ashton's spelling.
5 Constantinople, modern Istanbul.
6 Speed.
7 "Large, powerful horses ridden in battle and tournament" (*OED*, n.2, 1a).
8 Corrosive.

From whence our mighty Emperor Mahomet 5
Was driven to his country back with shame.[1]
No doubt thy father loves thee, Selimus,
To make thee regent of so great a land—
Which is not yet his own, or, if it were,
What dangers wait on him that should it steer! 10
Here the Polonian, he comes hurtling in
Under the conduct of some foreign prince[2]
To fight in honour of his crucifix.
Here the Hungarian with his bloody cross
Deals blows about to win Belgrade again.[3] 15
And after all, forsooth, Basilius,[4]
The mighty Emperor of Russia,
Sends in his troops of slave-born Muscovites,
And he will share with us or else take all.
In giving such a land so full of strife, 20
His meaning is to rid me of my life.
Now, by the dreaded name of Termagant[5]
And by the blackest brook[6] in loathsome hell,
Since he is so unnatural to me,
I will prove as unnatural as he. 25
Thinks he to stop my mouth with gold or pearl?
Or rusty[7] jades[8] fetched from Barbaria?[9]

---

1 In 1454 Mehmed II beseiged, but failed to capture, the city of Samandria, an obstacle between the Ottomans and Belgrade, which
   Mehmed beseiged by an alternative route in 1456 (Finkel 59).
2 Polish monarchs were elected, often from the ranks of high European aristocracy.
3 The Ottomans besieged Belgrade in 1440 and 1456 but did not capture it until 1521 (Imber 22, 26, 42).
4 Basil III (r. 1505–33).
5 Medieval and early modern writers often claimed that Muslims
   worshipped (at least) three gods: Mahound (Muhammad), Apollin
   (Apollo), and Termagant (Chew 389).
6 Hades has five rivers: Acheron, Cocytus, Lethe, Phleghethon, and
   Styx (Grimal 4, 257, 428).
7 Fat, stale, rancid (*OED*, adj.2).
8 "A horse of inferior breed" (*OED*, n.1, 1a).
9 The north coastal region of Africa, known as the Barbary Coast.
   Ortelius describes it thus: Africa is divided "into four chief parts:
   Barbary, Numidia, Libya, and the land of *Negros. Barbary*, which is
   accounted the best, they circumscribe with the Atlantic and Mediterranean seas, with mount *Atlas*, and with the region of *Barcha*
   bordering upon *Egypt*" (fol. 4). Later Ortelius adds (*continued*)

No, let his minion,[1] his philosopher,
Corcut and Acomat, be enriched with them.
I will not take my rest till this right hand   30
Hath pulled the crown from off his coward's head
And on the ground his bastards'[2] gore-blood shed.
Nor shall his flight to old Byzantium
Dismay my thoughts, which never learned to stoop.
March, Sinam, march in order after him!   35
Were his light steeds as swift as Pegasus[3]
And trod the airy pavement with their heels,
Yet Selimus would overtake them soon,
And though the heavens do ne'er so crossly frown,
In spite of heaven shall Selim wear the crown.   40

Exeunt.

[Scene 5
Çorlu[4]]

*Alarum[5] within. Enter Bajazet, Mustaffa, Cherseoli and the
Janissaries at one door, Selimus, Sinam, Ottrante, Occhiali, and
their soldiers at another.*

Bajazet. Is this thy duty, son, unto thy father—
So impiously to level[6] at his life?
Can thy soul, wallowing in ambitious mire,

---

that "Barbaria" is "divided into four kingdoms ... namely, *Morocco,
Fess, Telesine,* and *Tunis*" (fol. 114). The Barbary Coast was noted for
its swift horses and its pirates.
1 Favourite.
2 Ed. (Vitkus); bastards Q.
3 In classical myth, the winged horse who was born from Medusa's
   neck after Perseus cut her head off (Grimal 349).
4 Ashton narrates that "[n]ow was Bayazet come to Ciorle, which
   town is almost in the midway between Andrinople and Constantinople, when as lo the Tartarians with other ambushments of Selimus'
   horsemen (which were laid abroad in the plain) advanced themselves
   and by and by set upon Bayazet" (sig. G6r). The confrontation between Bajazet and Selimus at Çorlu took place in August 1511 (Finkel 101).
5 "[W]idely used signal ... for a call to *arms* in the form of *sound* produced offstage before and during a *battle*" (Dessen and Thomson 3).
6 Aim.

Seek for to reave[1] that breast with bloody knife
From whence thou hadst thy being, Selimus?   5
Was this the end for which thou join'dst thyself
With that mischievous traitor Ramirchan?
Was this thy drift to speak with Bajazet?
Well hoped I—but hope, I see, is vain—
Thou wouldst have been a comfort to mine age,   10
A scourge and terror[2] to mine enemies;
That this thy coming with so great an host
Was for no other purpose and intent
Than[3] for to chastise those base Christians
Which spoil my subjects' wealth with fire and sword.   15
Well hoped I the rule of Trebisond
Would have increased the valour of thy mind
To turn thy strength upon the[4] Persians,
But thou, like to a crafty polypus,[5]
Doest turn thy hungry jaws upon thyself,   20
For what am I, Selimus, but thyself?
When courage first crept in thy manly breast
And thou beganst to rule the martial sword,
How oft said thou the sun should change his course,
Water should turn to earth, and earth to heaven,   .   25
Ere thou wouldst prove disloyal to thy father!
O Titan,[6] turn thy breathless coursers back,
And enterprise[7] thy journey from the East;
Blush, Selim, that the world should say of thee
That by my death thou gain'dst the empery.[8]   30

---

1 Plunder, pillage, sack (*OED*, v.1, 1, 2).
2 Tamburlaine calls himself "the Scourge and Wrath of God, / The
   only fear and terror of the world" (1.3.3.44–45).
3 Ed. (Grosart 2); Then Q.
4 Ed. (Grosart 2); thy Q.
5 Greene's natural lore here is unusual. "Polypus" is Aristotle's name
   for the octopus (*OED*, n., 2), and in his prose works Greene most
   commonly refers to the polypus's ability to change colour and shape.
   In *Mamillia*, for example, Greene refers to male seducers who "with
   the polipe change themselves into the likeness of every object" (Grosart 2.257).
6 The Titans preceded the Olympian gods in classical myth. Helios
   was the Titan sun god.
7 Undertake.
8 Empire.

Selimus. Now let my cause be pleaded, Bajazet—
For father I disdain to call thee now.
I took not arms to seize upon thy crown,
For that, if once thou hadst been laid in grave,
Should sit upon the head of Selimus   35
In spite of Corcut and[1] Acomat.
I took not arms to take away thy life:
The remnant of thy days is but a span,
And foolish had I been to enterprise
That which the gout and death would do for me.   40
I took not arms to shed my brothers'[2] blood
Because they stop my passage to the crown,
For while thou liv'st Selimus is content
That they should live, but when thou once art dead
Which of them both dares Selimus withstand?   45
I soon should hew their bodies in piecemeal,
As easy as a man would kill a gnat.[3]
But I took arms unkind[4] to honour thee
And win again the fame that thou hast lost.
And thou thoughtst scorn Selim should speak with thee![5]   50
But had it been your darling Acomat,
You would have met him half the way yourself.
I am a prince, and, though your younger[6] son,
Yet are my merits better than[7] both theirs.
But you do seek to disinherit me,   55
And mean t'invest Acomat with your crown,
So he shall have a prince's due reward
That cannot show a scar received in field.
We that have fought with mighty Prester John[8]

---

1 Grosart 2 emends to "and of."
2 Ed. (Grosart 2); brothers Q.
3 Bloodthirsty though they may be, the sentiments Selimus expresses
   in lines 43 to 47 accord with the fratricidal law of succession established by Bayezid II's father Mehmed II, who decreed that upon his
   death an emperor's sons would have to battle it out with each other
   to determine who would succeed him (Finkel 38–39, 71). Neither
   seniority nor election by the deceased emperor was determinative.
4 Against kindred, unnatural.
5 wit Q BPL F HU 1 UI VAM 2 BD 2.
6 Youngest.
7 Ed. (Grosart 2); then Q.
8 Legendary priestly ruler over a Christian nation located in various
   parts of the world. According to Ortelius, "This *Prester John*, out of

And stripped th'Egyptian Sultan[1] of his camp,   60
Venturing life and living to honour thee,
For that same cause shall now dishonoured be.
Art thou a father? Nay, false Bajazet,
Disclaim the title which thou doest not merit.
A father would not thus flee from his son   65
As thou doest fly from loyal Selimus.
A father would not injure thus his son
As thou doest injure loyal Selimus.
Then, Bajazet, prepare thee to the fight.
Selimus, once thy son, but now thy foe,   70
Will make his fortunes by the sword,[2]
And, since thou fearst as long as I do live,
I'll also fear as long as thou doest live.

Exit Selimus and his company.

Bajazet. My heart is overwhelmed with fear and grief.
What dismal comet blazèd at my birth,[3]   75
Whose influence[4] makes my strong, unbridled sons
Instead of love to render hate to me?
Ah, bashaws, if that ever heretofore
Your emperor owed his safety unto you,
Defend me now 'gainst my unnatural son.   80
Non timeo mortem: mortis mihi displicet auctor.[5]

Exit Bajazet and his company.

---

   doubt, in this our age, is one of the greatest monarchs of the world,
whose kingdom lying between the two tropics, reacheth from the
Red Sea almost unto the Ethiopian ocean" (fol. 113).

1 Qansuh II Al-Ghawri (r. 1501–16) (Imber 40).

2 Grosart 2 adds "and shield" in order to render the line regular iambic pentameter.

3· In *Mamillia*, the enemies of the prodigal Pharicles interpret his
prodigality and expensive clothes as the "two blazing stars and careful comets which did always prognosticate [that] some such event
[Pharicles' ruin] should happen" (Grosart 2.150).

4 Power.

5 "I do not fear death. It is the author of my death who displeases
me" (Latin), an adaptation of lines 492–93 of Book VIII of Ovid's
Metamorphoses, "meruisse fatemur / illum, cur pereat; mortis mihi
displicet auctor," which Golding translates as "His tresspass I confess deserves the stopping of his breath: / But yet I do not like that I
be the author of his death" (639–40).

[Scene 6
Battlefield around Çorlu]

Alarum. Mustaffa beat[s] Selimus in, then Ottrante and Cherseoli
enter at diverse¹ doors.

Cherseoli. Yield thee, Tartarian, or thou shalt die.
Upon my sword's sharp point standeth pale Death²
Ready to rive³ in two thy caitiff⁴ breast.
  Ottrante. Art thou that knight that like a lion fierce
Tiring his stomach on a flock of lambs   5
Hast broke our ranks and put them clean⁵ to flight?
  Cherseoli. Ay,⁶ and unless thou look unto thyself,
This sword here,⁷ drunk in the Tartarian blood,
Shall make thy carcass as the outcast dung.
  Ottrante. Nay, I have matched a braver knight than⁸ you,   10
Strong Alemshae, thy master's eldest son,
Leaving his body naked on the plains,
And, Turk, the selfsame end for thee remains.

They fight. He [Ottrante] killeth Cherseoli and flieth.

[Scene 7
Battlefield around Çorlu]

Alarum. Enter Selimus.

Selimus. Shall Selim's hope be buried in the dust,
And Bajazet triumph over his fall?
Then, O thou blindful mistress of mishap,

---

1 Different.
2 "Behold my sword. What see you at the point?" (1.5.2.45), Tamburlaine asks the Virgins of Damascus before commanding his soldiers to slaughter them. "[T]here sits imperious Death" (48), he tells
   them.
3 Tear apart (*OED*, v.1, 1a).
4 Base, worthless, wretched (*OED*, adj., 3).
5 Completely.
6 Ed. (Grosart 2); I Q.
7 Ed. (Grosart 2); nere Q.
8 Ed. (Grosart 2); then Q.

Chief patroness of Rhamnus'[1] golden gates,[2]
I will advance my strong, revenging hand   5
And pluck thee from thy ever-turning wheel.[3]
Mars,[4] or Minerva,[5] Mahound, Termagant,
Or whosoe'er you are that fight 'gainst me,
Come and but show yourselves before my face,
And I will rend you all like trembling reeds.   10
Well, Bajazet, though Fortune smile on thee
And deck thy camp with glorious victory,
Though Selimus, now conquerèd by thee,
Is fain[6] to put his safety in swift flight,
Yet so he flies that, like an angry ram,   15
He'll turn more fiercely than[7] before he came.

Exit Selimus.

---

1 Ed.; Rhamus Q.
2 Rhamnus, in Greece, was the site of a temple dedicated to Nemesis, the goddess of destiny. According to classical writer Pausanius, the Greeks carved the temple's statue of Nemesis after they defeated the Persians at the battle of Marathon (490 BCE), from a block of marble the overconfident Persians had brought to the battle with them with the intention of carving from it a monument to their victory (*Description of Greece* I.33.2). In *1 Tamburlaine*, the similarly over-confident Cosroe declares that "she that rules in Rhamnus' golden gates / And makes a passage for all prosperous arms / Shall make me solely Emperor of Asia" (2.3.37–39). In *Locrine* (1595), Hubba imprecates "she that rules fair Rhamnus' golden gate" to "Grant us the honour of the victory" (sig. C3r).
3 Selimus seems to be conflating Nemesis with Fortune. Fortune with her wheel, upon which she turns human life, was a common image in the Renaissance. La Primaudaye writes that "They that have laboured most in painting out this feigned goddess ... put a wheel into her hands, which she turneth about continually, whereby that part which is above is presently turned downward, thereby giving us to understand that from her highest preferment she throweth down in one instant such as are most happy into the gulf of misery" (472). Machiavelli advises that "Fortune is a woman, and it is necessary, if you wish to master her, to conquer her by force" (*The Prince* 94).
4 Classical god of war.
5 Classical goddess of war (and wisdom).
6 Necessitated, obliged (*OED*, adj., 2b).
7 Ed. (Grosart 2); then Q.

[Scene 8
Battlefield around Çorlu]

*Enter Bajazet, Mustaffa, the soldier with the body of Cherseoli, and
Ottrante prisoner.*

   Bajazet. Thus have we gained a bloody victory,
And, though we are the masters of the field,
Yet have we lost more than[1] our enemies.
Ah, luckless fault[2] of my Cherseoli!
As dear and dearer wert thou unto me   5
Than[3] any of my sons, than[4] mine own self.
When I was glad, thy heart was full of joy,
And bravely hast thou died for Bajazet,
And though thy bloodless body here do lie,
Yet thy sweet soul, in heaven forever blessed,   10
Among the stars enjoys eternal rest.
What art thou, warlike man of Tartary,
Whose hap it is to be our prisoner?
   Ottrante. I am a prince, Ottrante is my name,
Chief captain of the Tartars'[5] mighty host.   15
   Bajazet. Ottrante? Was't not thou that slew my son?
   Ottrante. Ay,[6] and, if Fortune had but favoured me,
Had sent the sire to keep him company.
   Bajazet. Off with his head, and spoil[7] him of his arms,
And leave his body for the airy birds.   20

                      Exit one [the soldier] with Ottrante.

The unrevengèd ghost of Alemshae
Shall now no more wander on Stygian banks[8]

---

1 Ed. (Grosart 2); then Q.
2 Failure (*OED*, n., 5b).
3 Ed. (Grosart 2); then Q.
4 Ed. (Grosart 2); then Q.
5 Ed. (Grosart 2); Tartars Q.
6 Ed. (Grosart 2); I Q.
7 Despoil, strip.
8 In classical myth, the souls of the dead were ferried across either
    Styx or Acheron by the ferryman Charon in order to enter Hades.
    The souls of the dead who had not received a proper burial or who
    had not been avenged could not cross. In Thomas Kyd's *The Spanish
    Tragedy* (1586), the murdered Andrea's soul "descended straight /

But rest in quiet in th'Elysian fields.[1]
Mustaffa and you worthy men-at-arms
That left not Bajazet in greatest need,   25
When we arrive at Constantine's great tower,[2]
You shall be honoured of your emperor.

Exeunt all.

[Scene 9
Acomat's camp in Amasia]

Enter Acomat, Vizier, Regan, and a band of soldiers.

Acomat. Perhaps you wonder why Prince Acomat,
Delighting heretofore in foolish love,
Hath changed his quiet to a soldier's state
And turned the dulcet[3] tunes of Hymen's[4] song

To pass the flowing stream of Acheron: / But churlish Charon, only
boatman there, / Said that my rites of burial not performed, / I might
not sit amongst his passengers" (1.1.18–22). Surveying his slaughter
of the Sultan of Egypt's army at the conclusion of *1 Tamburlaine*,
Tamburlaine boasts that "Millions of souls sit on the banks of Styx,
/ Waiting the back return of Charon's boat" (5.2.399–400). In *Locrine*, the "corpses" of the suicides Locrine and Estrilda "pass foul
Styx in Charon's ferry-boat" (sig. K3v). In contrast, the unrevenged
ghost of Hamlet's father in Shakespeare's *Hamlet* (1600) wanders to
and from Purgatory, "Doomed for a certain term to walk the night /
And for the day confined to fast in fires / Till the foul crimes done in
my days of nature / Are burnt and purged away" (1.5.10–13).
1 In classical mythology, Elysium was the afterlife destination of the
souls of heroes and others favoured by the gods. "Hell and Elysium
swarm with ghosts of men / That I have sent from sundry foughten fields / To spread my fame through hell and up to heaven"
(1.5.2.401–03), Tamburlaine declares.
2 Constantinople (Byzantium). In Constantinople, according to Ashton, was "the strong tower wherein the Emperor's treasures were
lodged" (sig. H6r).
3 Soft, sweet. Vitkus emends to "dullest."
4 Hymen was the classical god of marriage and was "personified in
the bridal song" (Grimal 220). In the soliloquy with which he opens
scene 2 of Marlowe's *Massacre at Paris*, the Duke of Guise threatens
that "If ever Hymen loured at marriage rites" (1), he, Guise, will
turn the first scene's marriage between Margaret of Valois and Henri of Navarre into a massacre (and he does).

Into Bellona's[1] horrible outcries.   5
You think it strange, that whereas I have lived
Almost a votary to wantonness,
To see me now[2] lay off effeminate robes
And arm my body in an iron wall.
I have enjoyed quiet long enough   10
And surfeited with pleasure's surquidry.[3]
A field of dainties I have passèd through
And been a champion to fair Cytheree.[4]
Now, since this idle peace hath wearied me,
I'll follow Mars and war another while   15
And dye[5] my shield in dolorous vermeil.[6]
My brother Selim through his manly deeds
Hath lifted up his fame unto the skies,
While we like earthworms lurking in the weeds
Do live inglorious in all men's eyes.[7]   20
What lets[8] me, then, from this vain slumber rise
And by strong hand achieve eternal glory
That may be talked of in all memory?
And see how Fortune favours mine intent:
Heard you not, lordings, how Prince Selimus   25
Against our royal father armèd went
And how the Janissaries made him flee
To Ramir Emperor of Tartary?
This[9] his rebellion greatly profits me,
For I shall sooner win my father's mind   30

---

1 Bellona was a classical goddess of war and wife of Mars (Grimal 75–
   76). In Greene's *Orlando Furioso*, the king Marsillus declares that so
   much blood has been shed on the battlefield that "Mars, descending
   in his purple robe, / Vows with Bellona in whole heaps of blood / To
   banquet all the demigods of war" (sig. G4v).
2 Ed. (Grosart 2); low Q.
3 Excess, surfeit (*OED*, n., 2).
4 Venus, classical goddess of love.
5 Ed. (Grosart 2); die Q.
6 I.e., blood. Vermeil is a bright red colour.
7 Acomat's transition from Venus to Mars in lines 12 to 20 echoes
   the Prologue of Greene's *Alphonsus King of Aragon*: "[T]his my hand
   which used for to pen / The praise of love and Cupid's peerless power, / Will now begin to treat of bloody Mars, / Of doughty deeds and
   valiant victories" (sig. A3v) so that "Alphonsus' fame unto the heavens should climb" (sig. A3r).
8 Hinders, prevents.
9 Grosart 2 emends to "That."

To yield me up the Turkish Empire[1]—
Which if I have, I am sure I shall find
Strong enemies to pull me down again
That fain would have[2] Prince Selimus to reign.
Then civil discord and contentious war 35
Will follow Acomat's coronation.
Selim, no doubt, will broach[3] seditious jar,[4]
And Corcut too will seek for alteration.
Now to prevent all sudden perturbation,
We thought it good to muster up our power, 40
That danger may not take it unprovided.
   Vizier. I like Your Highness' resolution well,
For these should be the chief arts of a king:
To punish those that furiously rebel
And honour those that sacred counsel bring; 45
To make good laws, ill customs to expel;
To nourish peace from whence your riches spring;
And when good quarrels call you to the field,
T'excel your men in handling spear and shield.[5]
Thus shall the glory of your matchless name 50
Be registered up in immortal lines,
Whereas that prince that follows lustful game
And to fond toys his captive mind inclines
Shall never pass the temple of true fame,
Whose worth is greater than[6] the Indian mines.[7] 55

---

1 Grosart 2 emends to "empery."
2 I.e., would be glad to have.
3 Cause, raise.
4 Traitorous disturbance, rebellion, civil war.
5 All the elements of Vizier's description of the "chief arts of a king"
   (43) may be found in La Primaudaye's "Of the Office and Duty of
   a Prince," in *The French Academy.* The prince must "use great care
   and diligence that justice may be well administered, to the preser-
   vation of every man's right and to the punishment of the wicked"
   (657). He "must often hear" his councillors and "learn of them"
   (657). He must recognize that "the first duty of a good king towards
   his subjects is to maintain them in peace and concord" (657). In
   sum, "He must rule by good laws and by good example, judge by
   wisdom providence and justice, and defend by prowess, care and
   vigilance" (656).
6 Ed. (Grosart 2); then Q.
7 Though the allusion might be to the "Indian mines" of South and
   Central America that were in the early modern period being ex-
   ploited by the Spanish for silver, it is equally possible *(continued)*

But is Your Grace assurèd certainly
That Bajazet doth favour your request?
Perhaps you may make him your enemy:
You know how much your father doth detest
Stout obedience[1] and obstinacy.   60
I speak not this as if I thought it best
Your Highness should your right in it neglect
But that you might be close[2] and circumspect.
   Acomat. We thank thee, Vizier, for thy loving care.
As for my father Bajazet's affection,   65
Unless his holy vows forgotten are,
I shall be sure of it by his election.[3]
But[4] after Acomat's erection,[5]
We must forecast what things be necessary,
Lest that our kingdom be too momentary.   70
   Regan. First let my lord be seated in his throne,
Installed by great Bajazet's consent;
As yet your harvest is not fully grown
But in the green and unripe blade is pent.[6]
But when you once have got the regiment,[7]   75
Then may your lords more easily provide
Against all accidents that may betide.

---

that Acomat is looking eastward, following the gaze of *1 Tambur-laine*'s Cosroe, who after seizing the crown of Persia vows to "march to all those Indian mines / My witless brother to the Christians lost" (1.2.5.41–42). In Greene's *Orlando Furioso*, the twelve peers of France sail to India, "the rich and wealthy Indian clime / Sought too by greedy minds for hurtful gold" (sig. F2r). In Greene's *Alphonsus King of Aragon*, Alphonsus woos Iphigenia by promising her that "The Indian soil shall be thine at command, / Where every step thou settest on the ground, / Shall be received on the golden mines" (sig. H1v). In contrast, *Locrine* refers to the "wealthy mines / Found in the bowels of America" (sig. B2v).

1 Determined defiance (*OED*, stout, adj., 4b). Grosart 2 emends to "stout disobedience."
2 Secret.
3 Choice. Ashton narrates that after Selimus's rebellion, Bajazet "certified his son and heir Acomathes that he would in his lifetime give up his empire to him" (sig. G6v).
4 Ed. (Grosart 2); By Q.
5 I.e., establishment as emperor.
6 Confined.
7 Rulership.

Acomat. Then set we forward to Byzantium,
That we may know what Bajazet intends.
Advise thee, Acomat, what's best to do.   80
The Janissaries favour Selimus,
And they are strong, undaunted enemies,
Which will in arms 'gainst thy election rise.
Then wile[1] them to thy will with precious gifts
And store of gold: timely largition[2]   85
The steadfast persons from their purpose lifts—
But then beware lest Bajazet's affection
Change into hatred by such premunition,[3]
For then he'll[4] think that I am factious[5]
And imitate my brother Selimus.   90
Besides, a prince his honour doth debase
That begs the common soldiers'[6] suffrages,
And if the bashaws knew I sought their grace,
It would the more increase their insolentness.
To resist them were overhardiness,   95
And worse it were to leave my enterprise.
Well, howsoe'er, resolve to venture it:
Fortune doth favour every bold assay,
And 'twere a trick of an unsettled wit,
Because the bees have stings with them alway,   100
To fear[7] our mouths in honey to embay.[8]
Then resolution for me leads the dance,
And, thus resolved, I mean to try my chance.

Exeunt all.

---

1 Ed. (Grosart 2); will Q.
2 Largesse, gifts, bribes (*OED*, n.).
3 Preventative actions, precautionary measures (*OED*, n., 2).
4 Ed. (Grosart 2); he Q.
5 "Given to faction, mutinous, dissenting, partisan" (*OED*, adj., 2).
6 Ed. (Grosart 2); souldiers Q.
7 Ed. (Grosart 2); fare Q.
8 Plunge, drench, imbrue (*OED*, v.2, 1). "He is not worthy of the hon-
   eycomb, / That shuns the hives because the bees have stings" (sig.
   F1v), declares the Scythian prince Hubba in *Locrine*.

[Scene 10
Bajazet's court in Byzantium]

Enter Bajazet, Mustaffa, Cali Bashaw, Hali Bashaw, and the Janissaries.

    Bajazet. What prince soe'er trusts to his mighty power,
Ruling the reins of many nations,
And feareth not lest fickle Fortune lour,[1]
And[2] thinks his kingdom free from alterations,
If he were in the place of Bajazet, 5
He would but little by his sceptre set.[3]
For what hath rule that makes it acceptable?
Rather, what hath it not worthy of hate?
First of all is our state still mutable
And our continuance at the people's rate,[4] 10
So that it is a slender thread whereon
Depends the honour of a prince's throne.
Then do we fear, more than[5] the child new born,
Our friends, our lords, our subjects, and our sons.
Thus is our mind in sundry pieces torn 15
By care, by fear, suspicion, and distrust.
In wine, in meat, we fear pernicious poison;
At home, abroad, we fear seditious treason.
Too true that tyrant Dionysius
Did picture out the image of a king 20
When Damocles[6] was placèd in his throne
And o'er his head a threatening sword did hang,
Fastened up only by a horse's hair.[7]

---

1 Frown.
2 Ed; Ar Q; Or (Grosart 2).
3 I.e., he would consider his power and authority to be worth little
and untrustworthy. Raid notes a parallel passage in *Locrine*: "What
prince soe'er adorned with golden [crown] / Doth sway the regal
sceptre in his hand," the captured Estrild laments, "And thinks no
chance can ever throw him down, / Or that his state shall everlasting stand, / Let him behold poor Estrild in this plight" (sig. G3r).
Raid states that both passages are "indebted to Hecuba's lament in
[French humanist, c. 1545–90] Garnier's *La Troade*" (60).
4 Ratification, approval (*OED*, n.4).
5 Ed. (Grosart 2); then Q.
6 Ed. (Grosart 2); *Daniocles* Q.
7 In this classical moral story illustrating the cares of rule, the Syracu-
san tyrant Dionysius II places Damocles, one of his courtiers, in his

Our chiefest trust is secretly distrust,
For whom have we whom we may safely trust   25
If our own sons, neglecting awful[1] duty,
Rise up in arms against their loving fathers?
Their heart is all of hardest marble wrought
That can lay wait to take away their breath
From whom they first sucked this vital air.   30
My heart is heavy, and I needs must sleep.
Bashaws, withdraw yourselves from me awhile,
That I may rest my overburdened soul.

*They [Mustaffa, Cali Bashaw, and Hali Bashaw] stand aside
while the curtains are drawn.[2]*

Eunuchs, play me some music while I sleep.

Music[3] within.

Mustaffa. Good Bajazet, who would not pity thee,   35
Whom thine own son so vilely persecutes!
More mildly do th'unreasonablest[4] beasts
Deal with their dams than[5] Selimus with thee.
    Hali. Mustaffa, we are princes of the land
And love our emperor as well as thou,   40
Yet will we not for pitying his estate
Suffer our foes our wealth to ruinate.

---

throne for a day after Damocles praises the happiness that he thinks
must accompany Dionysius' position. A sword is suspended over the
throne by a horse hair, however, and Damocles begs to be allowed
to vacate his new seat (Cicero, *Tusculan Disputations* 5.21). In *England's Parnassus*, Allott reproduces lines 19 to 23 under the heading
"Kings" and attributes them to "R. Greene" (sig. L7v) (Grosart 2 x).
1 Full of awe, reverent.
2 Bajazet may withdraw into the discovery space behind the tiring
   house façade, across whose entrance curtains would then be drawn.
   Alternatively, a curtained bed might be thrust out onto the stage
   through the main doors, whose curtains would be drawn once Bajazet has gotten onto the bed. See Dessen and Thomson 62; Thomson.
3 What type of music or where offstage it was created is commonly left
   unspecified in stage directions, but Dessen and Thomson suggest
   that "the musicians are located *above* in a *music room*" (147).
4 Ed. (Grosart 2); vnreasonables Q.
5 Ed. (Grosart 2); then Q.

If Selim have played false with Bajazet
And overslipped the duty of a son,
Why, he was moved by just occasion.   45
Did he not humbly send his messenger
To crave access unto His Majesty?
And yet he could not get permission
To kiss his hands and speak his mind to him.
Perhaps he thought his agèd father's love   50
Was clean estranged from him and Acomat
Should reap the fruit that he had laboured for.
'Tis lawful for the father to take arms,
Ay,[1] and by death chastise his rebel son.
Why should it be unlawful for the son   55
To levy arms 'gainst his injurious sire?
    Mustaffa. You reason, Hali, like a sophister,[2]
As if 'twere lawful for a subject prince
To rise in arms 'gainst[3] his sovereign
Because he will not let him have his will.   60
Much less is't lawful for a man's own son.
If Bajazet had injured Selimus,
Or sought his death, or done him some abuse,
Then Selimus' cause had been more tolerable.
But Bajazet did never injure him,   65
Nor sought his death, nor once abusèd him,
Unless because he gives him not the crown,
Being the youngest of His Highness' sons.
Gave he not him an empire for his part,
The mighty empire of great Trebisond?   70
So that if all things rightly be observed,
Selim had more than[4] ever he deserved.
I speak not this because I hate the prince,
For, by the heavens, I love young Selimus
Better than[5] either of his brethren,   75
But, for[6] I owe allegiance to my king
And love him much that favours me so much,
Mustaffa, while old Bajazet doth live,

---

1 Ed. (Grosart 2); I Q.
2 Debater, rhetorician, one skilled in specious reasoning.
3 Grosart 2 emends to "against."
4 Ed. (Grosart 2); then Q.
5 Ed. (Grosart 2); then Q.
6 Because.

Will be as true to him as to himself.
    Cali. Why, brave Mustaffa, Hali and myself   80
Were never false unto His Majesty!
Our father Hali died in the field
Against the Sophy in His Highness' wars,
And we will never be degenerate.
Nor do we take part with Prince Selimus   85
Because we would depose old Bajazet
But for because we would not Acomat,
That[1] leads his life still in lascivious pomp,
Nor Corcut, though he be a man of worth,
Should be commander of our empire,[2]   90
For he that never saw his foeman's face
But always slept upon a lady's lap
Will scant endure to lead a soldier's life,
And he that never handled but his pen
Will be unskilful at the warlike lance.   95
Indeed, his wisdom well may guide the crown
And keep that safe his predecessors got,
But, being given to peace as Corcut is,
He never will enlarge the empire[3]—
So that the rule and power over us   100
Is only fit for valiant Selimus.
    Mustaffa. Princes, you know how mighty Bajazet
Hath honoured Mustaffa with his love.
He gave his daughter, beauteous Solyma,
To be the sovereign mistress of my thoughts,   105
He made me captain of the Janissaries,
And too unnatural should Mustaffa be
To rise against him in his dying age.
Yet know, you warlike peers,[4] Mustaffa is
A loyal friend unto Prince Selimus,   110
And, ere[5] his other brethren get the crown,
For his sake I myself will pull them down.
I love, I love them dearly, but the love
Which I do bear unto my country's good

---

1 Who.
2 Grosart 2 emends to "empery."
3 Grosart 2 emends to "empery."
4 Ed. (Grosart 2); peere Q.
5 Before.

Makes me a friend to noble Selimus.[1]   115
Only let Bajazet, while he doth live,
Enjoy in peace the Turkish diadem.
When he is dead and laid in quiet grave,
Then none but Selimus our help shall have.

Sound within. A Messenger enters, Bajazet awakens.

    Bajazet. How now, Mustaffa, what news have we there?   120
Is Selim up in arms 'gainst me again?
Or is the Sophy entered our confines?[2]
Hath the Egyptian snatched his crown again?
Or have the uncontrollèd Christians
Unsheathed their swords to make more war on us?   125
Such news or none will come to Bajazet.
    Mustaffa. My gracious lord, here's an ambassador
Come from your son, the Sultan Acomat.
    Bajazet. From Acomat? Oh, let him enter in.

Enter Regan.

Ambassador, how fares our loving son?   130
    Regan. Mighty commander of the warlike Turks,
Acomat Sultan of Amasia[3]
Greeteth Your Grace by me his messenger

He gives him a letter[, which Bajazet reads.]

And gratulates Your Highness' good success,
Wishing good fortune may befall you still.   135
    Bajazet. Mustaffa, read.

He [Bajazet] gives the letter to Mustaffa and speaks the rest to himself.

---

1 Raid notes a parallel between lines 113–15 and Thomas Kyd's *Cornelia* (1594), a translation of Robert Garnier's *Cornélie* (58). Lamenting his upcoming participation in Caesar's assassination, Brutus declares, "I love, I love him dearly. But the love / That men their country and their birthright bear / Exceeds all loves, and dearer is by far / Our country's love than friends or children are" (sig. G1r).
2 Territory.
3 Ottoman province bordering Trebisond on the southern coast of the Black Sea (Shaw xiv–xv).

Acomat craves thy promise, Bajazet,
To give the empire up into his hands
And make it sure to him in thy lifetime—
And thou shalt have it, lovely Acomat,   140
For I have been encumbered long enough
And vexed with the cares of kingly rule.
Now let the trouble of the empery
Be buried in the bosom of thy son.
Ah, Acomat, if thou have such a reign   145
So full of sorrow as thy father's was,
Thou wilt accurse the time, the day, and hour
In which thou was established Emperor.

Sound. [Enter] a Messenger from Corcut.

Yet more news?
    Messenger. Long live the mighty Emperor Bajazet!   150
Corcut the Sultan of Magnesia,
Hearing of Selim's worthy overthrow
And of the coming of young Acomat,
Doth certify Your Majesty by me
How joyful he is of your victory,   155
And therewithal he humbly doth require
Your Grace would do him justice in his cause.
His brethren, both unworthy such a father,
Do seek the empire while Your Grace doth live,
And that by indirect, sinister means.   160
But Corcut's mind, free from ambitious thoughts
And trusting to the goodness of his cause,
Joined unto Your Highness' tender love,
Only desires Your Grace should¹ not invest
Selim nor Acomat in the diadem,   165
Which appertaineth unto him by right,
But keep it to yourself the while you live;
And when it shall the great Creator please,
Who hath the spirits of all men in his hands,
To² call Your Highness to your latest home,   170
Then will he also sue to have his right.³

---

1 Grosart 2 emends to "would."
2 Ed.; Shall Q.
3 As Ashton relates, Corcut's "right" is based in part upon a promise Bajazet made to him during Bajazet's struggle with his brother Cem for the emperorship after Mehmed II's death *(continued)*

Bajazet. Like to a ship sailing without stars,[1]
Whom waves do toss one way and winds another,
Both without ceasing, even so my poor heart
Endures a combat betwixt[2] love and right.[3]   175
The love I bear to my[4] dear Acomat
Commands me give my suffrage unto him,
But Corcut's title, being my eldest son,
Bids me recall my hand and give it him.
Acomat, he would have it in my life,   180
But gentle Corcut, like a loving son,
Desires me live and die an emperor
And at my death bequeath my crown to him.
Ah, Corcut, thou, I see, lov'st me indeed.
Selimus sought to thrust me down by force,   185
And Acomat seeks the kingdom in my life,
And both of them are grieved thou[5] liv'st so long,
But Corcut numbereth not my days as they.
Oh, how much dearer loves he me than[6] they.
Bashaws, how counsel you your emperor?   190
    Mustaffa. My gracious lord, myself will speak for all,
For all, I know,[7] are minded as I am.
Your Highness knows the Janissaries' love,
How firm they mean to cleave to your behest,
As well you might perceive in that sad fight   195
When Selim set upon you in your flight.
Then we do all desire you on our knees
To keep the crown and sceptre to yourself.
How grievous will it be unto your thoughts,
If you should give the crown to Acomat,   200

---

in 1481. Upon Mehmed's death, the Janissaries installed Corcut as
Emperor until Bajazet could reach Byzantium to claim it for himself.
After taking the throne from his son, "Bayazet, like a kind and natural father, of his own free will, after he had received the Empire into
his own hands, promised that he would in time convenient restore
again the empire to his son Corcuthus" (sig. E7r).
1 Grosart 2 emends to "stars' sight."
2 Grosart 2 emends to "between."
3 The extended metaphor in lines 172–75 is a common conceit of
   Renaissance Petrarchan poetry. See p. 123, note 12.
4 Grosart 2 omits "my."
5 Bajazet may be addressing himself here.
6 Ed. (Grosart 2); then Q.
7 Ed. (Vitkus); all I know Q.

To see the brethren disinherited
To flesh their anger one upon another
And rend the bowels of this mighty realm.[1]
Suppose that Corcut would be well content,
Yet thinks Your Grace if Acomat were king   205
That Selim ere long would join league with him?
Nay, he would break from forth his Trebisond
And waste the empire all with fire and sword.
Ah, then too weak would be poor Acomat
To stand against his brother's puissance[2]   210
Or save himself from his enhancèd[3] hand,
While Isma'il and the cruel Persians,
And the great Sultan of th'Egyptians,
Would smile to see our force dismembered so.
Ay,[4] and perchance the neighbour Christians   215
Would take occasion to thrust out their heads.
All this may be prevented by Your Grace
If you will yield to Corcut's just request
And keep the kingdom to you while you live.
Meantime, we that Your Grace's subjects are   220
May make us strong to fortify the man
Whom at your death Your Grace shall choose as king.
    Bajazet. Oh, how thou speakest ever like thyself,
Loyal Mustaffa! Well were Bajazet
If all his sons did bear such love to him.   225
Though loath I am longer to wear the crown,
Yet for I see it is my subjects' will,
Once more will Bajazet be Emperor.
But we must send to pacify our son,
Or he will storm, as erst did Selimus.   230
Come, let us go unto our council, lords,[5]
And there consider what is to be done.

                                                    Exeunt all.

---

1 Ed. (Grosart 2); raigne Q.
2 Power.
3 Raised (*OED*, v., 3a).
4 Ed. (Grosart 2); I Q.
5 Ed. (Grosart 2); Lords Q.

[Scene 11
Acomat's camp, somewhere between Amasia and Byzantium]

*Enter Acomat, Regan, Vizier, and his soldiers. Acomat must read a
letter and then, rending it, say:*

    Acomat. Thus will I rend the crown from off thy head,
False-hearted and injurious Bajazet!
To mock thy son that lovèd thee so dear!
What? For because the head-strong Janissaries
Would not consent to honour Acomat,   5
And their base bashaws, vowed to Selimus,
Thought me unworthy of the Turkish crown,
Should he be ruled and overruled by them,
Under pretence of keeping it himself,
To wipe me clean for ever being king?   10
Doth he esteem so much the bashaws' words
And prize their favour at so high a rate
That for to gratify their stubborn minds
He casts away all care and all respects
Of duty, promise, and religious oaths?   15
Now, by the holy Prophet Mahomet,
Chief president[1] and patron of the Turks,
I mean to challenge now my right by arms
And win by sword that glorious dignity
Which he injuriously detains from me.   20
Haply[2] he thinks because that Selimus,
Rebutted by his warlike Janissaries,
Was fain to fly in haste from whence he came,
That Acomat, by his example moved,
Will fear to manage arms against his sire,   25
Or that my life, forepassed in pleasure's court,
Promises weak resistance in the fight,
But he shall know that I can use my sword
And like a lion seize upon my prey.
If ever Selim moved him heretofore,   30
Acomat means to move him ten times more.
    Vizier. 'Twere good Your Grace would to[3] Amasia
And there increase your camp with fresh supply.[4]

---

1 "Presiding god, guardian, or patron" (*OED*, n., 1b).
2 Perhaps.
3 Return to.
4 Troops.

Acomat. Vizier, I am impatient of delay,
And, since my father hath incensed[1] me thus,   35
I'll quench those kindled flames with his heart blood.
Not like a son but a most cruel foe
Will Acomat henceforth be unto him.
March to Natolia![2] There we will begin
And make a preface to our massacres.   40
My nephew Mahomet, son to Alemshae,[3]
Departed lately from Iconium,[4]
Is lodgèd there,[5] and he shall be the first
Whom I will sacrifice unto my wrath.

                                                    Exeunt all.

                        [Scene 12
                         Natolia]

*Enter the young Prince Mahomet, the Belierbey of Natolia, and one
or two soldiers.*

Mahomet. Lord Governor, what think you best to do?
If we receive the Sultan Acomat,
Who knoweth not but his bloodthirsty sword

---

1 Set on fire.
2 In this play Natolia is a city. Ortelius equates the region of Natolia
   with Asia Minor: "Natolia, sometime called Asia the Lesser," according to Ortelius, comes from "Anatolia, of the Greek word Ana-
   tole, which signifieth the East, under which name they comprehend
   all that part of Asia that is beyond Propontis (Mar di Marmora, it is
   now vulgarly called) and Hellespontus, or, Stretto di Gallipoli, the
   streits of Gallipoli, as at this day they term it: that is, to wit, all Ph-
   rygia, Galatia, Bithynia, Pontus, Lydia, Caria, Paphlagonia, Lycia,
   Magnesia, Cappadocia, and Comagena" (fol. 111). Anatolia today
   comprises a large part of modern Turkey.
3 Ashton calls Mahomet's father "Cleustiachus" (sig. G8v). The name
   "Alemshae" is not found in Ashton's account of Selimus's rebellion
   or reign. In Lonicerus's account in *Chronicorum Turcicorum* (1578),
   however, which may incorporate the Latin account by Paulo Giovius
   that Ashton is translating, one of Selimus's first acts after becoming
   emperor is "in fratris sui Alemsiaci filios Imperii legitimos succes-
   sores grassatus est," "to march on the sons of his own brother Alemshae, who were the legitimate successors to the Empire" (30).
4 Moden Konya, a city in central Anatolia and the administrative capital of the Ottoman Karaman province (Shaw xiv–xv).
5 Natolia.

Shall be embowelled in our countrymen.
You know he is displeased with Bajazet   5
And will rebel, as Selim did tofore,[1]
And would to God, with Selim's overthrow.
You know his angry heart hath vowed revenge
On all the subjects of his father's land.

    Belierbey. Young prince, thy uncle seeks to have thy life   10
Because by right the Turkish crown is thine.
Save thou thyself by flight or otherwise,
And we will make resistance as we can.
Like an Armenian tiger that hath lost
Her lovèd whelps,[2] so raveth Acomat,   15
And we must be subject to[3] his rage,
But you may live to venge your citizens.
Then fly, good prince, before your uncle come.

    Mahomet. Nay, good my lord, never shall it be said
That Mahomet the son of Alemshae   20
Fled from his citizens for fear of death.
But I will stay and help to fight for you,
And if you needs must die, I'll die with you,
And I among the rest with forward hand
Will help to kill a common enemy.   25

Exeunt all.

[Scene 13
Before the walls of Natolia]

Enter Acomat, Vizier, Regan, and the soldiers.

    Acomat. Now, fair Natolia, shall thy stately[4] walls
Be overthrown and beaten to the ground.
My heart within me for revenge still calls.
Why, Bajazet, thoughtst thou that Acomat
Would put up such a monstrous injury?   5
Then had I brought my chivalry in vain

---

1 Before.
2 The female tiger of Hyrcania and India, according to Pliny, "runs on end after her young ones" (*Natural History* 8.18) if they are stolen from her.
3 Grosart 2 emends to "unto."
4 Princely, noble, majestic (*OED*, adj.).

And to no purpose drawn my conquering blade,
Which, now unsheathed, shall not be sheathed again
Till it a world of bleeding souls hath made.
Poor Mahomet, thou thoughtst thyself too sure   10
In thy strong city of Iconium
To plant thy forces in Natolia,
Weakened so much before by Selim's sword.
Summon a parley to the citizens,
That they may hear the dreadful words I speak   15
And die in thought before they come to blows.
    All. A parley!

[*Enter*] *Mahomet, Belierbey, and soldiers on the walls.*[1]

    Mahomet. What craves our uncle Acomat of us?
    Acomat. That thou and all the city yield themselves,
Or, by the holy rites of Mahomet,   20
His wondrous tomb[2] and sacred Alcoran,[3]
You all shall die—and not a common death,
But even as monstrous as I can devise.

---

1 The walls of the city would be represented by the tiring house façade
at the back of the stage. Mahomet, Belierbey and the soldiers would
enter onto the balcony of the façade, commonly designated in stage
directions as "above." From this raised position above the main
stage, they would talk or "parley" with Acomat and his forces, who
are situated on the main stage.

2 Located in Medina. In one of his sources, Thomas Newton's *Notable Historie of the Saracens* (1575), Greene may have read the following about Mahomet's burial, which may account for the adjective
"wondrous": "His body without any princely furniture or ceremonial solemnity was shrined and lapped in a white sheet three times
double, and so being chested in an iron coffin, was after a homely
sort buried: where afterward his kinsfolks and allies edified a sump-
tuous and magnifical temple of brick work, and arched the same
with a vault so pargetted with lodestones (whose nature is to draw
iron unto it) that the iron coffin wherein Mahomet his body was
enclosed, was drawn up, even unto the top of the church and there
hangeth. For which cause that place is yet with great devotion and
pilgrimage worshipped of all the East" (sig. E4v). According to Tilley, "To be suspended like Mahomet's tomb between heaven and
earth" was proverbial (M13), but the earliest example he cites is
from Milton (1649). Chew (414) cites an example from 1589.

3 Qur'an.

Mahomet. Uncle, if I may call you by that name
Which[1] cruelly hunt for your nephew's blood, 25
You do us wrong thus to besiege our town,
That ne'er deserved such hatred at your hands,
Being your friends and kinsmen as we are.
    Acomat. In that thou wrongst me, that thou are my kinsman.
    Mahomet. Why, for[2] I am your nephew doest thou frown? 30
    Acomat. Ay,[3] that thou art so near unto the crown.
    Mahomet. Why, uncle, I resign my right to thee,
And all my title, were it ne'er so good.
    Acomat. Wilt thou? Then know assuredly from me,
I'll seal the resignation with thy blood. 35
Though Alemshae thy father loved me well,
Yet Mahomet his[4] son shall down to hell.
    Mahomet. Why, uncle, doth my life put you in fear?
    Acomat. It shall not, nephew, since I have you here.
    Mahomet. When I am dead, more hinderers shalt thou find. 40
    Acomat. When one's cut off, the fewer are behind.
    Mahomet. Yet think the gods do bear an equal[5] eye.
    Acomat. Faith, if they all were squint-eyed, what care I?
    Mahomet. Then, Acomat,[6] know we will rather die
Than[7] yield us up into a tyrant's hand. 45
    Acomat. Beshrew me but you be the wiser, Mahomet,
For if I do but catch you, boy, alive,
'Twere better for you run through Phlegethon.[8]
Sirs, scale the walls and pull the caitiffs down;
I give to you the spoil of all the town. 50

*Alarum. [Acomat, Vizier, and Regan exit, while Acomat's soldiers]
scale[9] the walls. Enter Acomat, Vizier, and Regan, with Mahomet.*

    Acomat. Now, youngster, you that bravedst us on the walls
And shook your plumèd crest against our shield,

---

1 Who.
2 Because.
3 Ed. (Grosart 2); I Q.
4 Ed. (Grosart 2); thy Q.
5 Impartial.
6 Ed. (Grosart 2); *Mahomet* Q.
7 Ed. (Grosart 2); Then Q.
8 River of fire in Hades.
9 Dessen and Thomson suggest that this bit of stage business is accomplished with ladders (188).

What wouldst thou give, or what wouldst thou not give,
That thou wert far enough from Acomat?
How like the villain[1] is to Bajazet!   55
Well, nephew, for thy father loved me well,
I will not deal extremely with his son.
Then hear a brief compendium[2] of thy death:
Regan, go cause a grove of steel-head spears
Be pitched thick under the castle wall,   60
And on them let this youthful captain fall.
   Mahomet. Thou shalt not fear me, Acomat, with death,
Nor will I beg my pardon at thy hands,
But as thou giv'st me such a monstrous death,
So do I freely leave to thee my curse.   65

Exit Regan with Mahomet.

Acomat. Oh, that will serve to fill my father's purse.

Alarum. Enter a soldier with Zonara, sister to Mahomet.

   Zonara. Ah, pardon me, dear uncle, pardon me.
   Acomat. No, minion,[3] you are too near a kin to me.
   Zonara. If ever pity enterèd thy breast
Or ever thou wast touched with woman's love,   70
Sweet uncle, spare wretched Zonara's life.
Thou once wast noted for a quiet prince,
Soft-hearted, mild, and gentle as a lamb;
Ah, do not prove a lion unto me.
   Acomat. Why, wouldst thou live when Mahomet is dead?   75
   Zonara. Ah, who slew Mahomet? Uncle, did you?
   Acomat. He that's prepared to do as much for you.
   Zonara. Doest thou not pity Alemshae in me?
   Acomat. Yes, that he wants so long thy company.
   Zonara. Thou art not, false groom, son to Bajazet.   80
He would relent to hear a woman weep,
But thou wast born in desert Caucasus,[4]

---

1 Used here (ironically) as a familiar term of affection.
2 Summary.
3 Favourite (used here ironically).
4 Region immediately north of Anatolia and east of the Black Sea. It
    includes the Caucasus mountain range.

And the Hyrcanian[1] tigers gave thee suck,[2]
Knowing thou wert a monster like themselves.
    Acomat. Let you her thus to rate[3] us? Strangle her.   85

They [*soldiers*] *strangle her.*

Now scour the streets and leave not one alive
To carry these sad news to Bajazet,
That all the citizens may dearly say,
"This day was fatal to Natolia."

                                          Exeunt all.

[Scene 14
Bajazet's court in Byzantium]

Enter Bajazet, Mustaffa, [*Aga,*] *and the Janissaries.*

    Bajazet. Mustaffa, if my mind deceive me not,
Some strange misfortune is not far from me.
I was not wont[4] to tremble in this sort.
Methinks I feel a cold run through my bones,
As if it hastened to surprise my heart;   5
Methinks some voice still whispereth in my ears
And bids me to take heed of Acomat.
    Mustaffa. 'Tis but Your Highness' overchargèd mind,
Which feareth most the things it least desires.

*Enter two soldiers, with the Belierbey of Natolia in a chair, and the
bodie*[*s*] *of Mahomet and Zonara in two coffins.*

    Bajazet. Ah, sweet Mustaffa, thou art much deceived.   10
My mind presages me some future harm—

---

1 Region in Persia.
2 Pomponius Mela describes the tigers of Hyrcania as "a cruel kind of
    wild beast, and so swift, that they be wont even with ease to overtake
    a horse man, that is gone away upon the spur" (76). In Marlowe's
    Dido Queen of Carthage, Dido exclaims to the departing Aeneas that
    "thou art sprung from Scythian Caucasus, / And tigers of Hyrcania
    gave thee suck" (5.1.158–59).
3 Berate, scold, upbraid.
4 Accustomed to.

And, lo, what doleful exequy[1] is here?
Our chief commander of Natolia?
What caitiff hand is it hath wounded thee,
And who are these covered in tomb-black hearse?   15
    Belierbey. These are thy nephews, mighty Bajazet,
The son and daughter of good Alemshae,
Whom cruel Acomat hath murdered thus.
These eyes beheld when from an airy tower
They hurled the body of young Mahomet,   20
Whereas[2] a band of armèd soldiers
Received him falling on their spears' sharp points.
His sister, poor Zonara,[3]
Entreating life and not obtaining it,
Was strangled by his barbarous soldiers.   25

Bajazet falls in a swoon and, being recovered, say[s]:

    Bajazet. O you dispensers of our hapless breath,
Why do you glut your eyes and take delight
To see sad pageants of men's miseries?
Wherefore have you prolonged my wretched life
To see my son, my dearest Acomat,   30
To lift his hands against his father's life?
Ah, Selimus, now do I pardon thee,
For thou didst set upon me manfully
And moved by an occasion, though unjust.
But Acomat, injurious Acomat,   35
Is ten times more unnatural to me.
Hapless Zonara, hapless Mahomet,
The poor remainder of my Alemshae,
Which of you both shall Bajazet most wail?
Ah, both of you are worthy to be wailed.   40
Happily dealt the froward[4] Fates with thee,
Good Alemshae, for thou didst die in field[5]
And so preventedst[6] this sad spectacle,
Pitiful spectacle of sad dreariment,

---

1 Funeral.
2 Where (*OED*, adv. and conj., 1).
3 Grosart 2 adds "luckless maid" to the end of the line.
4 Unreasonable, perverse, malevolent (*OED*, adj., 1). Grosart 2
   emends to "forward."
5 On the battlefield.
6 Avoided, escaped.

Pitiful spectacle of dismal death.[1]   45
But I have lived to see thee, Alemshae,
By Tartar pirates[2] all in pieces torn;
To see young Selim's disobedience;
To see the death of Alemshae's poor seed;
And, last of all, to see my Acomat   50
Prove a rebellious enemy to me.
    Belierbey. Ah, cease your tears, unhappy Emperor,
And shed not all for your poor nephews' death.
Six thousand of true-hearted citizens
In fair Natolia Acomat hath slain.   55
The channels run like riverets[3] of blood,
And I escaped with this poor company,
Bemangled and dismembered as you see,
To be the messenger of these sad news.
And now mine eyes fast swimming in pale death   60
Bid[4] me resign my breath unto the heavens.
Death stands before, ready for to strike.
Farewell, dear Emperor, and revenge our loss,
As ever thou doest hope for happiness.

He [*Belierbey*] *dies.*

    Bajazet. Avernus'[5] jaws and loathsome Taenarus,[6]   65

---

1   Before he commits suicide in order to avoid capture, Locrine declares, "Ne'er shall mine eyes behold that dismal hour, / Ne'er will I view that ruthful spectacle" (*Locrine* sig. K1v). Seeing his and her mother's bodies, Locrine's daughter later exclaims, "What doleful sight, what ruthful spectacle, / Hath Fortune offered to my hapless heart?" (sig. K2v).

2   As the *OED* documents, historically the literal meaning of "pirate" has been "a person who robs or plunders from ships, esp. at sea" (1a). The noun can be used figuratively, however, to mean "a person who goes about in search of plunder" (1b), wherever said plunder might be located. See the anonymous *Famous Victories of Henry V* for an extended dramatization of the battlefield as a site of the piratical plunder of the dead.

3   Rivulets.

4   Ed.; Bids Q.

5   In classical myth, the Italian volcano Avernus was considered the entrance to Hades. In Book VI of the *Aeneid*, Aeneas descends into the underworld through Avernus, having been told by the Cumaean Sibyl that "the way to Avernus is easy; / Night and day lie open the gates of death's dark kingdom" (126–27).

6   Another entrance to Hades, through which Orpheus descends into the underworld in pursuit of his dead bride Eurydice (Ovid,

From whence the damnèd ghosts do often creep
Back to the world to punish wicked men,
Black Demogorgon,[1] grandfather of night,
Send out thy Furies[2] from thy fiery hall,
The pitiless Erinyes[3] armed with whips,   70
And all the damnèd monsters of black hell,
To pour their plagues on cursèd Acomat.
How shall I mourn, or which way shall I turn,
To pour my tears upon my dearest friends?
Couldst thou endure,[4] false-hearted Acomat,   75
To kill thy nephew and his[5] sister thus
And wound to death so valiant a lord?

Metamorphoses X.13–15). *Locrine* mentions the "hell mouth
Tanarus" (sig. H4v).

1 According to Giovanni Boccaccio's (1313–75) *Genealogia Deorum
Gentilium*, Demogorgon is "deorum gentilium omnium patrem
principiumque" (Lib. I. Prohemium II.14), "the progenitor and
prince of all pagan gods." Boccaccio adds that Demogorgon means
"terre deus," or "God of the earth" and that "sanctum et terribile
nomen eius" (Lib. I. Prohemium III.11), "his name is holy and terrible." In Marlowe's *1 Tamburlaine*, the Sultan of Egypt describes
Tamburlaine as "as monstrous as Gorgon, Prince of Hell" (4.1.18).
In *The Faerie Queene*, Edmund Spenser (1552/53–99) describes the
magician Archimago as "A bold bad man, that dar'd to call by name
/ Great *Gorgon*, Prince of darknesse and dead night, / At which *Cocytus* quakes, and *Styx* is put to flight" (I.i.377–79). In 1.3 of Marlowe's
Doctor Faustus, Doctor Faustus invocates Demogorgon in his incantation to summon Mephostophilis, and in Greene's *Friar Bacon and
Friar Bungay* (1594), Friar Bacon calls Demogorgon "master of the
Fates" (11.108). He appears in an incantation again in Greene's *Orlando Furioso* as "Demogorgon qui noctis fata gubernas, / Qui regis
infernum, solemque, solumque, coelumque" (sig. G1v), "Demogorgon who rules the hurtful fates, who alone is rules hell and heaven,"
and in the same play is called "Demogorgon ruler of the Fates" (sig.
G4v). In *Locrine*, Locrine laments that "by Demogorgon's knife" his
father Brutus has been "bereft of life" (sig. B3v).
2 Goddesses of vengeance in classical myth, which names three Furies: Tisiphone, Megæra, and Alecto (Grimal 151).
3 The Furies. Grimal writes that they were "violent goddesses, whom
the Romans identified with their Furies.... They were analogous
with the Parcae, or Fates, who had no laws other than their own,
which even Zeus had to obey" (151). "That which the Fates appoint
must happen so," states Medea in Greene's *Alphonsus King of Aragon*, "Though heavenly Jove and all the gods say no" (sig. F1r).
4 Ed. (Grosart 2); endue Q.
5 Ed. (Grosart 2); thy Q.

And will you not, you all-beholding heavens,
Dart down on him your piercing lightning brand
Enrolled[1] in sulphur and consuming flames?   80
Ah, do not, Jove! Acomat is my son
And may perhaps by counsel be reclaimed
And brought to filial obedience.
Aga, thou art a man of perceant[2] wit.
Go thou and talk with my son Acomat   85
And see if he will any way relent.
Speak him fair,[3] Aga, lest he kill thee too.
And we, my lords, will in and mourn awhile
Over these princes' lamentable tombs.

Exeunt all.

[Scene 15
Acomat's camp outside Natolia]

Enter Acomat, Vizier, Regan, and their soldiers.

Acomat. As Tityus[4] in the country of the dead
With restless cries doth call upon high Jove
The while the vulture tireth[5] on his heart,
So, Acomat, revenge still gnaws thy soul.
I think my soldiers' hands have been too slow   5
In shedding blood and murdering innocents.
I think my wrath hath been too patient,

---

1 Wrapped up in.
2 Penetrating, sharp, keen, piercing (*OED*, adj.).
3 Gently, in a conciliatory fashion (often deceptively). In Marlowe's
   Edward the Second, threatened with the banishment of his beloved
   Gaveston, Edward in an aside declares, "It boots me not threaten,
   I must speak fair" (4.63). When counselling his daughter Abigall to
   pretend to want to become a nun in order to help his plan to recover
   his riches, Barabas in Marlowe's *Jew of Malta* advises her to "Entreat
   'em [the nuns] fair and give them friendly speech" (2.283). "Is it
   flattery in me, sir, to speak you fair?" Andrew asks his master Ateu-
   kin in Greene's *James IV* (1598).
4 For attacking one of his many lovers at the instigation of Juno, Jove
   struck the giant Tityus with a thunderbolt and consigned him to Hades, where vultures gnawed on his liver, which regenerated monthly
   (Grimal 457).
5 Pulls, tears, feeds upon (*OED*, v.2, 2a, 2b).

Since civil[1] blood quencheth not out the flames
Which Bajazet hath kindled in my heart.
    Vizier. My gracious lord, here is a messenger   10
Sent from your father the Emperor.

Enter Aga, and one with him.

    Acomat. Let him come in. Aga, what news with you?
    Aga. Great prince, thy father, mighty Bajazet,
Wonders Your Grace, whom he did love so much
And thought to leave possessor of the crown,   15
Would thus requite his love with mortal hate,
To kill thy nephews with revenging sword
And massacre his subjects in such sort.
    Acomat. Aga, my father, traitorous Bajazet,
Detains the crown injuriously from me,   20
Which I will have if all the world say nay.
I am not like the unmanured land,
Which answers not his honour's[2] greedy mind.
I sow not seeds upon the barren sand.
A thousand ways can Acomat soon find   25
To gain my will, which if I cannot gain,
Then purple blood my angry hands shall stain.
    Aga. Acomat,[3] yet learn by Selimus
That hasty purposes have hated ends.
    Acomat. Tush, Aga, Selim was not wise enough   30
To set upon[4] the head[5] at the first brunt.[6]
He should have done as I do mean to do:
Fill all the confines[7] with fire, sword, and blood,
Burn up the fields, and overthrow whole towns,
And, when he had endamagèd that way,   35
Then tear the old man piecemeal with my teeth
And colour my strong hands with his gore-blood.

---

1 Civic, of citizens, of countrymen.
2 Grosart 2 emends to "earers."
3 Grosart 2 emends to "Ah, Acomat."
4 To seize.
5 Forward momentum, advance against an opposing force (*OED*, n.1,
    55).
6 Assault, charge, attack (*OED*, n.1, 2b).
7 Territory.

Aga. O see, my lord, how fell[1] ambition
Deceives your senses and bewitches you.
Could you, unkind,[2] perform so foul a deed   40
As kill the man that first gave life to you?
Do you not fear the people's adverse fame?
   Acomat. It is the greatest glory of a king
When, though his subjects hate his wicked deeds,
Yet are they forced to bear them all with praise.[3]   45
   Aga. Whom fear constrains to praise their prince's deeds,
That fear eternal hatred in them feeds.[4]
   Acomat. He knows not how to sway the kingly mace
That loves to be great in his people's grace.
The surest ground for kings to build upon   50
Is to be feared and cursed of everyone.[5]
What though the world of nations me hate?
Hate is peculiar to a prince's state.[6]
   Aga. Where there's no shame, no care of holy law,
No faith, no justice, no integrity,   55
That state is full of mutability.
   Acomat. Bare faith, pure virtue, poor integrity
Are ornaments fit for a private man;
Beseems[7] a prince for to do all he can.[8]
   Aga. Yet know it is a sacrilegious will   60
To slay thy father, were he ne'er so ill.[9]

---

1 Treacherous, deceitful, false (*OED*, adj.1, 1b).
2 Unnatural.
3 According to Gentillet's eighth Machiavellian maxim of policy, "a prince need not care to be accounted cruel if so be that he can make himself be obeyed thereby" (253).
4 In *England's Parnassus*, Allott reproduces lines 46 and 47 under the heading "Fear" and attributes them to "R. Greene" (sig. G5r) (Gilbert 4).
5 Gentillet's ninth Machiavellian maxim of policy is that "it is better for a prince to be feared than loved" (253).
6 In *England's Parnassus*, Allott reproduces line 53 under the heading "Hate" and attributes it to "R. Greene" (sig. K1r) (Gilbert 4).
7 It befits, it is appropriate for.
8 Machiavelli states that "a man who wants to act virtuously in every way necessarily comes to grief among so many who are not virtuous. Therefore if a prince wants to maintain his rule he must learn how not to be virtuous, and to make use of this or not according to need" (*The Prince* 91). According to Gentillet's first Machiavellian maxim of religion, "a prince must ... desire to be esteemed devout, though he be not so indeed" (251).
9 Bad.

Acomat. 'Tis lawful, greybeard, for to do to him
What ought not to be done unto a father.
Hath he not wiped me from the Turkish crown?
Preferred he not the stubborn Janissaries   65
And heard the bashaws' stout petitions
Before he would give ear to my request?
As sure as day, mine eyes shall ne'er taste sleep
Before my sword have riven[1] his perjured breast.
    Aga. Ah, let me never live to see that day.   70
    Acomat. Yes, thou shalt live, but never see that day,
Wanting the tapers[2] that should give thee light.

[Acomat] pulls out his [Aga's] eyes.

Thou shalt not see so great felicity,
When I shall rend out Bajazet's dim eyes
And by his death install myself a king.   75
    Aga. Ah, cruel tyrant and unmerciful,
More bloody than[3] the Anthropophagi[4]
That fill their hungry stomachs with man's flesh!
Thou shouldst have slain me, barbarous Acomat,
Not leave me in so comfortless a life,   80
To live on earth and never see the sun.
    Acomat. Nay, let him die that liveth at his ease.
Death would a wretched caitiff greatly please.
    Aga. And thinkst thou, then, to 'scape unpunishèd?
No, Acomat, though both mine eyes be gone,   85
Yet are my hands left on to murder thee.
    Acomat. 'Twas well remembered. Regan, cut them off.

*They [Regan and the soldiers] cut off his [Aga's] hands and give
them [to] Acomat.*

Now in that sort[5] go tell thy Emperor
That if himself had but been in thy place

---

1 Torn apart (*OED*, rive, v.1, 1a).
2 Candles; figuratively, eyes.
3 Ed. (Grosart 2); then Q.
4 Literally, "Man-eaters." Pliny states that the Scythian Anthropophagi "use to drink out of the skulls of men's heads and to wear the
   scalps, hair and all, instead of mandilions or stomachers before their
   breasts" (*Natural History* 7.2).
5 Condition.

I would have used him crueller than[1] thee.   90
Here, take thy hands. I know thou lov'st them well.

[Acomat] opens his [Aga's] bosom[2] and puts them in.

Which hand is this? Right? Or left? Canst thou tell?
    Aga. I know not which it is, but 'tis my hand.
But, O thou[3] supreme Architect of all,
First mover[4] of those tenfold[5] crystal orbs[6]   95
Where all those moving and unmoving eyes[7]
Behold thy goodness everlastingly,
See, unto thee I lift these bloody arms—
For hands I have not for to lift to thee—
And in thy justice dart thy smouldering flame   100
Upon the head of cursèd Acomat!
O cruel heavens and injurious Fates,
Even the last refuge of a wretched man
Is took from me, for how can Aga weep
Or rain[8] a brinish shower of pearlèd tears,   105

---

1 Ed. (Grosart 2); then Q.
2 The space between Aga's chest and his garment (*OED*, n., 3a).
3 God.
4 Ultimate cause of motion. In medieval and Renaissance astronomy, based on the geocentric system of Ptolemy, God was the ultimate cause of motion (prime motor) of the universe.
5 Usually, as in Greene and Thomas Lodge's *A Looking Glass for London and England* (1594), the "orbs of heaven" are "ninefold" (sig. D4v).
6 The spheres of the Ptolemaic universe. In Ptolemaic astronomy God inhabits the ninth sphere of the heavens and is the source of the motion of all the other spheres, which are contained within the ninth sphere like concentric circles. The eighth sphere is the sphere of the fixed stars. The first through seventh spheres are the planetary spheres of the moon, Mercury, Venus, the sun, Mars, Jupiter, and Saturn, respectively. The earth is at the centre of the spheres. The writer of *The Compost of Ptholomeus Prince of Astronomers,* a frequently reprinted digest of Ptolemaic astronomy, calls the spheres "skies" and notes that some astronomers posit the existence of a number of immobile "skies" beyond the ninth (which they consider completely empty): "There [have] been some astrologians say that above these nine skies one is immobile, for it turneth not, and above it is one of crystal, over the which is the sky imperial, in the which is the throne of God" (sig. E1v).
7 Planets and stars.
8 Ed. (Vitkus); ruine Q.

Wanting the watery cisterns of his eyes?
Come, lead me back again to Bajazet,
The woefullest and sadd'st ambassador
That ever was dispatched to any king.
    Acomat. Why, so, this music pleases Acomat.   110
And would I had my doting father here,
I would rip up his breast and rend his heart,
Into his bowels thrust my angry hands,
As willingly and with as good a mind
As I could be the Turkish Emperor.   115
And by the clear declining vault of heaven,
Whither the souls of dying men do flee,
Either I mean to die the death myself
Or make that old false faitour[1] bleed his last,
For death no sorrow could unto me bring,   120
So Acomat might die the Turkish king.

                                  Exeunt all.

[Scene 16
Bajazet's court in Byzantium]

Enter Bajazet, Mustaffa, Cali, Hali, and Aga led by a soldier, who
[Aga], kneeling before Bajazet and holding his legs, shall say:

  · *Aga.* Is this the body of my sovereign?
Are these the sacred pillars that support
The image of true magnanimity?[2]
Ah, Bajazet, thy son, false Acomat,
Is full resolved to take thy life from thee.   5
'Tis true, 'tis true. Witness these handless arms,
Witness these empty lodges of mine eyes,
Witness the gods that from the highest heaven
Beheld the tyrant with remorseless heart
Pull[3] out mine eyes and cut off my weak hands.   10
Witness that[4] sun whose golden-coloured beams
Your eyes do see but mine can ne'er behold,
Witness the earth that sucked up my blood

---

1 Imposter, cheat (*OED*, n., 1). Grosart 2 emends to "traitor."
2 In *Locrine*, Locrine is called "the map of magnanimity" (sig. K2v).
3 Ed. (Grosart 2); Puld Q.
4 Grosart 2 emends to "the."

Streaming in rivers from my trunkèd[1] arms,
Witness the present that he sends to thee: 15
Open my bosom: there you shall it see.

Mustaffa opens his [Aga's] bosom and takes out his hands.

Those are the hands which Aga once did use
To toss the spear and in a warlike gyre[2]
To hurtle my sharp sword about my head.
Those[3] sends he to the woeful Emperor,   20
With purpose so to[4] cut thy hands from thee.
Why is my sovereign silent all this while?
    Bajazet. Ah, Aga, Bajazet fain would[5] speak to thee,
But sudden sorrow eateth up my words.
Bajazet, Aga, fain would weep for thee,   25
But cruel sorrow drieth up my tears.
Bajazet, Aga, fain would die for thee,
But grief hath weakened my poor agèd hands.
How can he speak whose tongue sorrow hath tied?
How can he mourn that cannot shed a tear?   30
How shall he live that, full of misery,
Calleth for Death, which will not let him die?
    Mustaffa. Let women weep, let children pour forth tears,[6]
And cowards spend the time in bootless[7] moan.
We'll load the earth with such a mighty host   35
Of Janissaries, stern-born sons of Mars,
That Phoeb[8] shall fly and hide him in the clouds
For fear our javelins thrust him from his wain.[9]
Old Aga was a prince among your lords,
His counsels always were true oracles,[10]   40
And shall he thus unmanly be misused,
And he unpunishèd that did the deed?

---

1 Truncated, cut short, lopped (*OED*, trunk, v.1).
2 Whirl, circular turn (*OED*, n., 1).
3 Grosart 2 emends to "these."
4 Ed. (Grosart 2); not in Q.
5 Would like to.
6 foor Q NLS 1 VAM 3 BD 2 HU 2 NLS 2.
7 Futile, useless.
8 Phoebus Apollo.
9 Chariot.
10 "My words are oracles" (3.3.102), Tamburlaine declares in *1 Tamburlaine*.

Shall Mahomet and poor Zonara's ghosts,
And the good governor of Natolia,
Wander in Stygian meadows unrevenged?[1]   45
Good Emperor, stir up thy manly heart
And send forth all thy warlike Janissaries
To chastise that rebellious Acomat.
Thou knowst we cannot fight without a guide,
And he must be one of the royal blood,   50
Sprung from the loins of mighty Ottoman,[2]
And who remains now but young Selimus?
So please Your Grace to pardon his offence
And make him captain of th'imperial host.

    Bajazet. Ay,[3] good Mustaffa, send for Selimus.   55
So I may be revenged, I care not how.
The worst that can befall me is but death,
That[4] would end my woeful misery.
Selimus, he must work me this good turn.
I cannot kill myself; he'll do't for me.   60
Come, Aga, thou and I will weep the while,
Thou for thy eyes and loss of both thy hands,
I for th'unkindness of my Acomat.

                          Exeunt all.

[Scene 17
Court of Ramirchan]

Enter Selimus and a Messenger with a letter from Bajazet.

    Selimus. Will Fortune favour me yet once again,
And will she thrust the cards into my hands?
Well, if I chance but once to get the deck
To deal about and shuffle as I would,
Let Selim never see the daylight spring   5
Unless I shuffle out myself a king.[5]
Friend, let me see thy letter once again,

---

1 See p. 82, note 8.
2 Osman I (r. 1280–1324), founder of the Ottoman Empire (Shaw 13).
3 Ed. (Grosart 2); I Q.
4 Grosart 2 emends to "'Tis that."
5 Guise in Marlowe's *Massacre at Paris* exclaims to himself, "Guise, since thou hast all the cards within thy hands / (*continued*)

That I may read these reconciling lines.

[*Selimus*] *reads the letter.*

Thou hast a pardon, Selim, granted thee.
Mustaffa and the forward Janissaries   10
Have sued to thy father Bajazet
That thou mayst be their captain general
Against th'attempts of Sultan Acomat.
Why, that's the thing that I requested most,
That I might once th'imperial army lead,   15
And, since it's offered me so willingly,
Beshrew me but I'll take their courtesy.
Soft, let me see, is there no policy[1]
T'entrap poor Selimus in this device?[2]
It may be that my father fears me yet,   20
Lest I should once again rise up in arms
And, like Antaeus quelled by Hercules,[3]
Gather new forces by my overthrow,[4]
And therefore sends for me under pretence
Of this and that, but when he hath me there   25
He'll make me sure for putting him in fear.
Distrust is good when there's cause of distrust.
Read it again. Perchance thou doest mistake.

[*Selimus*] *read[s].*

Oh, here's Mustaffa's signet set thereto.
Then, Selim, cast all foolish fear aside,   30
For he's a prince that favours thy estate

   To shuffle or cut, take this as surest thing: / That, right or wrong,
   thou deal thyself a king" (2.85–87).
1 Trick, stratagem, plan (*OED*, n.1, 3).
2 Plan, scheme, plot.
3 In classical myth, Antaeus was "A giant, son of Poseidon and Gaia
   (The Earth). He lived in Libya.... Antaeus was invulnerable so long
   as he kept in touch with his mother (that is, the ground), but Hera-
   cles, when he was passing through Libya in his search for the Gold-
   en Apples, fought with him and choked him to death by hoisting
   him on his shoulders" (Grimal 43).
4 During his fight with Hercules, Antaeus would recover his strength
   every time Hercules threw him to the ground.

And hateth treason worse than[1] death itself,
And hardly can I think he could be brought,
If there were treason, to subscribe his name.[2]
Come, friend, the cause requires we should be gone.   35
Now once again have at the Turkish throne!

Exeunt both.

[Scene 18
Bajazet's court at Byzantium[3]]

*Enter Bajazet leading Aga, Mustaffa, Hali, Cali, Selimus, the
Janissaries.*

    Bajazet. Come, mournful Aga, come and sit by me.
Thou hast been sorely grieved for Bajazet;
Good reason, then, that he should grieve for thee.
Give me thy arm. Though thou hast lost thy hands
And liv'st as a poor exile in this light,   5
Yet hast thou won the heart of Bajazet.
    Aga. Your Grace's words are very comfortable,
And well can Aga bear his grievous loss
Since it was for so good a prince's sake.
    Selimus. Father, if I may call thee by that name[4]   10
Whose life I aimed at with rebellious sword,
In all humility thy reformed son
Offers himself into Your Grace's hands
And at your feet layeth his bloody sword
Which he advanced against Your Majesty.   15
If my offence do seem so odious
That I deserve not longer time to live,
Behold, I open unto you my breast,
Ready prepared to die at your command.
But if repentance in unfeignèd heart   20
And sorrow for my grievous crime forepassed
May merit pardon at your princely hands,

---

1 Ed. (Grosart 2); then Q.
2 I.e., sign his name to the letter.
3 Bayezid II resigned his crown to Selimus I on 25 April 1512 (Shaw
    79).
4 In Greene's *Orlando Furioso*, the disgraced Angelica addresses her
    father similarly: "Father, if I may dare to call thee so" (sig. G4v).

Behold where poor inglorious Selimus
Upon his knees begs pardon of Your Grace.[1]
    Bajazet. Stand up, my son. I joy to hear thee speak,   25
But more to hear thou art so well reclaimed.
Thy crime was ne'er so odious unto me
But thy reformèd life and humble thoughts
Are thrice as pleasing to my agèd spirit.
Selim, we here pronounce thee by our will   30
Chief general of the warlike Janissaries.
Go, lead them out against false Acomat,
Which hath so grievously rebelled 'gainst me.
Spare him not, Selim. Though he be my son,
Yet do I now clean disinherit him   35
As common enemy to me and mine.
    Selimus. May Selim live to show how dutiful
And loving he will be to Bajazet.
[*Aside*] So now doth Fortune smile on me again
And in regard of former injuries   40
Offer me millions of diadems.
I smile to see how that the good old man
Thinks Selim's thoughts are brought to such an ebb
As he hath cast off all ambitious hope;
But soon shall that opinion be removed,   45
For if I once get 'mongst the Janissars
Then on my head the golden crown shall sit.
Well, Bajazet, I fear me thou wilt grieve
That e'er thou didst thy feigning son believe.

    Exit Selim[us] with all the rest save Bajazet[, Mustaffa,] and Aga.

    Bajazet. Now, Aga, all the thoughts that troubled me   50

---

1   In another Queen's Men play, *The Famous Victories of Henry V*, the
once-rebellious but now-penitent Prince Henry humbles himself
(sincerely) before his sick father, Henry IV, in similar terms, offering
his father his dagger, declaring himself unworthy to be considered a
son, and begging his father's pardon: "whereas you conjecture that
this hand and this dagger shall be armed against your life," he exclaims, "know, my belovèd father, far be the thoughts of your son—
'Son,' said I? An unworthy son for so good a father!—but far be the
thoughts of any such pretended mischief, and I most humbly render
it to your Majesty's hand. And live, my Lord and sovereign, forever,
and with your dagger at me show like vengeance upon the body of
that your son.... Pardon me, sweet father, pardon me" (6.45).

Do rest within the centre of my heart,
And thou shalt shortly joy as much with me
That[1] Acomat by Selim's consuming sword
Shall lose[2] that ghost which made thee lose[3] thy sight.

    Aga. Ah, Bajazet, Aga looks not for revenge   55
But will pour out his prayers to the heavens
That Acomat may learn by Selimus
To yield himself up to his father's grace.

Sound within, "Long live Selimus Emperor of Turks!"

    Bajazet. How now, what sudden triumph have we here?
    Mustaffa. Ah gracious lord, the captains of the host   60
With one assent have crowned Prince Selimus,
And here he comes with all the Janissaries
To crave his confirmation at thy hands.

*Enter Cali Bashaw, Selimus, Hali Bashaw, Sinam, and the
Janissaries.*

    Sinam. Bajazet, we the captains of thy host,
Knowing thy weak and too unwieldy age   65
Unable is longer to govern us,
Have chosen Selimus, thy younger son,
That he may be our leader and our guide
Against the Sophy and his Persians,
'Gainst the victorious Sultan Tonombey.[4]   70
There wants but thy consent, which we will have
Or hew thy body piecemeal with our swords.
    Bajazet. Needs must I give what is already gone.

---

1 Ed.; Then Q.
2 Ed.; leese Q; Grosart 2 emends to "leave."
3 Ed. (Grosart 2); leese Q.
4 Al-Ashraf Abu Al-Nasr Tuman bay (r. 1516–17), who historically
    became Egyptian Sultan Tuman bay II after Selimus I defeated and
    slew his predecessor at the Battle of Majr Dabiq in 1516 (Imber 40).
    According to Ashton, after their defeat at Majr Dabiq, the Mamluks
    "chose Tomonbeius, which was the admiral of Alexandria and a Cir-
    cassian born, to be their prince and sultan" (sig. L5r). Greene's To-
    nombey, however, is the son of the Sultan (see 30.3), unless Greene
    has decided to give royal father and son the same name, a move that
    Shakespeare will employ in a famous tragedy six years later.

He [Bajazet] takes off his crown.

Here, Selimus, thy father Bajazet,
Wearied with cares that wait upon a king,   75
Resigns the crown as willingly to thee
As ere my father gave it unto me.[1]

[Bajazet] sets it on his [Selimus's] head.

All. Long live Selimus, Emperor of Turks!
Bajazet. Live thou a long and a victorious reign,
And be triumpher of thine enemies.   80
Aga and I will to Dimoticum[2]
And live in peace the remnant of our days.

Exit Bajazet and Aga.

Selimus. Now sit I like the arm-strong son of Jove[3]
When, after he had all his monsters quelled,
He was received in heaven 'mongst the gods   85
And had fair Hebe[4] for his lovely bride.[5]

---

1 Bayezid II resigned his crown to Selimus I on 25 April 1512 (Shaw 79).
2 Demotica, a city in the Ottoman province of Adrianople and
   Bayezid's birthplace (Shaw 79).
3 I.e., Hercules. *Locrine* mentions "the arm-strong Hercules" twice
   (sig. E3v, sig. F4v). In the same play, the temporarily victorious Locrine boasts that "Now sit I like the mighty god of war" (sig. F3v).
4 Cupbearer of the gods and goddess of youth (Grimal 181).
5 Hercules was the son of Jove and the mortal queen Alcmena. Before
   his birth, Jove chose him to be the ruler of a vast empire, but Juno
   caused this promise of empire to be transferred to another, purely mortal man, Eurystheus. For Eurystheus, Hercules undertakes
   his famous twelve labours. Besides their seeming impossibility,
   what these labours have in common is their civilizing effect: Hercules defeats ravaging monsters or cleans things or restores to the
   gods their sacrifices. Hercules' labours, however, ironically increase
   Eurystheus' glory and strengthen his reign. Hercules dies a horrible death: unwittingly, his earthly wife Deianira sends to Hercules
   a shirt which she thinks is soaked in a love potion but is actually
   steeped in poison; the poison causes Hercules intolerable pain once
   he has put it on, and in his agony Hercules throws Deianira's servant
   Lichias into the sea, tears himself apart and then burns himself to
   death because he cannot get the shirt off. Only then is he installed
   amongst the gods and given Hebe as his bride (Grimal 193–207).

As many labours Selimus hath had
And now at length attainèd to the crown.
This is my Hebe, and this is my heaven.
Bajazet goeth to Dimoticum,   90
And there he purposes to live at ease,
But, Selimus, as long as he is on earth
Thou shalt not sleep in rest without some broil,
For Bajazet is inconstant as the wind.
To make that sure I have a platform[1] laid.   95
Bajazet hath with him a cunning Jew
Professing physic,[2] and so skilled therein
As if he had power over life and death;
Withal,[3] a man so stout and resolute
That he will venture anything for gold.   100
This Jew with some intoxicated[4] drink
Shall poison Bajazet and that blind lord.
Then, one of Hydra's heads is clean cut off.[5]
Go some[6] and fetch[7] Abraham the Jew.

Exit one [a Janissary] for Abraham.

Corcut, thy pageant next is to be played,   105
For though he be a grave philosopher,
Given to read Mahomet's dread laws,
And Razin's[8] toys, and Avicenna's[9] drugs,

Lines 83–86 echo Tamburlaine's exclamation after he and his followers crown Zenocrate Queen of Persia at the end of *1 Tamburlaine*:
"As Juno, when the giants were suppressed / That darted mountains
at her brother Jove, / So looks my love, shadowing in her brows / Triumphs and trophies for my victories" (5.2.446–49).

1 Plot, trap.
2 Medicine.
3 Additionally.
4 Poisoned.
5 In one of his twelve labours, Hercules defeats the Lernaean Hydra, a
   snake-like monster with multiple heads that instantly grow back when
   cut off. Hercules slays the Hydra by cutting its heads off and searing
   its neck stumps before the heads can regenerate (Grimal 197).
6 Someone.
7 Grosart 2 emends to "fetch here."
8 Abu Bakr al-Razi (865–925 CE) was a Persian physician and philosopher who held that "human reason alone could give certain knowledge, the path of philosophy was open to all uses, [and] the claims of
   revelation were false and religions were dangerous" (Hourani 78).
9 Abu Ali al-Husayn (980–1037 CE), known in medieval *(continued)*

Yet he may have a longing for the crown.
Besides, he may by devilish necromancy[1]   110
Procure my death or work my overthrow—
The Devil still[2] is ready to do harm.[3]
Hali, you and your brother presently
Shall with an army to Magnesia.
There you shall find the scholar at his book   115
And—hear'st thou, Hali?—strangle him.

Exeunt Hali and Cali.

Corcut once dead, then Acomat remains,
Whose death will make me certain of the crown.
These heads of Hydra are the principal;
When these are off, some other will arise,   120
As Amurath and Aladin, sons to Acomat,
My sister Solyma, Mustaffa's wife.
All these shall suffer shipwreck on a shelf[4]
Rather than[5] Selim will be drowned himself.

Enter Abraham the Jew.

Jew, thou art welcome unto Selimus.   125
I have a piece of service for you, sir,
But on your life be secret in the deed.
Get a strong poison, whose envenomed taste
May take away the life of Bajazet
Before he pass forth of Byzantium.   130
    Abraham. I warrant you, my gracious sovereign,
He shall be quickly sent unto his grave,
For I have potions of so strong a force
That whosoever touches them shall die.
[*Aside*][6] And would Your Grace would once but taste of them,   135

---

and early modern Europe as Avicenna, was a physician and major
Islamic philosopher whose synthesis of Platonic and Aristotelian
philosophies heavily influenced medieval scholasticism (*Oxford Dictionary of Philosophy* 32).
1 Black magic.
2 Always.
3 Proverbial (Tilley D276).
4 Sandbank, submerged ledge of rock (*OED*, n.2, 1a).
5 Ed. (Grosart 2); then Q.
6 Ed.; *Speakes aside* Q, on previous line and aligned right.

I could as willingly afford them you
As your agèd father Bajazet.
[*To Selimus*] My lord, I am resolved to do the deed.

Exit Abraham.

Selimus. So, this is well, for I am none of those
That make a conscience for to kill a man,   140
For nothing is more hurtful to a prince
Than[1] to be scrupulous and religious.[2]
I like Lysander's counsel passing[3] well—
If that I cannot speed[4] with lion's force,
To clothe my complots in a fox's skin[5]—   145
For th'only things that wrought our empery
Were open wrongs and hidden treachery.
Oh, th'are[6] two wings wherewith[7] I use[8] to fly
And soar above the common sort!
If any seek our wrongs to remedy,   150
With these I take his meditation short,[9]
And one of these shall still maintain my cause:
Or[10] fox's skin, or lion's rending paws.

Exeunt all.

---

1 Ed. (Grosart 2); Then Q.
2 According to Machiavelli, the prince "will find that some of the
   things that appear to be virtues will, if he practices them, ruin him,
   and some of the things that appear to be vices will bring him security and prosperity" (*The Prince* 92).
3 Very, extremely.
4 Succeed.
5 Lysander was a fourth-century BCE Spartan politician and general. In his *Lives*, Plutarch reports Lysander to have said, "when the
   lion's skin will not serve, we must help it with the case [skin] of a
   fox" (483). Machiavelli repeats Lysander's advice in *The Prince*: the
   prince "must learn from the fox and the lion; because the lion is
   defenceless against traps and a fox is defenceless against wolves.
   Therefore one must be a fox in order to recognize traps, and a lion to
   frighten off wolves. Those who simply act like lions are stupid" (99).
6 They are.
7 With which.
8 Am accustomed.
9 I.e., defeat his intention.
10 Either.

[Scene 19
On the road to Dimoticum, but still within the bounds of
Byzantium]

*Enter Bajazet, Aga in mourning cloaks,[1] Abraham the Jew with a
cup.*

   Bajazet. Come, Aga, let us sit and mourn awhile,
For Fortune never showed herself so cross[2]
To any prince as to poor Bajazet.
That woeful emperor first of my name,[3]
Whom the Tartarians locked in cage   5
To be a spectacle to all the world,[4]
Was ten times happier than[5] I am,[6]
For Tamburlaine,[7] the scourge of nations,
Was he that pulled him from his kingdom so,
But mine own sons expel me from the throne.   10
Ah, where shall I begin to make my moan,
Or what shall I first reckon in my plaint?
From my youth up I have been drowned in woe,
And to my latest[8] hour I shall be so.
You swelling seas of never-ceasing care,   15
Whose waves my weather-beaten ship do toss,
Your boisterous billows too unruly are
And threaten still my ruin and my loss.
Like hugy mountains do your waters rear
Their lofty tops and my weak vessel cross.   20

---

1 Presumably black (Dessen and Thomson 145).
2 Opposed.
3 Bayezid I (r. 1389–1402).
4 After defeating him in the Battle of Ankara in 1402, the Tartar con-
    queror Tamburlaine (d. 1405) placed Bayezid I in an iron cage, in
    which he was displayed in Tamburlaine's military camp. In Mar-
    lowe's *1 Tamburlaine*, Bajazeth eventually commits suicide by dash-
    ing out his brains on the cage's bars (5.2.240 s.d.).
5 Ed. (Grosart 2); then Q.
6 Vitkus emends to "am now."
7 Timur the Lame (d. 1405), according to Greene "the most bloody
    butcher in the world" (Grosart 2.81), the Tartar conqueror whose
    stunningly successful military conquests throughout Asia Marlowe
    dramatizes in his two *Tamburlaine* plays.
8 Last.

Alas, at length allay[1] your stormy strife
And cruel wrath within[2] me rages[3] rife,
Or else my feeble bark cannot endure
Your flashing buffets and outrageous blows
But while thy foamy flood doth it immure[4]   25
Shall soon be wrecked upon the sandy shallows.
Grief, my lewd[5] boatswain,[6] steereth[7] nothing sure,
But without stars 'gainst tide and wind he rows
And cares not though upon some rock we split,
A restless pilot for the charge[8] unfit.   30
But out, alas, the god that vails[9] the sea[10]
And can alone this raging tempest stent[11]
Will never blow a gentle gale of ease
But suffer my poor vessel to be rent.[12]
Then, O thou[13] blind procurer of mischance   35
That[14] stayst[15] thyself upon a turning wheel,[16]

---

1 Diminish.
2 I.e., wrath that within.
3 Grosart 2 emends to "raging."
4 Enclose, surround, engulf.
5 Foolish, unskilful, rude (*OED*, adj., 4).
6 Ship's deck officer (*OED*, n., 1).
7 Ed. (Vitkus); stirreth Q.
8 Duty.
9 Lowers, subdues, abases. "Then mayst thou think that Mars himself came down / To vail thy plumes and heave thee from thy pomp, / Proud that thou art" (sig. G3r), Orlando boasts to Sacrepant in Greene's *Orlando Furioso*. This usage not in *OED*. Grosart 2 emends to "rules."
10 In classical myth, the god who ruled the sea was Poseidon, but the reference here may be more generally to God.
11 "To extend, stretch out or set (a tent, sail, curtain, net, etc.) in its proper position" (*OED*, v.1, 1a).
12 Figuring himself as a boat tossed in the storm of his unruly and reckless emotions, Bajazet in lines 15 to 34 adapts a common Petrarchan conceit, an early English example of which is Wyatt's "My galley charged with forgetfulness," whose opening four lines are as follows: "My galley charged with forgetfulness / Thorough sharp seas, in winter nights doth pass / 'Tween rock and rock; and eke mine enemy, alas, / That is my lord, steereth with cruelness" (1–4). Lines 15 to 38 are divided by rhyme into a sonnet-like structure of two octaves (ababab cc; dedede ff) followed by two quatrains (ghgh; ijij).
13 Fortune.
14 Who.
15 Props, supports.
16 Selimus employs a similar image at 7.3–6.

Thy cruel hand, even when thou wilt, enhance[1]
And pierce my poor heart with thy thrillant[2] steel.
   Aga. Cease, Bajazet. Now it is Aga's turn.
Rest thou awhile and gather up more tears   40
The while poor Aga tells his tragedy.
When first my mother brought me to the world,
Some blazing comet ruled in the sky,
Portending miserable chance to me.
My parents[3] were but men of poor estate,[4]   45
And happy yet had wretched Aga been
If Bajazet had not exalted him.
Poor Aga, had it not been much more fair
T'have died among the cruel Persians
Than[5] thus at home by barbarous tyranny   50
To live and never see the cheerful day
And to want hands wherewith to feel the way?
   Bajazet. Leave weeping, Aga. We have wept enough.
Now Bajazet will ban[6] another while
And utter curses to the concave sky[7]   55
Which may infect the regions of the air
And bring a general plague on all the world.
Night, thou most ancient grandmother of all,
First made by Jove for rest and quiet sleep
When cheerful day is gone from th'earth's wide hall,   60
Henceforth thy mantle in black Lethe[8] steep[9]
And clothe the world in darkness infernal.
Suffer not once the joyful daylight peep
But let thy pitchy[10] steeds aye[11] draw thy wain
And coal-black silence in the world still[12] reign.   65

---

1 Lift, raise (*OED*, v., 1a).
2 Ed. (Grosart 2); chrillant Q. Thrilling (*OED*, adj.).
3 Relations.
4 Condition.
5 Ed. (Grosart 2); Then Q.
6 Curse.
7 In *Locrine*, the famished Humber vows to "ban my fill" and "utter curses to the concave sky / Which may infect the airy regions" (sig. F4v).
8 River of forgetfulness in Hades.
9 Ed. (Grosart 2); sleepe Q.
10 Black.
11 Ever, always, continually (*OED*, adv.).
12 Always.

Curse on my parents that first brought me up
And on the cradle wherein I was rocked;
Curse on the day when first I was created
The[1] chief commander of all Asia!
Curse on my sons that drive me to this grief, 70
Curse on myself that can find no relief,
And curse on him, an everlasting curse,
That quenched those lamps of ever-burning light
And took away my Aga's warlike hands!
And curse on all things under the wide sky! 75
Ah, Aga, I have cursed my stomach dry.
    Abraham. I have a drink, my lords, of noble worth,
Which soon will calm your stormy passions
And glad your hearts if so you please to taste it.
    Bajazet. And[2] who art thou that thus doest pity us? 80
    Abraham. Your Highness' humble servant, Abraham.
    Bajazet. Abraham, sit down and drink to Bajazet.
    Abraham. [*Aside*] Faith, I am old as well as Bajazet
And have not many months to live on earth.
I care not much to end my life with him. 85
[*To Bajazet and Aga*] Here's to you, lordings, with a full carouse.

He [Abraham] drinks [and passes the cup to Bajazet].

    Bajazet. Here, Aga, woeful Bajazet drinks to thee.

[*Bajazet drinks.*]

Abraham, hold the cup to him while he drinks.

[*Aga drinks while Abraham holds the cup.*]

    Abraham. Now know, old lords, that you have drunk your last.
This was a potion which I did prepare 90
To poison you, by Selimus' instigation,
And now it is dispersèd through my bones,
And glad I am that such companions
Shall go with me down to Proserpina.[3]

---

1 Grosart 2 emends to "To."
2 Ed. (Grosart 2); For Q.
3 Queen of Hades and wife of Pluto, god of the underworld.

He [*Abraham*] *dies.*

Bajazet. Ah, wicked Jew! Ah, cursèd Selimus!　　　　　　95
How have the Destins[1] dealt with Bajazet,
That none should cause my death but mine own son?
Had Isma'il and his warlike Persians
Pierced my body with their iron spears,
Or had the strong, unconquered Tonombey　　　　　　100
With his Egyptians took me prisoner
And sent me with his valiant Mamelukes[2]
To be a prey unto the crocodilus,
It never would have grieved me half so much.
But welcome, Death, into whose calmy[3] port　　　　　　105
My sorrow-beaten soul joys to arrive,
And now farewell, my disobedient sons,
Unnatural sons unworthy of that name.
Farewell, sweet life, and, Aga, now farewell
Till we shall meet in the Elysian fields.　　　　　　110

He [*Bajazet*] *dies.*[4]

Aga. What greater grief had mournful Priamus[5]
Than[6] that he lived to see his Hector[7] die,
His city[8] burnt down by revenging[9] flames,[10]

1　Destinies, or Fates, who were classical goddesses. There were three
　　Fates: Clotho, who spun the thread of life, Lachesis, who spooled it
　　out, and Atropos, who cut it.
2　Mamluks. The Mamluks ruled Egypt from 1250 until they were de-
　　feated by Selimus I in 1517 (Shaw 8, 84).
3　Grosart 2 emends to "calm."
4　Bajazet died 26 May 1512 (Shaw 79).
5　King of Troy.
6　Ed. (Grosart 2); Then Q.
7　Priam's eldest son, killed in single combat by the Greek hero Achil-
　　les during the Trojan War. Hector's death is narrated in Book XXII
　　of Homer's *Iliad*.
8　Troy.
9　The Greeks began the Trojan War to avenge the Trojan prince Paris'
　　kidnapping of Helen, the wife of Menelaus, King of Sparta.
10　After ten years of besieging Troy, the Greeks penetrated the city's
　　walls concealed in the large wooden horse they deceitfully offered
　　to the Trojans as a gift. They then sacked and burned the city. The
　　Trojan prince Aeneas recounts the event to the Carthaginian Queen

And poor Polites[1] slain before his face?[2]
Aga, thy grief is matchable to his, 115
For I have lived to see my sovereign's death;
Yet glad that I must breathe my last with him.
And now farewell, sweet light, which my poor eyes
These twice six months never did behold.
Aga will follow noble Bajazet 120
And beg a boon of lovely Proserpine,
That he and I may in the mournful fields[3]
Still weep and wail our strange calamities.

He [Aga] dies.

[Scene 20
Countryside around Smyrna]

*Enter Bullithrumble the shepherd running in haste and laughing to
himself.*[4]

Bullithrumble. Ha, ha, ha! "Married," quoth you? Marry,[5] an[6]
Bullithrumble were to begin the world again, I would set a tap
abroach[7] and not live in daily fear of the breach of my wife's Ten
Commandments. I'll tell you what, I thought myself as proper[8] a
fellow at wasters[9] as any in all our village, and yet when my wife 5
begins to play club's trump[10] with me, I am fain to sing:

Dido in Book II of Virgil's epic the *Aeneid*. Marlowe expands upon
Virgil's narrative in 2.1 of *Dido Queen of Carthage*.

1 Priam's youngest son, who is slain by Achilles' son Pyrrhus.
2 In Virgil's account of Pyrrhus' slaughter of Priam (*Aeneid* II.506–
67), Priam upbraids Pyrrhus for killing Polites in front of him and
therefore exhibiting an impiety not displayed by his father Achilles.
In reply, Pyrrhus swiftly murders Priam at the altar at which he has
sought refuge. In *Dido Queen of Carthage* Marlowe amplifies the violence of Virgil's account.
3 The Elysian fields. See p. 83, note 1.
4 As is frequently the case for clown characters in English Renaissance drama, Bullithrumble speaks in prose.
5 An expression of surprise or indignation (*OED*, int.).
6 Ed.; and Q. If.
7 I.e., open a tap (and thereby flood the world).
8 Decent, respectable (*OED*, adj., 2).
9 Fencing with clubs or cudgels (*OED*, n.2, 3).
10 "Club is trump," a card game, here used as a metaphor for a cud-
gelling. In Greene's prose romance *Pandosto* (1588), (*continued*)

What hap[1] had I to marry a shrew,
For she hath given me many a blow,
And how to please her, alas, I do not know.
From morn to even[2] her tongue ne'er lies,[3]   10
Sometimes she laughs, sometimes she cries,
And I can scarce keep her talons from my eyes.
When from abroad I do come in,
"Sir knave," she cries, "where have you been?"
Thus please or displease, she lays it on my skin.   15
Then do I crouch, then do I kneel,
And wish my cap were furred[4] with steel
To bear the blows that my poor head doth feel.
But, our Sir John,[5] beshrew thy heart,
For thou hast joined[6] us. We cannot part,   20
And I, poor fool, must ever bear the smart.

I'll tell you what, this morning while I was making me ready she
came with a holly wand[7] and so blessed my shoulders that I was
fain to run through a whole alphabet of faces. Now at the last,
seeing she was so cramuk[8] with me, I began to swear all the criss-   25
cross-row[9] over, beginning at great A, little a, 'til I came to w, x, y
and, snatching up my sheep-hook and my bottle and my bag, like
a desperate fellow ran away, and here now I'll sit down and eat
my meat.

While he is eating, enter Corcut and his Page, disguised like
mourners.

---

the shepherd's wife "began to crow against her goodman, and, taking up a cudgel ... swore solemnly that she would make clubs trumps
if he brought any bastard brat within her doors" (Grosart 4.267).
In *Locrine*, the clown Strumbo has a similar comic speech, in which
his shrewish wife "began to play knave's trumps" and "set her Ten
Commandments in my face" (sig. H2r) because he came home late
drunk.
1 Chance.
2 Evening.
3 Lies still, is quiet.
4 Lined.
5 The parson.
6 Married.
7 Branch, stick.
8 "Perverse, contrary, cantankerous" (Grosart 2 99).
9 Christ-cross-row, i.e., the alphabet as displayed in elementary school
   texts ("hornbooks") for children, so called because of the cross preceding the letter "a" (*OED*, n.).

Corcut. O hateful, hellish snake of Tartary,[1]   30
That feedest on the souls[2] of noblest men,
Damned Ambition, cause of all misery,
Why doest thou creep from out thy loathsome fen
And with thy poison animatest friends
To[3] gape and long one for the other's ends?   35
Selimus, couldst thou not content thy mind
With the possession of the sacred throne,
Which thou didst get by father's death unkind,
Whose poisoned ghost before high God doth groan,
But thou must seek poor Corcut's overthrow,   40
That never injured thee, so, nor so?
Old Hali's sons with two great company
Of barded[4] horse were sent from Selimus
To take me prisoner in Magnesia,
And death I am sure should have befell to me   45
If they had once but set their eyes on me.
So, thus disguised, my poor page and I
Fled fast to Smyrna,[5] where in a dark cave
We meant t'await th'arrival of some ship
That might transfreight us safely unto Rhodes.[6]   50
But see how Fortune crossed my enterprise:

---

1 Tartarus was the deepest level of hell in classical myth. Here the
   Titans were imprisoned after being defeated by the Olympian gods
   (Grimal 433). Son of Tartarus and Gaia (Earth), Typhon is the
   "snake" of Tartarus, a giant serpent-like monster who battled Jove
   for supreme rulership of the universe and therefore is a personifica-
   tion of ambition. Jove finally defeated Typhon with his thunderbolts
   and then crushed him under the volcanic Mount Etna (Grimal 461–
   62). A version of Typhon's assault on Jove can be found in Ovid,
   Metamorphoses V.405–423. Greene provides his own in *Orlando Furioso*: "The son of Saturn in his wrath / Pashed all the mountains at
   Typheus' head, / And topsy-turvy turned the bottom up" (sig. C2v).
   Typhon was the father of the Hydra (see p. 119, note 5 and p. 120,
   line 119).
2 Ed.; soule Q.
3 Ed. (Vitkus); And Q.
4 Armoured (*OED*, n.2, 1).
5 City on the Aegean coast of Anatolia.
6 Island off the southwest coast of Anatolia. The Hospitallers of St.
   John conquered Rhodes in 1310, and for the next two centuries the
   island was a key offensive and defensive outpost in the Crusades. In
   1522 Suleiman I (r. 1520–66), Selimus's son, attacked the island; by
   the end of the year its defenders surrendered and left (Riley-Smith
   278–81).

Bostangi Bashaw,[1] Selim's son-in-law,
Kept all the sea coasts with his brigantines,[2]
That[3] if we had but ventured on the sea
I presently had been his prisoner.   55
These two days have we kept us in the cave,
Eating such herbs as the ground did afford,
And now through hunger are we both constrained
Like fearful snakes to creep out step by step
And see if we may get us any food.   60
And in good time! See, yonder sits a man
Spreading a hungry dinner on the grass.

Bullithrumble spies them and puts up his meat.

Bullithrumble. These are some felonians that seek to rob me.
Well, I'll make myself a good deal valianter than[4] I am indeed,
and if they will needs creep into kindred with me, I'll betake me   65
to my old occupation and run away.
    Corcut. Hail, groom.[5]
    Bullithrumble. Good Lord, sir, you are deceived. My
name's Master Bullithrumble. [*Aside*] This is some cozening,
coney-catching cross-biter[6] that would fain persuade me he   70
knows me and so, under a 'tence[7] of familiarity and acquaintance, uncle[8] me of victuals.

---

1 Selimus later had Bostangi "beheaded for the extortion he did in the
   province whereas he made him governor" (Ashton sig. N2r).
2 "A small vessel equipped both for sailing and rowing, swifter and
   more easily manœuvred than larger ships, and hence employed for
   purposes of piracy, espionage, reconnoitring, etc." (*OED*, n., 1).
3 So that.
4 Ed. (Grosart 2); then Q.
5 Boy, man-servant (*OED*, n.1, 1, 3).
6 In 1591 Greene published a pamphlet entitled *A Notable Discovery of Cosenage Now Daily Practiced by Sundry Lewd Persons Called
   Cony-Catchers and Cross-Biters*, ostensibly an attempt to expose some
   of the scams by which the rogues of the London underworld cheat-
   ed (cozened) and robbed their unsuspecting victims (conies). In the
   pamphlet, Greene defines the "cony-catching law" as "cosenage
   by cards" (37) and the "cross-biting law" as "cosenage by whores"
   (36). In the short tales Greene tells, the cony, usually a naive character, is caught and stripped of his money at cards by the male cony-
   catcher(s), often with cross-biting help from a female prostitute.
7 Pretence.
8 Cheat.

Corcut. Then, Bullithrumble, if that be thy name—

Bullithrumble. My name, sir? O Lord, yes, and if you will not
believe me, I will bring my godfathers and godmothers, and they   75
shall swear it upon the font-stone[1] and upon the church book[2]
too, where it is written. [*Aside*] Mass, I think he be some Justice
of Peace,[3] *ad quorum* and *omnium populorum*,[4] how he 'samines[5]
me. [*To Corcut*] A Christian, yes, marry am I, sir, yes, verily and
do believe. An[6] it please you, I'll go forward in my catechism.   80

Corcut. Then, Bullithrumble, by that blessèd Christ
And by the tomb where he was burièd,
By sovereign hope which thou conceiv'st in him,
Whom, dead, as ever-living thou adorest—

Bullithrumble. O Lord, help me! I shall be torn in pieces with   85
devils and goblins![7]

Corcut. By all the joys thou hop'st to have in heaven,
Give some meat to poor, hunger-starvèd men.

Bullithrumble. [*Aside*] Oh, these are, as a man should say, beggars. Now will I be as stately[8] to them as if I were Master Pig-   90
wiggen, our constable. [*To Corcut and the Page*] Well, sirs, come
before me. Tell me, if I should entertain you, would you not
steal?

Page. If we did mean so, sir, we would not make your worship
acquainted with it.   95

---

1 Christening font.
2 Parish register, in which the names of newborns were recorded after
   christening.
3 In early modern England, Justices of the Peace were local government magistrates who "had wide summary powers over a range of
   misdemeanours and some civil jurisdiction over disputes between
   masters and apprentices and cases of bastardy" (Braddick 31). Each
   county had multiple Justices of the Peace, who collectively constitut-
   ed the Commission of the Peace, the Bench, which met quarterly to
   try cases and determine local administrative matters (Braddick 31).
4 "Belonging to the Quorum" and "of all the people" (Latin). The
   Quorum was "a select body of (usually eminent) justices of the
   peace, every member of which had to be present to constitute a de-
   ciding body" (*OED*, n., 1).
5 Examines.
6 Ed.; and Q.
7 Bullithrumble believes that by invoking Christ in this fashion Corcut has begun a magical incantation to summon demons.
8 Haughty, arrogant, imperious (*OED*, adj., 3a).

Bullithrumble. A good, well-nutrimented[1] lad. Well, if you will keep my sheep truly and honestly, keeping your hands from lying and slandering and your tongues from picking and stealing, you shall be Master Bullithrumble's servitors.

Corcut. With all our hearts.   100

Bullithrumble. Then come on and follow me. We will have a hog's cheek and a dish of tripes and a society of puddings, and to field. "A society of puddings": did you mark that well used metaphor? Another would have said, "a company of puddings." If you dwell with me long, sirs, I shall make you as eloquent as our   105 parson himself.

Exeunt Corcut and Bullithrumble.

Page. Now is the time when I may be enriched.
The brethren that were sent by Selimus
To take my lord, Prince Corcut, prisoner,
Finding him fled, proposed large rewards   110
To them that could declare where he remains.
Faith, I'll to them and get the portagues,[2]
Though by the bargain Corcut lose his head.

Exit Page.

[Scene 21
Bajazet's tomb in Byzantium]

*Enter Selimus, Sinam Bashaw, the corpses of Bajazet[3] and Aga,
with funeral pomp,[4] Mustaffa, and the Janissaries.*

Selimus. [*Aside*][5] Why, thus must Selim blind his subjects'[6] eyes
And strain his own to weep for Bajazet.
They will not dream[7] I made him away

---

1 Sacrepant calls Orlando's page Orgalio a "well-nutrimented knave" (sig. C1r) in Greene's *Orlando Furioso*.

2 Portuguese coins worth approximately £4 each (*Stanford Dictionary of Anglicised Words and Phrases* 643).

3 Ed. (Grosart 2); *Mustaffa* Q.

4 "[A] public procession involving a *hearse/bier*, *mourning* figures, and appropriate accoutrements and *music*" (Dessen and Thomson 98).

5 Ed.; Q prints To himselfe on line 5.

6 Ed. (Grosart 2); subiect Q.

7 Grosart 2 emends to "dream that."

When thus they see me with religious pomp
To celebrate his tomb-black mortuary.[1]   5
And though my heart, cast in an iron mould,
Cannot admit the smallest dram of grief,
Yet, that I may be thought to love him well,
I'll mourn in show, though I rejoice indeed.
[*To the corpses*][2] Thus, after he hath five long ages lived,   10
The sacred phoenix of Arabia
Loadeth his wings with precious perfumes
And on the altar of the golden sun
Offers himself a grateful sacrifice.[3]
Long didst thou live triumphant, Bajazet,   15
A fear unto thy greatest enemies,
And, now that Death the conqueror of kings
Dislodgèd hath thy never-dying soul
To flee unto the heavens from whence she came
And leave her frail earthly[4] pavilion,   20
Thy body in this ancient monument,
Where our great predecessors sleep in rest,[5]

---

1 Ed. (Grosart 2); mortarie Q. Funeral (*OED*, n., 2).
2 Ed.; printed below line 9, aligned right, in Q.
3 Pliny writes that "The birds of Arabia and India are for the most
   part of diverse colours.... But the Phoenix of Arabia passeth all others.... He is as big as an eagle; for colour, as yellow and bright as
   gold (namely, all about the neck); the rest of the body a deep red
   purple; the tail azure blue, intermingled with feathers, of rose car-
   nation colour; and the head bravely adorned with a crest and pen-
   nache finely wrought, having a tuft and plume thereupon, right fair
   and goodly to be seen.... Never man was known to see him feeding
   and in Arabia he is held a sacred bird, dedicated unto the Sun. He
   liveth 660 years, and when he groweth old and begins to decay, he
   builds himself a nest with the twigs and branches of the canell or
   cinnamon and frankincense trees, and when he hath filled it with
   all sort of sweet aromatical spices, yieldeth up his life thereupon....
   Of his bones and marrow there breedeth at first, as it were, a little
   worm, which afterwards proveth to be a pretty bird. And the first
   thing that this young new phoenix doth is to perform the obsequies
   of the former phoenix late deceased, to translate and carry away his
   whole nest into the City of the Sun near Panchaea, and to bestow it
   full devoutly there upon the altar" (*Natural History* 10.2).
4 Ed. (Grosart 2); earth Q.
5 In Q, the following line interrupts Selimus's speech to instruct the
   reader to "Suppose the Temple of Mahomet." In the early modern period, mosques were commonly called temples. According to
   Ashton, "At his father's burial, he [Selimus] prepared a (*continued*)

Thy woeful son Selimus thus doth place.
Thou wert the phoenix of this age of ours
And diedst wrapped in the sweet perfumes   25
Of thy magnific deeds, whose lasting praise
Mounteth to highest heaven with golden wings.[1]
Princes, come bear your emperor company
In, till the days of mourning be o'erpassed,
And then we mean to rouse false Acomat   30
And cast him forth of Macedonia.[2]

Exeunt all.

[Scene 22
Countryside around Smyrna]

Enter Hali, Cali, Corcut's Page, and one or two soldiers.

Page. My lords, if I bring you not where Corcut is then let me
be hanged, but if I deliver him up into your hands then let me
have the reward due to so good a deed.
Hali. Page, if thou show us where thy master is,
Be sure thou shalt be honoured for the deed   5
And high exalted above other men.[3]

Enter Corcut and Bullithrumble.

Page. That same is he that, in disguisèd robes,
Accompanies yon shepherd to the fields.
Corcut. The sweet content that country life affords
Passeth the royal pleasures of a king,   10
For there our joys are interlaced with fears,

---

great rout of mourners with all pomp and solemnity, and further-
more set up a tomb very rich and precious to behold, sparing here
for no cost, that by this vain and feigned holiness he might cloak the
most cruel and manifest murder of his father" (sig. I3r). Historically, Bayezid II was buried in a tomb he himself commissioned and
had built between 1501 and 1506. The tomb is in Istanbul, in the
Bayezid II mosque (Curatola 150, 198).
1 See p. 133, note 3.
2 Region in northern Greece.
3 The gallows is "a place of great promotion" (sig. G2v), the servant
Andrew wryly tells the assassin Jacques in Greene's *James IV.*

But here no fear nor care is harbourèd
But a sweet calm of a most quiet state.[1]
Ah, Corcut, would thy brother Selimus
But let thee live, here shouldst thou spend thy life,   15
Feeding thy sheep among these grassy lands.
But, sure, I wonder where my page is gone.
   Hali. Corcut!
   Corcut. Ay me, who nameth me?
   Hali. Hali, the governor of Magnesia.   20
Poor prince, thou thoughtst in these disguisèd weeds
To mask unseen—and happily[2] thou mightst,
But that thy page betrayèd thee to us.
And be not wroth[3] with us, unhappy prince,
If we do what our sovereign commands: 25
'Tis for thy death that Selim sends for thee.
   Corcut. Thus I, like poor Amphiaraus, sought
By hiding my estate[4] in shepherd's coat
T'escape the angry wrath of Selimus;
But as his wife, false Eriphyle, did   30
Betray his safety for a chain of gold,
So my false page hath vilely dealt with me.[5]
[*To the Page*] Pray God that thou mayst prosper so as she.[6]
Hali, I know thou sorrowest for my case,

---

1 Grosart compares lines 8 to 12 with the following from Greene's
  Farewell to Folly: "Sweet are the thoughts that savour of content, /
  The quiet mind is richer than a crown; / Sweet are the nights in careless slumber spent, / The poor estate scorns Fortune's angry frown;
  / Such sweet content, such minds, such sleep, such bliss / Beggars
  enjoy, when princes often miss" (Grosart 2 xiii). Grosart calls this "a
  characteristically Greeneian repetition" (xiii).
2 Perhaps.
3 Ed. (Grosart 2); wrath Q. Angry.
4 State, condition, status (*OED*, n., 1, 3).
5 In classical myth, Polyneices is exiled from Thebes by his brother
  Eteocles and mounts a campaign against Thebes to recover it. He
  attempts to persuade the seer Amphiaraus to join the expedition,
  but Amphiaraus is reluctant to do so because he foresees that he
  will die if he does. Polyneices seduces Amphiaraus' wife Eriphyle to
  persuade Amphiaraus by giving her the necklace of Harmonia, and
  Amphiaraus finally and fatally joins (Apollodorus, *Library of Greek
  Mythology* 3.6).
6 Eriphyle was murdered by her two sons (*Library of Greek Mythology*
  3.6).

But it is bootless. Come, and let us go.   35
Corcut is ready since it must[1] be so.
  Cali. Shepherd.
  Bullithrumble. That's my profession, sir.
  Cali. Come, you must go with us.
  Bullithrumble. Who I? Alas, sir, I have a wife and seventeen   40
cradles rocking, two ploughs going, two barns filling, and a great
herd of beasts feeding, and you should utterly undo me to take
me to such a great charge.[2]
  Cali. Well, there is no remedy.

> *Exeunt all, but Bullithrumble stealing from them closely away.*

  Bullithrumble. The more's the pity. "Go with you," quoth he!   45
Marry, that had been the way to preferment: down Holborn,[3] up
Tyburn.[4] Well, I'll keep my best joint from the strappado[5] as well
as I can hereafter. I'll have no more servants.

> *Exit [Bullithrumble,] running away.*

[Scene 23
Selimus' court in Byzantium]

Enter Selimus, Sinam Bashaw, Mustaffa, and the Janissaries.

  Selimus. Sinam, we hear our brother Acomat
Is fled away from Macedonia
To ask for aid of Persian Isma'il
And the Egyptian Sultan, our chief foes.
  Sinam. Herein, my lord, I like his enterprise,   5

---

1 Ed. (Grosart 2); it is must Q.
2 Expense.
3 "One of the main thoroughfares of London, running west from the
   corner of Newgate Street and Old Bailey to Drury Lane" (Sugden
   252).
4 Tyburn was "the place of execution for Middlesex criminals" (Sugden 535); "[p]risoners from Newgate and the Tower were taken to
   Tyburn for execution along Holborn, and Holborn Hill was nicknamed Heavy Hill in consequence" (Sugden 252). The gallows site
   is now Marble Arch.
5 A form of torture in which the victim's shoulder joints were dislocat-
   ed through the use of a pulley mechanism (*OED*, n., 1).

For if they give him aid, as sure they will,
Being Your Highness' vowèd enemies,
You shall have just cause for to war on them
For giving succour[1] 'gainst you to your foe.
You know they are two mighty potentates[2]   10
And may be hurtful neighbours to Your Grace,
And to enrich the Turkish diadem
With two so worthy kingdoms as they are
Would be eternal glory to your name.
    Selimus. By heavens, Sinam, th'art a warrior   15
And worthy councillor unto a king.

Sound within. Enter Cali and Hali, with Corcut and his Page.

How now, what news?
    Cali. My gracious lord, we here present to you
Your brother Corcut, whom in Smyrna coasts
Feeding a flock of sheep upon a down[3]   20
His traitorous page betrayed to our hands.
    Selimus. Thanks, ye bold brethren, but for that false part
Let the vile page be famishèd to death.

                [*Exit Cali and Hali with the Page.*]

    Corcut. Selim, in this I see thou art a prince,
To punish treason with condign[4] reward.   25
    Selimus. Oh, sir, I love the fruit that treason brings,
But those that are the traitors, them I hate.
But, Corcut, could not your philosophy
Keep you safe from my Janissaries' hands?
We thought you had old Gyges' wondrous ring,[5]   30
That so you were invisible to us.
    Corcut. Selim, thou dealst unkindly with thy brother,
To seek my death and make a jest of me.

---

1   Aid.
2   Rulers, kings.
3   Hill.
4   Fitting, appropriate, merited (*OED*, adj., 3a).
5   Plato recounts the myth of Gyges' ring in Book II of the *Republic*:
    a Lydian shepherd, Gyges, stumbles across a magical ring that has
    the power to render its wearer invisible; he then "seduced the queen,
    and with her help attacked and murdered the king and seized the
    throne" (105–06).

Upbraidst thou me with my philosophy?
Why, this I learned by studying learnèd arts: 35
That I can bear my fortune as it falls
And that I fear no whit thy cruelty,
Since thou wilt deal no otherwise with me,
Than[1] thou hast dealt with agèd Bajazet.
    Selimus. By heavens, Corcut, thou shalt surely die   40
For slandering Selim with my father's death.
    Corcut. Then let me freely speak my mind this once,
For thou shalt never hear me speak again.
    Selimus. Nay, we can give such losers leave to speak.[2]
    Corcut. Then, Selim, hear thy brother's dying words   45
And mark them well, for ere thou die thyself
Thou shalt perceive all things will come to pass
That Corcut doth divine[3] before his death.
Since my vain flight from fair Magnesia,
Selim, I have conversed with Christians   50
And learned of them the way to save my soul
And please the anger of the highest God.
'Tis he that made this pure crystalline vault[4]
Which hangeth over our unhappy heads.
From thence he doth behold each sinner's fault,   55
And though our sins under his[5] feet he treads
And for a while seem for to wink at us,
It is but[6] to recall us from our ways.
But if we do like headstrong sons neglect
To hearken to our loving father's voice,   60
Then in his anger will he us reject
And give us over to our wicked choice.
Selim, before His Dreadful Majesty
There lies a book written with bloody lines
Where our offences all are registered,   65
Which if we do not hastily repent,
We are reserved to lasting punishment.
Thou, wretched Selimus, hast greatest need

---

1   Ed. (Grosart 2); Then Q.
2   Proverbial (Tilley L458).
3   Prophesy, foretell.
4   The heavens.
5   Ed.; our Q.
6   Ed. (Vitkus); not in Q. Grosart 2 emends the line by adding "ill"
    after "our."

To ponder these things in thy secret thoughts,
If thou consider what strange massacres 70
And cruel murders thou hast caused be done.
Think on the death of woeful Bajazet.
Doth not his ghost still haunt thee for revenge?
Selim, in Çorlu didst thou set upon
Our agèd father in his sudden flight; 75
In Çorlu shalt thou die a grievous death,
And if thou wilt not change thy greedy mind
Thy soul shall be tormented in dark hell,
Where woe, and woe, and never-ceasing woe
Shall sound about thy ever-damnèd soul.[1] 80
Now, Selim, I have spoken, let me die;
I never will entreat thee for my life.
Selim, farewell. Thou God of Christians,
Receive my dying soul into thy hands.[2]

[*Selimus*] *strangles him.*[3]

Selimus. What, is he dead? Then Selimus is safe 85
And hath no more corrivals[4] in the crown,
For, as for Acomat, he soon shall see
His Persian aid cannot save him from me.
Now, Sinam, march to fair Amasia's[5] walls,
Where Acomat's stout[6] queen immures herself, 90
And girt[7] the city with a warlike siege,
For since her husband is my enemy,
I see no cause why she should be my friend.
They say young Amurath and Aladin,

---

1 Ashton concludes his account of Selimus's reign by stating that Selimus "died in the year of our Lord MDXX [1520] in the month of September, in the same village of Cyurlu whereas he first set upon his father.... The which thing certes happened not without the plain judgement of God that whereas before he committed that unworthy crime, in the same place likewise he should receive a worthy punishment" (sig. M8v).
2 Echoing Christ's last words on the cross: "Father, into thy hands I commend my spirit" (Luke 23:46).
3 Historically, Corcut was strangled 13 March 1513 in Bursa (Finkel 103).
4 Rival claimants, competitors.
5 Ed. (Grosart 2); *Amasia* Q.
6 Proud, fierce, brave, resolute (*OED*, adj., 1).
7 Surround.

Her bastard brood, are come to succour her,   95
But I'll prevent this their officiousness
And send their souls[1] down to their grandfather.
Mustaffa, you shall keep Byzantium,
While I and Sinam girt Amasia.

Exit Selimus, Sinam, Janissaries all save one.

    Mustaffa. It grieves my soul that Bajazet's fair line   100
Should be eclipsèd thus by Selimus,
Whose cruel soul will never be at rest
Till none remain of Ottoman's fair race
But he himself. Yet for[2] old Bajazet
Loved Mustaffa dear unto his death,   105
I will show mercy to his family.
Go, sirrah, post to Acomat's young sons
And bid them as they mean to save their lives
To fly in haste from fair Amasia,
Lest cruel Selim put them to the sword.   110

Exit one [the Janissary] to Amurath and Aladin.

And now, Mustaffa, prepare thou thy neck,
For thou art next to die by Selim's hands.
Stern Sinam Bashaw grudgeth still at thee,
And crabbed Hali stormeth at thy life,
All repine[3] that thou art honoured so,   115
To be the brother of their emperor.

Enter Solyma.

But wherefore comes my lovely Solyma?
    Solyma. Mustaffa, I am come to seek thee out.
If ever thy distressèd Solyma
Found grace and favour in thy manly heart,   120
Fly hence with me unto some desert[4] land,
For if we tarry here we are but dead.
This night when fair Lucina's[5] shining wain

---

1 Ed. (Grosart 2); soule Q.
2 Because.
3 Complain.
4 Deserted, empty.
5 The moon's.

Was past the chair[1] of bright Cassiopey,[2]
A fearful vision appeared to me.   125
Methought, Mustaffa, I beheld thy neck,
So often folded in my loving arms,
In foul disgrace of bashaw's fair degree[3]
With a vile halter basely compassèd,[4]
And while I poured my tears on thy dead corpse,   130
A greedy lion with wide-gaping throat
Seized on my trembling body with his feet,
And in a moment rent me all to naught.[5]
Fly, sweet Mustaffa, or we be but dead.
   Mustaffa. Why should we fly, beauteous Solyma?   135
Moved by a vain and fantastic dream?
Or if we did fly, whither should we fly?
If to the farthest part of Asia,
Knowst thou not, Solyma, kings have long hands?
Come, come, my joy, return again with me   140
And banish hence these melancholy thoughts.

Exeunt.

[Scene 24
Somewhere in Amasia]

Enter Aladin, Amurath, [*and*] *the Messenger.*

   Aladin. Messenger, is it true that Selimus
Is not far hence encampèd with his host?

---

1 Throne.
2 Wife of the Ethiopian King Cephus, Cassiopeia was turned into a
   constellation by the gods because she boasted that her daughter An-
   dromeda was more beautiful than Juno (Grimal 91).
3 Rank (*OED*, n., 4b).
4 In early modern England, aristocrats were beheaded while common-
   ers were hanged. In Solyma's dream, Mustaffa's hanging degrades
   him socially. Early modern Turkish custom, however, reversed the
   socio-symbolic significance of the two modes of execution. See p.
   153, note 9.
5 Raid notes a parallel between lines 123–33 and lines 1256–60 of
   Robert Garnier's *La Troade*, a French translation of classical Latin dramatist Seneca's tragedy *Troades*. Because the dream image is
   Garnier's addition to Seneca's original, Raid suggests that it indicates "the direct influence of Garnier" (61) on Greene's play.

And means he to disjoin[1] the hapless sons
From helping our distressèd mother's town?
    Messenger. 'Tis true, my lord, and if you love your lives   5
Fly from the bounds of his dominions,
For he, you know, is most unmerciful.
    Amurath. Here, messenger, take this for thy reward.

[*Amurath gives the messenger money.*]

                                    Exit Mess[enger].

But we, sweet Aladin, let us depart
Now, in the quiet silence of the night,   10
That ere the windows of the morn be ope
We may be far enough from Selimus.
I'll to Egypt.
    Aladin. I to Persia.

                                      Exeunt.

[Scene 25
Selimus' court in Byzantium[2]]

Enter Selimus, Sinam, Hali, Cali, [and the] Janissaries.

    Selimus. But is it certain, Hali, they are gone
And that Mustaffa moved them to fly?
    Hali. Certain, my lord. I met the messenger
As he returned from young Aladin[3]
And learned of him[4] Mustaffa was the man   5
That certified the princes of your will.
    Selimus. It is enough. Mustaffa shall abye[5]

---

1 Prevent.
2 Although in the previous scene the Messenger suggests that Selimus
   is already on the move and encamped in Amasia, Mustaffa, who at
   23.98 was charged to remain in Byzantium, is in this scene ready at
   hand for Selimus to summon and execute. Moreover, at the end of
   this scene Selimus exclaims, "now to fair Amasia let us march" (70).
   These two facts suggest that Selimus is still in Byzantium. The apparent discrepancy might be the result of anticipatory license in the
   Messenger's report to Aladin and Amurath.
3 Ed. (Grosart 2); *Alinda* Q.
4 Ed. (Grosart 2); them Q.
5 Pay for (*OED*, v., 1).

At a dear price his pitiful[1] intent.
Hali, go fetch Mustaffa and his wife,

Exit Hali.

For though she be sister to Selimus,   10
Yet loves she him better than[2] Selimus,
So that if he do die at our command
And she should live, soon would she work a mean
To work revenge for her Mustaffa's death.

Enter Hali, Mustaffa, and Solyma.

[*To Mustaffa*] False of thy faith and traitor to thy king,   15
Did we so highly always honour thee,
And doest thou thus requite our love with treason?
For why shouldst thou send to young Aladin[3]
And Amurath, the sons of Acomat,
To give them notice of our secrecies,   20
Knowing they were my vowèd enemies?
      Mustaffa. I do not seek to lessen[4] my offence,
Great Selimus, but truly do protest
I did it not for hatred of Your Grace,
So help me God and holy Mahomet,   25
But for I grieved to see the famous stock
Of worthy Bajazet fall to decay.
Therefore I sent the princes both away.
Your Highness knows Mustaffa was the man
That saved you in the battle of Çorlu,   30
When I and all the warlike Janissaries
Had hedged your person in a dangerous ring.
Yet I took pity on your danger there
And made a way for you to 'scape by flight.
But those your bashaws have incensed you,   35
Repining at Mustaffa's dignity.
Stern Sinam grinds his angry teeth at me,
Old Hali's sons do bend their brows at me
And are aggrieved that Mustaffa hath

---

1 I.e., motivated by pity.
2 Ed. (Grosart 2); then Q.
3 Ed. (Grosart 2); *Alinda* Q.
4 Ed. (Grosart 2); lesson Q.

Showed himself a better man than[1] they.   40
And yet the Janissars mourn for me:
They know Mustaffa never provèd false.
Ay,[2] I have been as true to Selimus
As ever subject to his sovereign,
So help me God and holy Mahomet.   45
    Selimus. You did it not because you hated us
But for you loved the sons of Acomat.
Sinam, I charge thee quickly strangle him.
He loves not me that loves mine enemies.
As for your holy protestation,   50
It cannot enter into Selim's ears.
For why, Mustaffa? Every merchantman
Will praise his own ware, be it ne'er so bad.
    Solyma. For Solyma's sake, mighty Selimus,
Spare my Mustaffa's life and let me die,   55
Or, if thou wilt not be so gracious,
Yet let me die before I see his death.
    Selimus. Nay, Solyma, yourself shall also die
Because you may be in the selfsame fault.
Why stayst thou, Sinam? Strangle him, I say!   60

Sinam strangles him [*Mustaffa*].

    Solyma. Ah, Selimus! He made thee Emperor,
And wilt thou thus requite his benefits?
Thou art a cruel tiger and no man,
That couldst endure to see before thy face
So brave a man as my Mustaffa was   65
Cruelly strangled for so small a fault.
    Selimus. Thou shalt not after live[3] him, Solyma.
'Twere pity thou shouldst want the company
Of thy dear husband. Sinam, strangle her.

[*Sinam strangles Solyma.*]

And now to fair Amasia let us march.   70
Acomat's wife and her unmanly host

---

1   Ed. (Grosart 2); then Q.
2   Ed. (Grosart 2); I Q.
3   Grosart 2 emends to "live after."

Will not be able to endure our sight,
Much less make strong resistance in hard fight.

Exeunt.

[Scene 26
Acomat's camp on Mount Orminius, in the environs of
Yenisehir[1]]

Enter Acomat, Tonombey, Vizier, Regan, and their soldiers.

Acomat. Welcome, my lords, into my native soil,
The crown whereof by right is due to me,
Though Selim by the Janissaries' choice
Through usurpation keep the same from me.
You know contrary to my father's mind   5
He was enthronized by the bashaws' will
And, after his installing, wickedly
By poison made good Bajazet to die,
And strangled Corcut, and exilèd me.
These injuries we come for to[2] revenge   10
And raise his siege from fair Amasia's[3] walls.
    Tonombey. Prince of Amasia and the rightful heir
Unto the mighty Turkish diadem,
With willing heart great Tonombey hath left
Egyptian Nilus and my father's court   15
To aid thee in thy undertaken war,
And by the great Usancassano's[4] ghost,
Companion unto mighty Tamburlaine,
From whom my father lineally descends,
Fortune shall show herself too cross to me   20
But we will thrust Selimus from his throne
And revest[5] Acomat in the empery.

---

1 Yenisehir is a district in the Ottoman province of Karasi and the
   modern Turkish province of Bursa, in northwestern Anatolia, east of
   Byzantium and west of Amasia (Shaw xiv–xv).
2 In order to.
3 Ed.; *Amasia* Q.
4 In Marlowe's *Tamburlaine* plays, Usumcasane is one of Tamburlaine's three chief companions and by *2 Tamburlaine* has been
   crowned by Tamburlaine the King of Morocco (1.3.128).
5 Re-establish.

Acomat. Thanks to the[1] uncontrollèd Tonombey.
But let us haste us to Amasia
To succour my besiegèd citizens.   25
None but my queen is overseer there,
And too too weak is all her policy
Against so great a foe as Selimus.

                                                        Exeunt all.

[Scene 27
Before the walls of Amasia]

Enter Selimus, Sinam, Hali, Cali, and the Janissaries.

Selimus. Summon a parley, sirs, that we may know
Whether these mushrooms here will yield or no.

*A parley. [Enter the] Queen of Amasia and her soldiers on the
walls.*

Queen. What cravest thou, bloodthirsty[2] parricide?
Is't not enough that thou hast foully slain
Thy loving father, noble Bajazet,   5
And strangled Corcut, thine unhappy brother,
Slain brave Mustaffa and fair Solyma
Because they favoured my unhappy sons,
But thou must yet seek for more massacres?
Go, wash thy guilty hands in lukewarm blood,   10
Enrich thy soldiers with robberies,
Yet do the heavens still bear an equal eye,
And vengeance follows thee even at the heels.
   Selimus. Queen of Amasia, wilt thou yield thyself?
   Queen. First shall the overflowing Euripus[3]   15
Of swift Euboea stop his restless course
And Phoeb's[4] bright globe bring the day from the West
And quench his hot flames in the Eastern Sea.

---

1 Grosart 2 emends to "thee."
2 Grosart 2 emends to "thou bloodthirsty."
3 The Euripus Strait separates the Aegean island of Euboea from the
   Greek mainland. *Locrine* refers to the "lightfoot Euripus" (sig. H4r).
4 Phoebus Apollo's.

Thy[1] bloody sword, ungracious Selimus,
Sheathed in bowels of thy dearest friends,   20
Thy wicked guard which still attends on thee,
Fleshing themselves in murder, lust, and rape:
What hope of favour, what security,
Rather what death do they not promise me?
Then think not, Selimus, that we will yield,   25
But look for strong[2] resistance at our hands.
    Selimus. Why, then, you never-daunted Janissaries,
Advance your shields and uncontrollèd spears,
Your conquering hands in foemen's blood embay,
For Selimus himself will lead the way.   30

Alarum, [Selimus with his soldiers] beats them off the walls.
Alarum.

[Scene 28
Before the walls of Amasia]

Enter Selimus, Sinam, Hali, Cali, [and the] Janissaries, with
Acomat's Queen prisoner.

    Selimus. Now, sturdy dame, where are your men of war
To guard your person from my angry sword?
What? Though you[3] braved[4] us on your city walls,
Like to that Amazonian[5] Menalippe,
Leaving the banks of swift-streamed Thermodon   5
To challenge combat with great Hercules,[6]
Yet Selimus hath plucked your haughty plumes,[7]

---

1 Grosart 2 emends to "The."
2 Grosart 2 emends to "stronger."
3 Ed. (Grosart 2); not in Q.
4 Defied.
5 Ed. (Grosart 2); *Amanonian* Q.
6 Eurystheus commands Hercules to obtain for his daughter the girdle
   of the Amazonian Queen Hippolyta. In battle in front of Hippolyta's
   palace on the Thermodon River, Hercules slaughters the Amazons and
   captures the Amazonian warrior Menalippe but lets her go free in exchange for the girdle (Diodorus Siculus, *Library of History* 4.16.1–4).
7 In Greene's *George a Green, Pinner of Wakefield* (1599), George threatens to beat three rebellious English lords and "pull all your plumes"
   (sig. D3r). In Greene's *Friar Bacon and Friar Bungay*, Prince Edward
   asks himself, "shall thy plumes be pull'd by Venus down?" (viii.115).

Nor can your spouse, rebellious Acomat,
Nor Aladin[1] or Amurath, your sons,
Deliver you from our victorious hands.   10
    Queen. Selim, I scorn thy threatenings as thyself,
And though ill hap[2] hath given me to thy hands,
Yet will I never beg my life of thee.
Fortune may chance to frown as much on thee,
And Acomat, whom thou doest scorn so much,   15
May take thy base Tartarian concubine[3]
As well as thou hast took his loyal queen.
Thou hast not Fortune tied in a chain,[4]
Nor doest thou like a wary pilot sit
And wisely steer[5] this all-containing barge.[6]   20
Thou art a man as those whom thou hast slain,
And some of them were better far than[7] thou.
    Selimus. Strangle her, Hali, let her scold no more.

[*Hali strangles the Queen.*]

Now let us march to meet with Acomat.
He brings with him that great Egyptian bug,[8]   25
Strong Tonombey,[9] Usancassano's son,
But we shall soon with our fine-tempered swords

---

1 Ed. (Grosart 2); *Alinda* Q.
2 Luck.
3 Selimus's wife, the Crimean Tartar Khan's daughter, Hafsa Hatun,
   whom he married in 1511 (Clot 26).
4 Echoing Tamburlaine's boast to Theridamas in 1.2 of *1 Tamburlaine*:
   "I hold the Fates bound fast in iron chains / And with my hand turn
   Fortune's wheel about" (174–75). Greene's Tamburlaine-like Alphonsus boasts to the Turkish Emperor Amurath in *Alphonsus King
   of Aragon* that "I clap up Fortune in a cage of gold, / To make her
   turn her wheel as I think best" (sig. G3r). "The Scythian Emperor,"
   Humber boasts in *Locrine*, "Leads Fortune tied in a chain of gold, /
   Constraining her to yield unto his will" (sig. C3r).
5 Ed. (Vitkus); *stir* Q.
6 I.e., the universe.
7 Ed. (Grosart 2); *then* Q.
8 In *2 Tamburlaine*, Tamburlaine describes his followers Theidamas,
   Techelles and Usumcasane as "bugs" that "Will make the hair stand
   upright on your heads / And cast your crowns in slavery at their feet"
   (3.5.146–48).
9 Neither Ashton nor Greene's other possible sources place Tuman
   bay at the battle of Yenisehir with Acomat.

Engrave our prowess on their burgonets[1]
Were they as mighty and as fell[2] of force
As those old earth-bred brethren[3] which once   30
Heaped[4] hill on hill to scale the starry sky,[5]
When Briareus,[6] armed with a hundred hands,
Flung forth a hundred mountains at great Jove,[7]
And when the monstrous giant Monichus[8]
Hurled Mount Olympus at great Mars his[9] targe[10]   35
And darted cedars at Minerva's shield.[11]

Exeunt all.

---

1 Helmets.

2 Deadly, destructive (*OED*, adj. 1, 4a).

3 The Giants, sons of Gaia (Earth) and Ouranos (Sky), "born from the blood of ... Uranus' wound when he was castrated by Cronus [his son]" (Grimal 170).

4 Ed. (Grosart 2); Heape Q.

5 In *Metamorphoses* Ovid recounts that during the Iron Age, after Jupiter had established his rule, "Men say that giants went about the realm of heaven to win / To place themselves to reign as Gods and lawless lords therein. / And hill on hill they heaped up aloft into the sky, / Till God Almighty from the heaven did let his thunder flie" (I.173–76). The giants were pinned and crushed under the mountains toppled by Jupiter's thunder; their occasional stirrings result in volcanic eruptions. See also Apollodorus, *Library* 1.6.1–3.

6 After giving birth to the Titans and the Cyclops, Earth and Sky had three more offspring, the Hundred-Handers, "Mighty and violent, unspeakable / Kottos and Gyes and Briareus, / Insolent children, each with a hundred arms / On his shoulders, darting about, untouchable, / And each had fifty heads, standing upon / His shoulders, over the crowded mass of arms, / And terrible strength was in their mighty forms" (Hesiod, *Theogony* 147–54).

7 In Hesiod, Briareus and his brothers defend the Olympians against the Titans (*Theogony* 709–20).

8 Monichus is in fact not a giant but a centaur who, in the Battle of the Lapiths and Centaurs, encourages his daunted fellow centaurs to attack a seemingly invincible Lapith by piling upon him the trees from Mount Pelion and Mount Othris (Ovid, *Metamorphoses* XII.551–92): "Whelm blocks and stones and mountains whole upon his hard brain pan, / And press ye out his lively ghost with trees" (562–63), Monichus exclaims.

9 Great Mars's.

10 Shield.

11 With some variance, lines 31 to 36 recur in the anonymous *Locrine*, which has been attributed to Greene by some scholars: "Heap hills on hills to scale the starry sky, / When Briareus, armed with a hundred hands, / Flung forth a hundred mountains at (*continued*)

[Scene 29
Yenisehir[1]]

*Alarum. Enter Selimus, Sinam, Cali, Hali, and the Janissaries at
one door and Acomat, Tonombey, Regan, Vizier, and their soldiers
at another.*

   Selimus. What, are the urchins[2] crept out of their dens,
Under the conduct of this porcupine?
Doest thou not tremble, Acomat, at us,
To see how courage masqueth[3] in our looks
And white-winged Victory[4] sits on our swords?   5
Captain of Egypt, thou that vauntst[5] thyself
Sprung from great Tamburlaine the Scythian[6] thief,[7]
Who bade thee enterprise this bold attempt
To set thy feet within the Turkish confines
Or lift thy hands against our majesty?   10
   Acomat. Brother of Trebisond, your squarèd[8] words
And broad-mouthed[9] terms can never conquer us.

---

   great Jove, / And when the monstrous giant Monichus / Hurled
Mount Olympus at great Mars his targe, / And shot huge cedars at
Minerva's shield" (sig. D4v).
1 Selimus defeated his brother at Yenisehir on 15 April 1513 (Shaw
    80). Ashton gives 25 April as the date, but this is according to the
    Julian calendar, which is ten days in front of the Gregorian.
2 Hedgehogs (*OED*, n., 1a).
3 Ed.; masketh Q. Displays itself.
4 In classical and Renaissance art and literature, the goddess Nike,
    or Victory, is winged to signify her rapidly shifting and unstable na-
    ture. Ovid, for example, describes the war between King Minos and
    Nisus King of Alcathoe as follows: "the war hung wavering still /
    In fickle Fortune's doubtful scales, and long with fleeting wings /
    Between them both flew Victory" (*Metamorphoses* VIII.14–16). In
    1 Tamburlaine, Tamburlaine boasts that "when she sees our bloody
    colours spread, / Then Victory begins to take her flight, / Resting
    herself upon my milk-white tent" (3.3.159–61).
5 Boasts.
6 Ed. (Grosart 2); *Scythia* Q.
7 An epithet that Tamburlaine's opponents frequently apply to him in
    1 Tamburlaine. The play opens with a discussion amongst the Persian
    king and his councillors about how to prevent the continuing depre-
    dations within their territory of "Tamburlaine, that sturdy Scythian
    thief" (1.1.36).
8 Blunt.
9 Freely spoken.

We come resolved to pull the Turkish crown,
Which thou doest wrongfully detain from me,
By conquering sword[1] from off thy coward crest.   15
    Selimus. Acomat, since the quarrel toucheth none
But thee and me, I dare and challenge thee.
    Tonombey. Should he accept the combat of a boy,
Whose unripe years and far unriper wit,
Like to the bold, foolhardy Phaeton,   20
That sought to rule the chariot of the sun,[2]
Hath moved thee t'undertake an empery?
    Selimus. Thou that resolvest in peremptory terms
To call him boy that[3] scorns to cope[4] with thee,
But[5] thou canst better use thy bragging blade   25
Than[6] thou canst rule thy overflowing tongue,
Soon shalt thou know that Selim's mighty arm
Is able to overthrow poor Tonombey.[7]

Alarum. Tonombey beats Hali and Cali in.[8] *Selim[us] beats*
Tonombey in. Alarum.

---

1 The Prologue to *1 Tamburlaine* refers to Tamburlaine's "conquering sword" (6); Tamburlaine himself vaunts that "kings shall crouch
   unto our conquering swords" (1.2.220); in *Locrine*, Albanact boasts
   of "our conquering swords" (sig. D2v).
2 Phaeton, the son of the sun god Apollo and the mortal Clymene,
   asks to guide his father's chariot through the sky as proof of his divine parentage but cannot control the horses and brings the sun too
   close to the earth, at whose request Jove destroys the chariot with a
   thunderbolt, also killing Phaeton. See Ovid, *Metamorphoses* I.944–
   II.415. Rozett remarks that "Phaeton is the classical embodiment
   of Elizabethan pride and aspiration; his desire literally to rise above
   human limitations is an emblem of the ambitions of Tamburlaine,
   Faustus, and a host of aspiring minds" (114).
3 Who.
4 Fight with (*OED*, v.2, 2).
5 Unless.
6 Ed. (Grosart 2); Then Q.
7 "But thou better use thy bragging blade, / Than thou doest rule thy
   overflowing tongue," Humber warns Albanact in *Locrine*, "Superbi-
   ous Britton, thou shalt know too soon, / The force of Humber and
   his Scythians" (sig. D4v).
8 Off the stage.

[Scene 30
Battlefield of Yenisehir]

Enter Tonombey.

Tonombey. The field is lost, and Acomat is taken.
Ah, Tonombey, how canst thou show thy face
To thy victorious sire, thus conquerèd?
A matchless knight is warlike Selimus,
And, like a shepherd 'mongst a swarm of gnats,[1]   5
Dings down the flying Persians with their swords.
Twice I encountered with him hand to hand
And twice returned foiled and ashamed,
For never yet since I could manage arms
Could any match with mighty Tonombey   10
But this heroic Emperor Selimus.
Why stand I still and rather do not fly
The great occision[2] which the victors make?

Exit Tonombey.

[Scene 31
Battlefield of Yenisehir]

*Alarum. Enter Selimus, Sinam Bashaw with Acomat prisoner,
Hali, Cali, [and the] Janissaries.*

Selimus. Thus, when the coward Greeks fled to their ships,[3]
The noble Hector,[4] all besmeared in blood,
Returned in triumph to the walls of Troy.
A gallant trophy, bashaws, have we won,
Beating the never-foiled Tonombey   5
And hewing passage through the Persians
As when a lion raving[5] for his prey

---

1   In Book I of the *Faerie Queene*, Spenser compares the Redcrosse Knight
    fighting the serpent-like spawn of Error to a "gentle Shepheard"
    (1.i.23.1) brushing off a "cloud of combrous gnattes" (1.i.23.5).
2   Slaughter, carnage (*OED*, n.). Grosart 2 emends to "occasion."
3   During the Trojan War, the Greeks would retreat to their ships
    when they were losing a battle.
4   The Trojan King Priam's eldest son and Troy's champion.
5   Grosart 2 emends to "rav'ning."

Falleth upon a drove of hornèd bulls[1]
And rends them strongly in his kingly paws
Or Mars, armed in his adamantine[2] coat,[3]   10
Mounted upon his fiery-shining wain,
Scatters the troops of warlike Thracians[4]
And warms cold Hebrus[5] with hot streams of blood.[6]
Brave Sinam, for thy noble prisoner
Thou shalt be general of my Janissaries   15
And Belierbey[7] of fair Natolia.
Now, Acomat, thou monster of the world,
Why stoopst thou not with reverence to thy king?
    Acomat. Selim, if thou have gotten victory,
Then use it to thy contentation.   20
If I had conquered, know assuredly
I would have said as much and more to thee.
Know I disdain them as I do thyself
And scorn to stoop or bend my lordly knee
To such a tyrant as is Selimus.   25
Thou slewst my queen without regard or care
Of love or duty or thine own good name.
Then, Selim, take that which thy hap[8] doth give.
Disgraced, displaced, I longer loath to live.
    Selimus. Then, Sinam, strangle him.

[*Sinam strangles Acomat.*][9]

---

1   Ed. (Grosart 2); balls Q.
2   Inpenetrable, unbreakable (*OED*, adj., 1a).
3   Armour.
4   Thrace was a region on the west coast of the Black Sea, in modern Romania and Bulgaria.
5   River in Thrace.
6   The temporarily victorious Locrine uses a similar image when he boasts that "Now sit I like the mighty god of war, / When, armed with his coat of adamant, / Mounted his chariot drawn with mighty bulls, / He drove the Argives over Xanthus' streams" (sig. F3v).
7   Governor.
8   Fortune, luck, success.
9   After recounting Acomat's execution (he "was hanged in a bowstring, in like manner as his brother Corcuth was tofore"), Ashton provides the following explanation for why the two brothers "were hanged rather than headed [beheaded]": "The Turks do think it is a thing unworthy of the majesty of the Turkish emperors that any drop of the Ottomans' blood should be shed on the ground" (sig. I5v). Though Greene has the two brothers strangled rather than hanged, the effect is the same.

Now he is dead,   30
Who doth remain to trouble Selimus?
Now am I king alone and none but I,
For, since my father's death until this time,
I never wanted[1] some competitors.
Now, as the weary wandering traveller   35
That hath his steps guided through many lands,
Through boiling soil of Africa and Ind,[2]
When he returns unto his native home,
Sits down among his friends and with delight
Declares the travels he hath overpassed,   40
So mayst thou, Selimus, for thou hast trod
The monster-guarded[3] paths that lead to crowns.
Ha, ha! I smile to think how Selimus
Like the Egyptian ibis[4] hath expelled
Those swarming armies of swift-wingèd snakes   45
That sought to overrun my territories.
When sweltering heat the earth's green children[5] spoils,
From forth the fens of venomous Africa
The generation[6] of those flying snakes
Do band themselves in troops and take their way   50
To Nilus' bounds; but those industrious birds,
Those ibides, meet them[7] in set array[8]
And eat them up like to a swarm of gnats,
Preventing such a mischief from the land.
But see how unkind Nature deals with them: 55
From out their eggs rises the basilisk,
Whose only sight[9] kills millions of men.[10]

---

1 Lacked.
2 India.
3 Ed. (Grosart 2); monster-garden Q.
4 In Egyptian mythology the god Thoth was associated with the ibis,
   a heron-like bird. Pliny writes that "The Egyptians ... have recourse
   in their prayers and invocations to their birds named Ibis, what time
   as they be troubled and annoyed with serpents" (*Natural History*
   X.28). In *Pandosto*, Greene alludes to "the bird ibis in Egypt, which
   hateth serpents yet feedeth on their eggs" (Grosart 4.306).
5 I.e., plant life, greenery.
6 Offspring, progeny.
7 Grosart 2 emends to "them less."
8 Battle formation.
9 Sight alone.
10 According to Pliny, the basilisk is a small Egyptian serpent with a
   "white spot ... like a coronet or diadem" on its head; "there is not

When Acomat lifted his ungracious hands
Against my agèd father Bajazet,
They sent for me, and I like Egypt's bird   60
Have rid that monster and his fellow mates.
But as from ibis springs the basilisk,
Whose only touch[1] burneth up stones and trees,[2]
So Selimus hath proved a cockatrice[3]
And clean consumèd all the family   65
Of noble Ottoman, except himself.
And now to you, my neighbour emperors,
That[4] durst[5] lend aid to Selim's enemies—
Sinam, those sultans of the Orient,
Egypt and Persia, Selimus will quell   70
Or he himself will sink to lowest hell.
This winter will we rest and breathe ourselves,
But soon as Zephyrus' sweet-smelling blast[6]
Shall gently[7] creep over the flowery meads,[8]
We'll have a fling at the Egyptian crown   75
And join it unto ours or lose our own.[9]

Exeunt.

---

one that looketh upon his eyes, but dyeth presently" (*Natural History*
8.21). "No physic [medicine] prevails against the gaze of the basilisks" (Grosart 6.45), Greene asserts in *Menaphon* (1589).

1 Touch alone.
2 Pliny states that the basilisk "killeth all trees and shrubs not only
   that he toucheth, but that he doth breathe upon also: as for grass and
   herbs, those he findeth and burneth up, yea and breaketh stones in
   sunder, so venomous and deadly is he" (*Natural History* 8.21).
3 Basilisk.
4 Who.
5 Dared.
6 Zephyr was the west wind, a mild breeze (*OED*, n., 1, 2). In classical myth, Zephyrus is one of the four chief Anemoi, sons of the
   wind god Aeolus and Eos, goddess of the dawn. The other three
   are Boreas (the north wind), Eurus (the east wind), and Notus (the
   south wind) (Grimal 77).
7 Ed. (Grosart 2); greatly Q.
8 Meadows.
9 Historically, Selim I began his invasion of Mamluk Egypt in 1516.
   By January 1517 he had conquered Cairo and subordinated Egypt to
   Ottoman rule. Tuman bay (Tonombey) was captured and executed
   in April 1517 (Shaw 84).

Conclusion.

[Enter Conclusion.][1]

Conclusion. Thus have we brought victorious Selimus
Unto the crown of great Arabia.
Next shall you see him with triumphant sword[2]
Dividing kingdoms into equal shares
And give them to his[3] warlike followers.   5
If this first part, gentles, do like you well,
The second part shall greater murders tell.

[Exit.]

FINIS.

---

1 Prologues and conclusions were common in English Renaissance
   plays. Both parts of *Tamburlaine* begin with a prologue, for example, and *Doctor Faustus* has a concluding Chorus. The printed text
   of *Selimus* has unimaginatively named the play's concluding chorus
   "Conclusion," perhaps merely for the sake of the reader's conve-
   nience, as the character remains unnamed to the audience.
2 The Prologue to *1 Tamburlaine* announces that "you shall hear the
   Scythian Tamburlaine / Threatening the world with high astound-
   ing terms / And scourging kingdoms with his conquering sword"
   (4–6).
3 Ed. (Grosart 2); their Q.

Appendix A: Robert Greene, Greene's Groatsworth of Wit, Bought with a Million of Repentance *(1592)*

["The fire of my light is now at the last snuff," Greene laments at the end of this pamphlet, which was published after his death in 1592. The pamphlet contains a rich mixture of genres, including an element of autobiography, which Greene makes explicit at the end of this narrative featuring a protagonist named Roberto who falls in with actors, becomes famous as a playwright, but approaches death in misery. The pamphlet is also a key if controversial document in both literary history and the history of atheistic and Machiavellian thinking in Elizabethan culture, containing Greene's notorious and oft-quoted denunciation of the "upstart crow" and his admonition of Marlowe to repent of his atheism and Machiavellianism.]

The Printer to the Gentle Readers

I have published here, gentlemen, for your mirth and benefit *Greene's Groatsworth of Wit*. With sundry of his pleasant discourses ye have been before delighted, but now hath death given a period to his pen. Only this happened into my hands, which I have published for your pleasures. Accept it favourably because it was his last birth, and not least worth, in my poor opinion. But I will cease to praise that which is above my conceit and leave itself to speak for itself, and so abide your learned censuring.

Yours,
W. W.[1]

---

1 The printer, William Wright.

To the Gentlemen Readers

Gentlemen. The swan sings melodiously before death, that in all his lifetime useth but a jarring sound. Greene, though able enough to write, yet deeplier searched[1] with sickness than ever heretofore, sends you his swan-like song, for that he fears he shall never again discover to you youth's pleasures. However yet sickness, riot, incontinence have at once shown their extremity, yet if I recover you shall all see more fresh sprigs than ever sprang from me directing you how to live, yet not dissuading ye from love. This is the last I have writ, and, I fear me, the last I shall write. And howsoever I have been censured for some of my former books, yet, gentlemen, I protest they were as I had special information.[2] But passing them, I commend this to your favourable censures, that like an embrion without shape, I fear me, will be thrust into the world. If I live to end it, it shall be otherwise; if not, yet will I commend it to your courtesies, that you may as well be acquainted with my repentant death as you have lamented my careless course of life. But as *nemo ante obitum felix*,[3] so *acta exitus probat*.[4] Beseeching therefore so to be deemed hereof as I deserve, I leave the work to your likings and leave you to your delights.

Greene's Groatsworth of Wit

In an island bounded with the ocean, there was sometime a city situated, made rich by merchandise[5] and populous by long peace; the name is not mentioned in the Antiquary,[6] or else worn out by time's antiquity. What it was it greatly skills[7] not, but therein thus it happened. An old new-made gentleman herein dwelt, of no small credit, exceeding wealth, and large conscience. He had gathered from many to bestow upon one, for, though he had two sons, he esteemed but one, that, being as himself brought up to

---

1 Afflicted.
2 Greene often claimed to have inside knowledge of the Elizabethan underworld in such cony-catching pamphlets as *A Notable Discovery of Cosenage Now Daily Practiced by Sundry Lewd Persons Called Cony-Catchers and Cross-Biters* (1591).
3 "No one before his death should be called happy" (Latin).
4 "The ends justify the means" (Latin).
5 Mercantile activity.
6 Chronicles, history.
7 Matters.

be a gold's bondman,[1] was therefore held heir apparent of all his ill-gathered goods.

The other was a scholar and married to a proper gentlewoman and therefore least regarded, for 'tis an old-said saw: "To learning and law there's no greater foe than they that nothing know." Yet was not the father altogether unlettered, for he had good experience in a *noverint*[2] and by the universal terms therein contained had driven many a young gentleman to seek unknown countries; wise he was, for he bore office in his parish and sat as formally in his fox-furred gown as if he had been a very upright-dealing burgess. He was religious too, never without a book at his belt and a bolt[3] in his mouth, ready to shoot through his sinful neighbor.

And Latin he had somewhere learned, which, though it were but little, yet was it profitable, for he had this philosophy written in a ring, "Tu tibi cura,"[4] which precept he curiously observed, being in self-love so religious as he held it no point of charity to part with anything of which he living might make use.

But as all mortal things are momentary and no certainty can be found in this uncertain world, so Gorinius (for that shall be this usurer's name) after many a gouty pang that had pinched his exterior parts, many a curse of the people that mounted into heaven's presence, was at last with his last summons by a deadly disease arrested, whereagainst when he had long contended and was by physicians given over, he called his two sons before him and, willing to perform the old proverb, "*qualis vita finis ita*,"[5] he thus prepared himself and admonished them. "My sons—for so your mother said ye were, and so I assure myself one of you is, and of the other I will make no doubt—you see the time is come which I thought would never have approached, and we must now be separated, I fear, never to meet again. This sixteen years daily have I lived vexed with disease, and, might I live sixteen more, however miserably, I should think it happy. But death is relentless and will not be entreated, witless and knows not what good my gold might do him, senseless and hath no pleasure in the delightful places I would offer him. In brief, I think he hath with this fool my eldest son been brought up in the university and therefore accounts that in riches is no virtue. But thou, my son," laying then his hand

---

1 Usurer, money-lender.
2 Legal writ, bond (*OED* 2).
3 Arrow.
4 "Let yourself be your greatest concern" (Latin). Proverbial.
5 "As the life, so the end" (Latin).

on the younger's head, "have thou another spirit. For without wealth, life is a death. What is gentry if wealth be wanting[1] but base servile beggary. Some comfort yet it is unto me to think how many gallants sprung of noble parents have crouched to Gorinius to have sight of his gold—O gold, desired gold, admired gold!— and have lost their patrimonies to Gorinius because they have not returned by their day[2] that adored creature! How many scholars have written rhymes in Gorinius's praise and received, after long capping[3] and reverence, a sixpenny reward in sign of my superficial liberality! Briefly, my young Lucanio, how I have been reverenced thou seest, when honester men, I confess, have been set far off. For to be rich is to be anything: wise, honest, worshipful—or what not? I tell thee, my son, when I came first to this city my whole wardrobe was only a suit of white sheepskins, my wealth an old groat,[4] my wonning[5] the whole world. At this instant—O grief to part with it!—I have in ready coin threescore[6] thousand pound, in plate and jewels fifteen thousand, in bonds and specialties[7] as much, in land nine hundred pound by the year, all which, Lucanio, I bequeath to thee, only I reserve for Roberto, thy well-read brother, an old groat, being the stock I first began with, wherewith I wish him to buy a groatsworth of wit, for he, in my life, hath reproved my manner of life and therefore, at my death, shall not be contaminated with corrupt gain."

Here, by the way, gentlemen, must I digress to show the reason of Gorinius's present speech. Roberto being come from the academy to visit his father, there was a great feast provided, where, for table talk, Roberto, knowing his father and most of the company to be execrable usurers, inveighed mightily against that abhorred vice, insomuch that he urged tears from diverse of their eyes and compunction[8] in some of their hearts. Dinner being past, he comes to his father, requesting him to take no offence at his liberal speech, seeing what he had uttered was truth. "Angry, son?," said he, "No, by my honesty (and that is somewhat, I may say to you) but use it still, and if thou canst persuade any of my neighbours from lending upon usury I should have the more

---

1 Lacking.
2 The day that the payment of their loan from Gorinius is due.
3 Removing or replacing a hat in respect.
4 Coin worth four pennies (*OED*, n., 2a).
5 Dwelling, house (*OED*).
6 Sixty. A score equals twenty.
7 Bonds (*OED*, n., 5b).
8 Contrition, remorse, repentance.

customers." To which when Roberto would have replied, he shut himself into his study and fell to tell[1] over his money.

This was Roberto's offence. Now return we to sick Gorinius, who, after he had thus unequally distributed his goods and possessions, began to ask his sons how they liked his bequests. Either seemed agreed, and Roberto urged him with nothing more than repentance of his sins. "To thine own," said he, "fond boy, and come, my Lucanio, let me give thee good counsel before my death. As for you, sir, your books are your counsellors, and therefore to them I bequeath you. Ah, Lucanio, my only comfort, because I hope thou wilt as thy father be a gatherer, let me bless thee before I die. Multiply in wealth, my son, by any means thou mayst, only fly alchemy, for therein are more deceits than her beggarly artists have words, and yet are the wretches more talkative than women. But my meaning is, thou shouldest not stand on conscience in causes of profit but heap treasure upon treasure for the time of need. Yet seem to be devout, else shalt thou be held vile. Frequent holy exercises, grave company, and above all use the conversation of young gentlemen, who are so wedded to prodigality that once in a quarter[2] necessity knocks at their chamber doors. Proffer them kindness to relieve their wants but be sure of good assurance. Give fair words till days of payment come, and then use my course: spare none. What though they tell of conscience (as a number will talk)? Look but into the dealings of the world, and thou shalt see it is but idle words. Seest thou not many perish in the streets and fall to theft for need, whom small succour would relieve? Then where is conscience, and why art thou bound to use it more than other men? Seest thou not daily forgeries, perjuries, oppressions, rackings of the poor, raisings of rents, enhancing of duties, even by them that should be all conscience, if they meant as they speak. But, Lucanio, if thou read well this book"—and with that he reached him Machiavel's works at large—"thou shalt see what 'tis to be so fool-holy as to make scruple of conscience where profit presents itself. Besides, thou hast an instance by thy threadbare brother here, who, willing to do no wrong, hath lost his child's right, for who would wish anything to him that knows not how to use it? So much, Lucanio, for conscience. And yet—I know not what's the reason—but somewhat stings me inwardly when I speak of it."

---

1 Count.
2 Three-month term in the legal and financial year (*OED*, n., 2b).

"Ay, father," said Roberto, "it is the worm of conscience, that urges you at the last hour to remember your life, that eternal life may follow your repentance." "Out, fool!," said this miserable father, "I feel it now, it was only a stitch.[1] I will forward with my exhortation to Lucanio. As I said, my son, make spoil of young gallants by insinuating thyself amongst them, and be not moved to think their ancestors were famous but consider thine were obscure and that thy father was the first gentleman of the name. Lucanio, thou art yet a bachelor and so keep thee till thou meet with one that is thy equal—I mean in wealth. Regard not beauty: it is a bait to entice thine neighbour's eye, and the most fair are commonly most fond.[2] Use not too many familiars,[3] for few prove friends, and as easy it is to weigh the wind as to dive into the thoughts of worldly glozers.[4] I tell thee, Lucanio, I have seen fourscore winters, besides the odd seven, yet saw I never him that I esteemed my friend but gold, that desired creature, whom I have so dearly loved and found so firm a friend as nothing to me, having it, hath been wanting. No man but may think dearly of a true friend, and so do I of it, laying it under sure locks and lodging my heart therewith. But now—ah, my Lucanio!—now must I leave it, and to thee I leave it with this lesson: love none but thyself, if thou wilt live esteemed."

So, turning him to his study, where his chief treasure lay, he loud cried out in the wise man's words, "*O mors quam amara*,[5] O death, how bitter is thy memory to him that hath all pleasures in this life!" And so with two or three lamentable groans he left his life and, to make short work, was by Lucanio his son interred, as the custom is, with some solemnity. But, leaving him that hath left the world to him that censureth of every worldly man, pass we to his sons and see how his long-laid-up store is by Lucanio looked into. The youth was of condition simple, shamefast, and flexible to any counsel, which, Roberto, perceiving and pondering how little was left to him, grew into an inward contempt of his father's unequal legacy and determinate resolution to work Lucanio all possible injury. Hereupon thus converting the sweetness of his study to the sharp thirst of revenge, he (as envy is seldom idle) sought out fit companions to effect his unbrotherly

---

1 Cramp.
2 Foolish.
3 Close companions.
4 Flatterers (*OED* 2).
5 "O death, how bitter" (Latin).

resolution. Neither in such a case is ill company far to seek, for the sea hath scarce so many jeopardies as populous cities have deceiving Sirens,[1] whose eyes are adamants,[2] whose words are witchcrafts, whose doors lead down to death. With one of these female serpents Roberto consorts, and they conclude, whatever they compassed,[3] equally to share their contents. This match made, Lucanio was by his brother brought to the bush,[4] where he had scarce pruned his wings but he was fast limed[5] and Roberto had what he expected. But, that we may keep form, you shall hear how it fortuned.

Lucanio being on a time very pensive, his brother broke with him in these terms. "I wonder, Lucanio, why you are disconsolate, that want not anything in the world that may work your content. If wealth may delight a man, you are with that sufficiently furnished. If credit may procure any comfort, your word, I know well, is as well accepted as any man's obligation. In this city are fair buildings and pleasant gardens, and cause of solace. Of them I am assured you have your choice. Consider, brother, you are young; then plod not altogether in meditating on our father's precepts, which, howsoever they savoured of profit, were most unsavoury to one of your years applied. You must not think but sundry merchants of this city expect your company, sundry gentlemen desire your familiarity, and by conversing with such you will be accounted a gentleman, otherwise a peasant if you live obscurely. Besides, which I had almost forgot and then had all the rest been nothing, you are a man by nature furnished with all exquisite proportion, worthy the love of any courtly lady, be she never so amorous. You have wealth to maintain her, of women not little longed for; words to court her you shall not want, for myself will be your secretary. Briefly, why stand I to distinguish ability in peculiarities when in one word it may be said which no man can gainsay: Lucanio lacketh nothing to delight a wife, nor anything but a wife to delight him." My young master, being this clawed and puffed up with his own praise, made no longer delay but, having on his holiday hose, he tricked himself up and, like a fellow that meant good sooth, he clapped his brother on the shoulder and said, "Faith, brother Roberto, an[6] ye say the word let's go

---

1 Mythical mermaids who lure seafarers to their deaths.
2 Magnets (*OED*, n., 2a).
3 Gained.
4 Led into the trap (bird-hunting terminology).
5 Caught with birdlime.
6 If.

seek a wife while 'tis hot, both of us together. I'll pay well, and I dare turn you loose to say as well as any of them all." "Well, I'll do my best," said Roberto, "and since ye are so forward, let's go now and try your good fortune."

With this forth they walk, and Roberto went directly toward the house where Lamilia (for so we call the courtesan) kept her hospital,[1] which was in the suburbs of the city, pleasantly seated and made more delectable by a pleasant garden wherein it was situated. No sooner come they within ken[2] but Mistress Lamilia like a cunning angler[3] made ready her change of baits, that she might effect Lucanio's bane.[4] And to begin, she discovered from her window her beauteous, enticing face, and, taking a lute in her hand that she might the rather allure, she sung this sonnet with a delicious voice:

Lamilia's Song

> Fie, fie, on blind fancy,
> It hinders youth's joy.
> Fair virgins, learn by me
> To count love a toy.
> When Love learned first the ABC of delight,
> And knew no figures nor conceited phrase,
> He simply gave to due desert her right.
> He led not lovers in dark, winding ways,
> He plainly willed to love or flatly answered no,
> But now who lists[5] to prove shall find it nothing so.
> Fie, fie, then, on fancy,
> It hinders youth's joy.
> Fair virgins, learn by me
> To count love a toy.
> For since he learned to use the poet's pen,
> He learned likewise with smoothing words to feign,
> Witching chaste ears with trothless[6] tongues of men,
> And wrongèd faith with falsehood and disdain.
> He gives a promise now, anon[7] he sweareth no.

---

1 "A house of entertainment" (*OED*, n., 4).
2 Sight.
3 Fisherman.
4 Harm, doom, destruction.
5 Wishes.
6 Truthless, false.
7 Then.

Who listeth for to prove shall find his changings so.
　　Fie, fie, then, on fancy,
　　It hinders youth's joy.
　　Fair virgins, learn by me
　　To count love a toy.

While this painted sepulcher was shadowing her corrupting guilt, hyena-like alluring to destruction, Roberto and Lucanio under her window kept even pace with every stop[1] of her instrument, but especially my young ruffler,[2] that beforetime, like a bird in a cage, had been prentice for three lives or one and twenty years at least to extreme Avarice, his deceased father. Oh, 'twas a world to see how he sometime simpered it, striving to set a countenance on his new-turned face, that it might seem of wainscot[3] proof to behold her face without blushing. Anon he would stroke his bow-bent leg, as if he meant to shoot love arrows from his shins, then wiped his chin—for his beard was not yet grown—with a gold-wrought handkercher, when of purpose he let fall a handful of angels.[4] This golden shower was no sooner rained but Lamilia ceased her song, and Roberto, assuring himself the fool was caught, came to Lucanio, that stood now as one that had stared Medusa[5] in the face, and awaked him from his amazement with these words: "What, in a trance, brother? Whence spring these dumps? Are ye amazed at this object? Or long ye to become Love's subject? Is there not difference between this delectable life and the imprisonment you have all your life hitherto endured? If the sight and hearing of this harmonious beauty work in you effects of wonder, what will the possession of so divine an essence, wherein beauty and art dwell in their perfect excellence?" "Brother," said Lucanio, "let's use few words. An she be no more than a woman, I trust you'll help me to win her, and, if you do, I say no more but I am yours till death us depart, and what is mine shall be yours, world without end. Amen."

Roberto, smiling at his simpleness, helped him to gather up his dropped gold and without any more circumstance led him to Lamilia's house, for of such places it may be said as of hell: "*noctes*

1　Note.
2　Rogue, scallywag.
3　Oak panelling.
4　Gold coins.
5　In classical myth, a Gorgon whose face turned its beholder into stone.

atque dies patet atri ianua ditis,"[1] so their doors are ever open to entice youth to destruction. They were no sooner entered but Lamilia herself like a second Helen[2] court-like begins to salute Roberto, yet did her wandering eye glance often at Lucanio. The effect of her entertainment consisted in these terms, that to her simple house signor Roberto was welcome, and his brother the better welcome for his sake, albeit his good report, confirmed by his present demeanour, were of itself enough to give him deserved entertainment in any place how honourable soever. Mutual thanks returned, they lead this prodigal child into a parlour garnished with goodly portraitures of amiable personages, near which an excellent consort of music[3] began at their entrance to play. Lamilia, seeing Lucanio shamefast, took him by the hand and tenderly wringing him used these words: "Believe me, gentleman, I am very sorry that our rude entertainment is such as no way may work your content, for that I have noted since your first entering that your countenance hath been heavy, and the face, being the glass of the heart, assures me that the same is not quiet. Would ye with anything hear that might content you, say but the word, and assure ye of present diligence to effect your full delight." Lucanio, being so far in love as he persuaded himself without her grant he could not live, had a good meaning to utter his mind, but, wanting fit words, he stood like a truant that lacked a prompter[4] or a player[5] that, being out of his part at his first entrance, is fain to have the book[6] to speak what he should perform. Which Roberto perceiving, replied thus in his behalf: "Madam, the sun's brightness dazzleth the beholder's eyes, the majesty of gods amazeth human men, Tully,[7] prince of orators, once fainted though his cause were good, and he that tamed monsters[8] stood amated at beauty's ornaments. Then blame not

---

1 "Night and day, black hell's gates lie open" (Latin). The quote is from Virgil's *Aeneid* 6.127 and continues, "sed rovacare gradum superasque evadare ad auras, / hoc opus, hic labor est" (128–29), "But to retrace one's steps and return to the sunshine, / this the work, this the labour is."

2 In classical myth, Trojan prince Paris' kidnapping of Helen, the stunningly beautiful wife of the Greek king Menelaus, was the cause of the Trojan war.

3 Group of musicians.

4 Someone to give him his lines to speak.

5 Actor.

6 Play book, script.

7 Marcus Tullius Cicero (106–43 BCE), Roman orator.

8 Hercules.

this young man though he replied not, for he is blinded with the beauty of your sun-darkening eyes, made mute with the celestial organ of your voice and fear of that rich ambush of amber-coloured darts whose points are levelled against his heart." "Well, signor Roberto," said she, "however you interpret their sharp level, be sure they are not bent to do him hurt, and, but that modesty blinds us poor maidens from uttering the inward sorrow of our minds, perchance the cause of grief is ours however men do colour, for as I am a virgin I protest"—and therewithal she tainted her cheeks with a vermilion blush—"I never saw gentleman in my life in my eye so gracious as is Lucanio; only this is my grief, that either I am despised, for that he scorns to speak, or else, which is my greater sorrow, I fear he cannot speak." "Not speak, gentlewoman?," quoth Lucanio, "That were a jest indeed! Yes, I thank God I am sound of mind and limb, only my heart is not as it was wont. But, an you be as good as your word, that will soon be well, and so, craving ye of more acquaintance, in token of my plain meaning receive this diamond, which my old father loved dearly," and with that delivered her a ring wherein was a pointed diamond of wonderful worth, which she accepting with a low congé,[1] returned him a silk ribbon for a favour, tied with a true love's knot, which he fastened under a fair jewel on his beaver belt.

After this Diomedes and Glaucus *permutatio*,[2] my young master waxed crank[3] and, the music continuing, was very forward in dancing, to show his cunning and so, desiring them to play on a hornpipe, laid on the pavement lustily with his leaden heels, curvetting[4] like a steed of signor Rocco's[5] teaching, and wanted nothing but bells to be a hobbyhorse in a morris.[6] Yet was he soothed in his folly, and whatever he did Lamilia counted excellent. Her praise made him proud, in so much that if he had not

---

1 Bow, curtsey.
2 Diomedes and Glaucus are heroes fighting on opposite sides during the Trojan War. When they meet on the battlefield, they discover they are related, refuse to fight each other, and exchange (*permutatio*) gifts instead (*Iliad* 6.232–36).
3 Lively, spritely, merrily (*OED*, adj., 1).
4 Ed.; corvetting Q. Prancing, capering, leaping (*OED* 1).
5 Greene may be referring here to Rocco Bonetti (d. 1590), the famous Italian fencing master who moved to England around 1570 and whose new style of fencing replaced the older English style of sword-fighting (Wallace 187).
6 Morris dance, a traditional English folk dance.

been entreated he would rather have died in his dance than left off to show his mistress delight. At last reasonably persuaded, seeing the table furnished, he was content to cease and settle him to his victuals, on which, having before labored, he set lustily, especially of woodcock pie, wherewith Lamilia, his carver,[1] plentifully plied him. Full dishes having furnished empty stomachs, and Lucanio thereby got leisure to talk, falls to discourse of his wealth, his lands, his bonds, his ability, and how himself with all he had was at madam Lamilia's disposing, desiring her afore his brother to tell him simply what she meant. Lamilia replied, "My sweet Lucanio, how I esteem of thee mine eyes do witness, that like handmaids have attended thy beauteous face ever since I first beheld thee. Yet, seeing love that lasteth gathereth by degrees his liking, let this for that suffice: if I find thee firm, Lamilia will be faithful; if fleeting, she must of necessity be unfortunate, that, having never seen any whom before she could affect, she should be of him injuriously forsaken." "Nay," said Lucanio, "I dare say my brother here will give his word for that." "I accept your own," said Lamilia, "for with me your credit is better than your brother's." Roberto broke off their amorous prattle with this speech: "Since either of you are of other so fond at the first sight, I doubt not but time will make your love more firm. Yet, madam Lamilia, although my brother and you be thus forward, some cross chance may come, for *multa cadunt inter calicem supremaque labe.*[2] And for a warning to teach you both wit, I'll tell you an old wives' tale." "Before ye go on with our tale," quoth mistress Lamilia, "let me give ye a caveat by the way, which shall be figured in a fable."

Lamilia's Fable

"The fox on a time came to visit the gray,[3] partly for kindred, chiefly for craft, and, finding the hole empty of all other company saving only one badger, enquired the cause of his solitariness. He described the sudden death of his dam[4] and sire with the rest of his consorts.[5] The fox made a Friday[6] face, counterfeiting sorrow but, concluding that death's stroke was inevitable,

---

1 Server.
2 "There is many a slip betwixt cup and lip" (Latin).
3 Badger (*OED*, n., 2b).
4 Mother.
5 Companions.
6 In the church calendar, Friday was a day of fasting and repentance.

persuaded him to seek some fit mate wherewith to match. The badger soon agreed, so forth they went and in their way met with a wanton ewe straggling from the fold. The fox bade the badger play the tall stripling and strut on his tiptoes, for, quoth he, 'this ewe is lady of all these lands and her brother chief bellwether[1] of sundry flocks.' To be short, by the fox's persuasion there would be a perpetual league between her harmless kindred and all other devouring beasts, for that the badger was to them all allied. Seduced, she yielded, and the fox conducted them to the badger's habitation, where, drawing her aside under colour[2] of exhortation, pulled out her throat to satisfy his greedy thirst. Here I should note, a young whelp that viewed their walk informed the shepherds of what happened. They followed and trained the fox and badger to the hole. The fox afore had craftily conveyed himself away; the shepherds found the badger raving for the ewe's murder; his lamentation being held for counterfeit, was by the shepherds' dogs werried.[3] The fox escaped, the ewe was spoiled, and ever since between the badgers and dogs hath continued a mortal enmity. And now be advised, Roberto," quoth she, "go forward with your tale, seek not by sly imitation to turn our mirth to sorrow." "Go to, Lamilia," quoth he, "you fear what I mean not, but, however ye take it, I'll forward with my tale."

Roberto's Tale

"In the north parts there dwelt an old squire that had a young daughter his heir, who had, as I know, madam Lamilia, you have had, many youthful gentlemen that long time sued to obtain her love. But she, knowing her own perfections, as women are by nature proud, would not to any of them vouchsafe favour, insomuch that, they perceiving her relentless, showed themselves not altogether witless but left her to her fortune when they found her frowardness.[4] At last it fortuned, among other strangers a farmer's son visited her father's house, on whom at the first sight she was enamoured, he likewise on her. Tokens of love passed

---

1 Chief male sheep. Wethers are castrated rams.
2 Pretext.
3 "Seized by the throat with the teeth and torn or lacerated; killed or injured by biting and shaking. Said e.g. of dogs or wolves attacking sheep, or of hounds when they seize their quarry" (*OED*, worry, v., 3a).
4 Ill-humoured stubbornness, disdain.

between them, either acquainted other's parents of their choice, and they kindly gave their consent. Short tale to make, married they were, and great solemnity was at the wedding feast. A young gentleman that had long been suitor to her, vexing that the son of a farmer should be so preferred, cast in his mind by what means, to mar their merriment, he might steal away the bride. Hereupon he confers with an old beldam[1] called Mother Gunby dwelling thereby, whose counsel having taken, he fell to his practice and proceeded thus. In the afternoon, when dancers were very busy, he takes the bride by the hand and, after a turn or two, tells her in her ear he had a secret to impart unto her, appointing her in any wise in the evening to find a time to confer with him. She promised she would, and so they parted. Then goes he to the bridegroom and with protestations of entire affect, protests that the great sorrow he takes at that which he must utter, whereon depended his especial credit, if it were known the matter by him should be discovered. After the bridegroom's promise of secrecy, the gentleman tells him that a friend of his received that morning from the bride a letter, wherein she willed him with some sixteen horse to await her coming at a park side, for that she detested him in her heart as a base country hind, with whom her father compelled her to marry. The bridegroom, almost out of his wits, began to bite his lip. 'Nay,' sayeth the gentleman, 'if you will by me be advised, you shall salve her credit, win her by kindness, and yet prevent her wanton complot.' 'As how?', said the bridegroom. 'Marry, thus,' said the gentleman, 'In the evening (for, till the guests be gone, she intends not to gad) get you on horseback and seem to be of the company that attends her coming. I am appointed to bring her from the house to the park and from thence fetch a winding compass of a mile about but to turn unto old Mother Gunby's house, where her lover, my friend, abides. When she alights, I will conduct her to a chamber far from his lodging, but when the lights are out and she expects her adulterous copemate, yourself, as reason is, shall prove her bedfellow, where privately you may reprove her and in the morning early return home without trouble. As for the gentleman my friend, I will excuse her absence to him by saying she mocked me with her maid instead of herself, whom when I knew at her alighting I disdained to bring her into his presence.' The bridegroom gave his hand it should be so.

---

1 Old woman, grandmother, hag (*OED*, n., 1a, 3).

Now by the way you must understand this Mother Gunby had a daughter, who all that day sat heavily at home with a willow[1] garland, for that the bridegroom, if he had dealt faithfully, should have wedded her before any other. But men, Lamilia, are inconstant. Money nowadays makes the match, or else the match is marred.

But to the matter. The bridegroom and the gentleman thus agreed, he took his time, conferred with the bride, persuaded her that her husband, notwithstanding his fair show at the marriage, had sworn to his old sweetheart, their neighbor Gunby's daughter, to be that night her bedfellow, and if she would bring her father, his father, and other friends to the house at midnight, they should find it so.

At this the young gentlewoman, inwardly vexed to be by a peasant so abused, promised if she saw likelihood of his slipping away that then she would do according as he directed.

All this thus sorting, the old woman's daughter was trickly attired ready to furnish this pageant, for her old mother provided all things necessary.

Well, supper past, dancing ended, and the guests would home, and the bridegroom, pretending to bring some friends of his home, got his horse, and to the park side he rode and stayed with the horsemen that attended the gentleman.

Anon came Marian like mistress bride and mounted behind the gentleman, away they post, fetch their compass, and at last alight at the old wife's house, where suddenly she is conveyed to her chamber and the bridegroom sent to keep her company, where he had scarce devised how to begin his exhortation but the father of his bride knocked at the chamber door. At which, being somewhat amazed, yet thinking to turn it to a jest, since his wife, as he thought, was in bed with him, he opened the door, saying, 'Father, you are heartily welcome. I wonder how you found us out here. This device to remove ourselves was with my wife's consent, that we might rest quietly without the maids and bachelors disturbing.' 'But where's your wife,' said the gentleman. 'Why, here in bed,' said he. 'I thought,' quoth the other, 'my daughter had been your wife, for sure I am today she was given you in marriage.' 'You are merrily disposed,' said the bridegroom, 'What, think you I have another wife?' 'I think but as you speak,' quoth the gentleman, 'for my daughter is below, and you say your wife

---

1   The willow tree symbolized an unrequited lover's grief (*OED*, n., 1d).

is in the bed.' 'Below?', said he, 'You are a merry man,' and with that, casting on a night gown, he went down, where, when he saw his wife, the gentleman his father, and a number of his friends assembled, he was so confounded that how to behave himself he knew not; only he cried out that he was deceived. At this the old woman arises and, making herself ignorant of the whole matter, inquires the cause of that sudden tumult. When she was told the new bridegroom was found in bed with her daughter, she exclaimed against so great an injury. Marian was called *in quorum*;[1] she justified, it was by his allurement; he, being condemned by all their consents, was adjudged unworthy to have the gentlewoman unto his wife and compelled, for escaping of punishment, to marry Marian; and the young gentleman, for his care in discovering the farmer's son's lewdness, was recompensed with the gentlewoman's ever-during love."

Quoth Lamilia, "And what of this?" "Nay, nothing," said Roberto, "but that I have told you the effects of sudden love. Yet the best is, my brother is a maidenly bachelor, and, for yourself, you have not been troubled with many suitors." "The fewer the better," said Lucanio, "but, brother, I con[2] you little thanks for this tale. Hereafter, I pray you use other table talk." "Let's, then, end talk," quoth Lamilia, "and you, signor Lucanio, and I will go to chess." "To chess?," said he, "What mean you by that?" "It is a game," said she, "that the first danger is but a check, the worst, the giving of a mate." "Well," said Roberto, "that game ye have been at already, then, for you checked him first with your beauty and gave yourself for mate to him by your bounty." "That's well taken, brother," said Lucanio, "so have we passed our game at chess." "Will ye play at tables, then?," said she? "I cannot," quoth he, "for I can go no further with my game, if I be once taken." "Will ye play, then, at cards?" "Ay," said he, "so it be at one-and-thirty." "That fool's game?," said she. "We'll all to hazard," said Roberto, "and, brother, you shall make one for an hour or two." "Content," quoth he. So to dice they went, and fortune so favoured Lucanio that, while they continued square play, he was no loser. Anon, cozenage[3] came about, and his angels, being double-winged, flew clean from before him. Lamilia, being the

---

1 "Into the group" (Latin). The phrase has legal connotations: in this period, "quorum" denoted the collective body of the Justices of the Peace (*OED*, n., 1).
2 Owe.
3 Cheating.

winner, prepared a banquet, which finished, Roberto advised his brother to depart home and to furnish himself with more crowns lest he were outcracked with newcomers.

Lucanio, loath to be out-countenanced, followed his advice, desiring to attend his return, which he before had determined unrequested. For as soon as his brother's back was turned, Roberto begins to reckon with Lamilia to be a sharer as well in the money deceitfully won as in the diamond so willfully given. But she, *secundum mores meretrices*,[1] jested thus with the scholar: "Why, Roberto! Are you so well read and yet show yourself so shallow-witted to deem women so weak of conceit that they see not into men's demerits? Suppose, to make you my stale[2] to catch the woodcock your brother, that, my tongue overrunning mine intent, I spoke of liberal reward. But what I promised—there's the point. At least what I part with I will be well advised. It may be you will thus reason: had Roberto not trained[3] Lucanio unto Lamilia's lure, Lucanio had not now been Lamilia's prey; therefore, since by Roberto she now possesseth the prize, Roberto merits an equal part. Monstrous absurd if so you reason! As well you may reason thus: Lamilia's dog hath killed her a deer, therefore his mistress must make him a pasty.[4] No, poor, penniless poet, thou art beguiled in me, and yet I wonder how thou couldst, thou hast been so often beguiled. But it fareth with licentious men as with the chased boar in the stream, who, being greatly refreshed with swimming, never feeleth any smart until he perish recurelessly wounded with his own weapons. Reasonless Roberto, that hast attempted to betray thy brother, irreligiously forsaken thy wife, deservedly been in thy father's eye an abject, thinkst thou Lamilia so loose to consort with one so lewd? No, hypocrite, the sweet gentleman thy brother I will till death love and thee, while I live, loath. This share Lamilia gives thee; other gettst thou none."

As Roberto would have replied, Lucanio approached, to whom Lamilia discoursed the whole deceit of his brother and never rested intimating malicious arguments till Lucanio utterly refused Roberto for his brother and forever forbade him his house. And when he would have yielded reasons and formed excuse, Lucanio's impatience, urged by her importunate malice, forbade all reasoning with them that was reasonless and so, giving him Jack

---

1 "As is the habit of whores" (Latin).
2 Hunting lure, decoy.
3 Drawn.
4 Meat pie.

Drum's entertainment,[1] shut him out of doors—whom we will follow, and leave Lucanio to the mercy of Lamilia. Roberto in an extreme ecstasy rent his hair, cursed his destiny, blamed his treachery, but most of all exclaimed against Lamilia and, in her, against all enticing courtesans, in these terms:

> What meant the poets in invective[2] verse
> To sing Medea's shame[3] and Scylla's[4] pride,
> Calypso's[5] charms, by which so many died?
> Only for this: their vices they rehearse,
> That curious wits which in this world converse
> May shun the dangers and enticing shows
> Of such false Sirens, those home-breeding foes
> That from the eyes their venom do disperse.
> So soon kills not the basilisk[6] with sight,
> The viper's tooth is not so venomous,
> The adder's tongue not half so dangerous,
> As they that bear the shadow of delight,
> Who chain blind youths in trammels of their hair
> Till waste bring woe, and sorrow haste despair.

With this he laid his head on his hand and leaned his elbow on the earth, sighing out sadly, "*Heu, patior telis vulnera facta meis!*"[7]

On the other side of the hedge sat one that heard his sorrow, who, getting over, came towards him and broke off his passion. When he approached, he saluted Roberto in this sort. "Gentleman," quoth he, "(for so you seem) I have by chance heard you discourse some part of your griefs, which appeareth to be more

---

1 Throwing him out.
2 Satirical.
3 In classical myth, Medea is abandoned by Jason after helping him to obtain the Golden Fleece in exchange for his promise to marry her.
4 Mythical female sea monster who lured sailors to their death by shipwreck.
5 Nymph who in Homer's *Odyssey* seduces Odysseus into staying with her on her island for seven years when he should have been returning home to his wife Penelope.
6 According to Pliny, the basilisk is a small Egyptian serpent with a "white spot ... like a coronet or diadem" on its head; "there is not one that looketh upon his eyes, but dyeth presently" (*Natural History* 8.21). "No physic [medicine] prevails against the gaze of the basilisks" (Grosart 6.45), Greene asserts in *Menaphon* (1589).
7 "Woe is me, I suffer wounds inflicted by my own weapons!" (Latin).

than you will discover or I can conceive. But if you vouchsafe such simple comfort as my ability may yield, assure yourself that I will endeavor to do the best that either may procure you profit or bring you pleasure, the rather for that I suppose you are a scholar, and pity it is that men of learning should live in lack.

Roberto, wondering to hear such good words, for that this iron age[1] affords few that esteem of virtue, returned him thankful gratulations and, urged by necessity, uttered his present grief, beseeching his advice how he might be employed. "Why, easily," quoth he, and greatly to your benefit, for men of my profession get by scholars their whole living." "What is your profession?," said Roberto. "Truly, sir," said he, "I am a player." "A player?," quoth Roberto, "I took you rather for a gentleman of great living, for if by outward habit men should be censured, I tell you, you would be taken for a substantial man." "So am I where I dwell," quoth the player, "reputed able at my proper[2] cost to build a windmill. What though the world once went hard with me, when I was fain[3] to carry my playing fardel[4] a-foot-back? *Tempora mutantur.*[5] I know you know the meaning of it better than I, but I thus conster[6] it, 'it's otherwise now,' for my very share in playing apparel[7] will not be sold for two hundred pounds." "Truly," said Roberto, "'tis strange that you should so prosper in that vain practice, for it seems to me your voice is nothing gracious." "Nay, then," said the player, "I mislike your judgement. Why, I am as famous for Delphrigus and the King of Faeries as ever was any of my time.[8] The twelve labours of Hercules have I terribly

---

1   Classical myth divided world history into four ages: golden, silver, bronze, and iron.
2   Own.
3   Obliged of necessity.
4   Bundle.
5   "Times have changed" (Latin).
6   Construe, translate.
7   Costumes.
8   Delphrigus and the King of Faeries were roles in popular plays of the type that the plays of University Wits were rendering out of fashion. Addressing "the Gentleman Students of Both Universities," Thomas Nashe in his preface to Greene's *Menaphon* writes of "Sundry other sweet gentlemen I know that have vaunted their pens in private devices and tricked up a company of taffeta fools with their feathers, whose beauty, if our poets had not pieced with the supply of their periwigs, they might have anticked it until this time up and down the country with the King of Faeries and dined every day at the pease porridge ordinary with Delphrigus" (sig. A2v).

thundered on the stage and played three scenes of the Devil in *The Highway to Heaven*." "Have ye so?," said Roberto, "Then, I pray you, pardon me." "Nay, more," quoth the player, "I can serve to make a pretty speech, for I was a country author, passing at a moral, for 'twas I that penned *The Moral of Man's Wit*, *The Dialogue of Dives*,[1] and for seven years' space was absolute interpreter[2] to the puppets. But now my almanack is out of date: 'The people make no estimation / Of morals, teaching, education!' Was not this pretty for a plain time extempore? If ye will, ye shall have more." "Nay, it's enough," said Roberto, "but how mean you to use me?" "Why, sir, in making plays," said the other, "for which you shall be well paid, if you will take the pains."

Roberto, perceiving no remedy, thought best, in respect of his present necessity, to try his wit and went with him willingly, who lodged him at the town's end in a house of retail, where what happened to our poet you shall after hear. There, by conversing with bad company, he grew *a malo in peius*,[3] falling from one vice to another. And so, having found a vein to finger crowns, he grew cranker than Lucanio, who by this time began to droop, being thus dealt with by Lamilia. She, having bewitched him with her enticing wiles, caused him to consume in less than two years that infinite treasure gathered by his father with so many a poor man's curse. His lands sold, his jewels pawned, his money wasted, he was cashiered by Lamilia, that had cozened him of all. Then walked he like one of Duke Humphry's squires, in a threadbare cloak, his hose drawn out with his heels, his shoes unseamed, lest his feet should sweat with heat. Now, as witless as he was, he remembered his father's words, his unkindness to his brother, his carelessness of himself. In this sorrow he sat down penniless on a[4] bench, where, when Opus and Usus[5] told him by chimes in his stomach it was time to fall unto meat, he was fain with the chameleon to feed upon the air and make patience his best repast.

While he was at his feast, Lamilia came flaunting by, garnished with the jewels whereof she beguiled him, which sight served to close his stomach after his cold cheer. Roberto, hearing of his

---

1 In a parable that Jesus tells in the Gospel of Luke, Dives is a rich man who goes to hell, while Lazarus, a poor beggar who sat outside Dives' gates, goes to heaven (Luke 16:19–31).
2 Puppet-master.
3 "From bad to worse" (Latin).
4 Ed. "on a" not in Q.
5 Need and Custom (Latin).

brother's beggary, albeit he had little remorse of his miserable state, yet did seek him out, to use him as a property,[1] whereby Lucanio was somewhat provided for. But, being of simple nature, he served but for a block to whet Roberto's wit on, which, the poor fool perceiving, he forsook all other hopes of life and fell to be a notorious pandar,[2] in which detested course he continued till death. But Roberto now famoused for an arch-playmaking-poet, his purse like the sea sometime swelled, anon like the same sea fell to a low ebb, yet seldom he wanted, his labours were so well esteemed. Marry, this rule he kept, whatever he fingered aforehand was the certain means to unbind a bargain, and being asked why he so slightly dealt with them that did him good, "It becomes me," said he, "to be contrary to the world, for commonly, when vulgar men receive earnest,[3] they do perform; when I am paid anything aforehand, I break my promise." He had shift of lodgings, where in every place his hostess writ up the woeful remembrance of him, his laundress, and his boy, for they were ever his in household, beside retainers in sundry other places. His company were lightly the lewdest persons in the land, apt for pilfery, perjury, forgery, or any villainy. Of these he knew the casts to cog[4] at cards, cozen[5] at dice; by these he learned the legerdemains[6] of nips, foists, cony-catchers, cross-biters, lifts, high lawyers, and all the rabble of that unclean generation of vipers.[7] And pithily could he paint out their whole courses of craft. So cunning he was in all crafts as nothing rested in him almost but craftiness. How often the gentlewoman his wife laboured vainly to recall him is lamentable to note, but as one given over to all lewdness he communicated her sorrowful lines among his loose trulls,[8] that jested at her bootless[9] laments. If he could any way get credit on scores, he would then brag his creditors carried stones, comparing every round circle to a groaning 'O' procured by a painful burden. The shameful end of sundry his consorts deservedly punished for their amiss wrought no compunction in his heart, of which one,

---

1 Stage prop.
2 Pimp.
3 Advance payment.
4 Cheat.
5 Cheat.
6 Tricks.
7 On cony-catchers and cross-biters, see p. 130, note 6. Nips, foists, lifts, and high lawyers are other criminal types.
8 Female companions.
9 Futile, unheeded.

brother to a brothel he kept, was trussed under a tree as round as a ball.

To some of his swearing companions thus it happened. A crew of them sitting in a tavern carousing, it fortuned an honest gentleman and his friend to enter their room. Some of them being acquainted with him, in their domineering drunken vein would have no nay but down he must needs sit with them. Being placed, no remedy there was but he must needs keep even company with their unseemly carousing, which, he refusing, they fell from high words to sound strokes, so that with much ado the gentleman saved his own and shifted from their company. Being gone, one of these tipplers forsooth lacked a gold ring, the other swore they saw the gentleman take it from his hand. Upon this, the gentleman was indicted before a judge; these honest men are deposed, whose wisdom weighing the time of the brawl, gave light to the jury, what power wine-washing poison had; they according unto conscience found the gentleman not guilty, and God released by that verdict the innocent. With his accusers thus it fared: one of them for murder was worthily executed; the other never since prospered; the third sitting not long after upon a lusty horse, the beast suddenly died under him—God amend the man!

Roberto, every day acquainted with these examples, was notwithstanding nothing bettered but, rather, hardened into wickedness. At last was that place[1] justified, "God warneth men by dreams and visions in the night and by known examples in the day, but, if he return not, He comes upon him with judgement that shall be felt." For now, when the number of deceits caused Roberto be hateful almost to all men, his immeasurable drinking had made him the perfect image of a dropsy,[2] and the loathsome scourge of lust tyrannized in his bones. Lying in extreme poverty and having nothing to pay but chalk, which now his host accepted not for current,[3] this miserable man lay comfortlessly languishing, having one groat left, the just proportion of his father's legacy, which, looking on, he cried, "Oh, now it is too late, too late, to buy wit with this, and therefore will I see if I can sell to careless youth what I negligently forgot to buy."

Dear gentlemen, break I off Roberto's speech, whose life in most parts agreeing with mine, found one self[4] punishment as I

---

1 Commonplace, scriptural maxim.
2 Dropsy is a disease caused by excess water in the body's cavities or connective tissue (*OED*, n., 1a).
3 Currency.
4 Same.

have done. Hereafter, suppose me the said Roberto, and I will go on with that he promised. Greene will send you now his groats-worth of wit, that never showed a mite's-worth in his life. And though no man now be by to do me good, yet ere I die I will by my repentance endeavor to do all men good:

> Deceiving world, that with alluring toys
> Hath made my life the subject of thy scorn
> And scorneth now to lend thy fading joys.
> To length my life, whom friends have left forlorn,
> How well are they that die ere they be born
> > And never see thy sleights, which few men shun
> > Till unawares they helpless are undone!

> Oft have I sung of Love and of his fire,
> But now I find that poet was advised
> Which made full feasts increasers of desire
> And proves weak Love was with the poor despised.
> For when the life with food is not sufficed,
> > What thought of Love, what motion of delight,
> > What pleasance can proceed from such a wight?[1]

> Witness my want, the murderer of my wit;
> My ravished sense, of wonted fury reft,
> Wants such conceit as should in poems fit
> Set down the sorrow wherein I am left.
> But therefore have high heavens their gifts bereft,
> > Because so long they lent them me to use
> > And I so long their bounty did abuse

> Oh, that a year were granted me to live,
> And for that year my former wits restored!
> What rules of life, what counsel would I give,
> How should my sin with sorrow be deplored!
> But I must die of every man abhorred.
> > Time loosely spent will not again be won;
> > My time is loosely spent, and I undone.

O horrenda fames,[2] how terrible are thy assaults! But *vermis conscientiae*,[3] more troubling are thy stings. Ah, gentlemen that live

---

1 Person.
2 "Evil reputation" (Latin).
3 "Worm of conscience" (Latin).

to read my broken and confused lines, look not that I should, as I was wont, delight you with vain fantasies, but gather my follies all together and, as ye would deal with so many parricides, cast them into the fire. Call them Telegones,[1] for now they kill their father, and every lewd line in them written is a deep piercing wound to my heart; every hour spent by any in reading them brings a million of sorrows to my soul. Oh, that the tears of a miserable man—for never any man was yet more miserable—might wash their memory out with my death, and that those works with me together might be interred! But since they cannot, let this my last work witness against them with me how I detest them. Black is the remembrance of my black works, blacker than night, blacker than death, blacker than hell.

Learn wit by my repentance, gentlemen, and let these few rules following be regarded in your lives.

1. First, in all your actions set God before your eyes, for the fear of the Lord is the beginning of wisdom.[2] Let His word be a lantern to your feet and a light unto your paths,[3] then shall you stand as firm rocks and not be moved.[4]
2. Beware of looking back, for God will not be mocked,[5] and of him that hath received much, much shall be demanded.[6]
3. If thou be single and can abstain, turn thy eyes from vanity, for there is a kind of women bearing the faces of angels but the hearts of devils, able to entrap the elect[7] if it were possible.
4. If thou be married, forsake not the wife of thy youth to follow strange flesh,[8] for whoremongers and adulterers the Lord will judge. The door of a harlot leadeth down to death, and in her

---

1 In classical myth, Telegonus unwittingly kills his father, Odysseus, in a fight.
2 "The fear of the Lord is the beginning of wisdom" (Psalm 111:10).
3 "Thy word is a lamp unto my feet, and a light unto my path" (Psalm 119:105).
4 Ed.; mocked Q. "They that trust in the Lord shall be as mount Zion, which cannot be removed, but abideth for ever" (Psalm 125:1).
5 "Be not deceived; God is not mocked: for whatsoever a man soweth, that shall he also reap" (Galatians 6:7).
6 "For unto whomsoever much is given, of him shall be much required" (Luke 12:48).
7 Those chosen ("elected") by God to go to heaven.
8 "Let thy fountain be blessed: and rejoice with the wife of thy youth," for "why wilt thou, my son, be ravished with a strange woman, and embrace the bosom of a stranger" (Proverbs 5:18, 20).

lips there dwells destruction. Her face is decked with odours, but she bringeth a man to a morsel of bread and nakedness, of which myself am instance.

5. If thou be left rich, remember those that want and so deal that by thy willfulness thyself want not. Let not taverners and victuallers[1] be thy executors, for they will bring thee to a dishonourable grave.

6. Oppress no man, for the cry of the wronged ascendeth to the ears of the Lord,[2] neither delight to increase by usury, lest thou lose thy habitation in the everlasting tabernacle.

7. Beware of building thy house to thy neighbour's hurt, for the stones will cry to the timber, "We were laid together in blood," and those that so erect houses, calling them by their names, shall lie in the grave like sheep, and death shall gnaw upon their souls.

8. If thou be poor, be also patient and strive not to grow rich by indirect means, for goods so gotten shall vanish like smoke.

9. If thou be a father, master, or teacher, join good example with good counsel, else little avail precepts, where life is different.

10. If thou be a son or servant, despise not reproof, for though correction be bitter at the first, it bringeth pleasure in the end.

Had I regarded the first of these rules or been obedient to the last, I had not now at my last end been left thus desolate. But now, though to myself I give *consilium post facta*,[3] yet to others they may serve for timely precepts. And therefore, while life gives leave, I will send warning to my old consorts, which have lived as loosely as myself. Albeit weakness will scarce suffer me to write, yet to my fellow scholars about this city will I direct these few ensuing lines.

To those gentlemen his quondam[4] acquaintance, that spend their wits in making plays, R.G. wisheth a better exercise and wisdom to prevent his extremities.

---

1 "Keeper[s] of an eating-house, inn, or tavern" (*OED*, n., 1a).
2 Many biblical verses express this sentiment, of which the following is an example: "Ye shall not afflict any widow, or fatherless child. | If thou afflict them in any wise, and they cry at all unto me, I will surely hear their cry" (Exodus 22:22–23).
3 "Advise after the fact" (Latin).
4 Former.

If woeful experience may move you, gentlemen, to beware, or unheard-of wretchedness entreat you to take heed, I doubt not but you will look back with sorrow on your time past and endeavor with repentance to spend that which is to come. Wonder not—for with thee will I first begin—thou famous gracer of tragedians,[1] that Greene, who hath said with thee, like the fool in his heart, "There is no God,"[2] should now give glory unto His greatness, for penetrating is His power, His hand lies heavy upon me, He hath spoken unto me with a voice of thunder, and I have felt He is a God that can punish enemies. Why should thy excellent wit, His gift, be so blinded that thou shouldst give no glory to the giver? Is it pestilent Machiavellian policy that thou hast studied? Oh, peevish folly! What are his rules but mere confused mockeries, able to extirpate in small time the generation of mankind? For if *sic volo, sic iubeo*[3] hold in those that are able to command and if it be lawful *fas et nefas*[4] to do anything that is beneficial, only tyrants should possess the earth, and they, striving to exceed in tyranny, should each to other be a slaughterman, till the mightiest outliving all, one stroke were left for death, that in one man's life should end. The broacher of this diabolical atheism[5] is dead and in his life had never the felicity he aimed at, but, as he began in craft, lived in fear and ended in despair. *Quam inscrutabilia sunt Dei iudicia!*[6] This murderer of many brethren had his conscience seared like Cain;[7] this betrayer of him that gave his life for him inherited the portion of Judas;[8] this apostate perished as ill as Julian.[9] And wilt thou, my friend, be his disciple? Look but to me, by him persuaded to that liberty, and thou shalt find it an

---

1 Christopher Marlowe.
2 "The fool hath said in his heart, There is no God" (Psalm 14:1).
3 "Thus I desire, thus I command" (Latin).
4 "Right or wrong" (Latin).
5 Machiavelli.
6 "How inscrutable are the judgements of God" (Latin). "O the depth of the riches both of the wisdom and knowledge of God! How unsearchable are his judgements, and his ways past finding out!" (Romans 11:33).
7 Cain, the eldest son of Adam, murdered his brother Abel, for which God condemned him to perpetual exile and placed a mark on his forehead (Genesis 4:1–15).
8 Judas received thirty pieces of silver for betraying Jesus but hanged himself later out of remorse (Matthew 27:3–5).
9 Roman Emperor Julian (r. 361–63 CE) attempted to replace Christianity with Neoplatonism as the Roman Empire's religion.

infernal bondage. I know the least of my demerits merit this miserable death, but willful striving against known truth exceedeth all the terrors of my soul. Defer not, with me, till this last point of extremity, for little knowst thou how in the end thou shalt be visited.

With thee I join young Juvenal,[1] that biting satirist, that lastly with me together writ a comedy.[2] Sweet boy, might I advise thee, be advised and get not many enemies by bitter words. Inveigh[3] against vain men, for thou canst do it, no man better, no man so well. Thou hast a liberty to reprove all and name none, for, one being spoken to, all are offended; none being blamed, no man is injured. Stop shallow water still running, it will rage, or tread on a worm and it will turn. Then blame not scholars vexed with sharp lines if they reprove thy too much liberty of reproof.

And thou no less deserving than the other two, in some things rarer, in nothing inferior, driven, as myself, to extreme shifts, a little have I to say to thee.[4] And were it not an idolatrous oath, I would swear by sweet Saint George[5] thou art unworthy better hap, since thou dependest on so mean a stay.[6] Base-minded men all three of you, if by my misery you be not warned, for unto none of you, like me, sought those burs to cleave—those puppets, I mean, that spoke from our mouths, those anticks[7] garnished in our colours.[8] Is it not strange that I, to whom they all have been beholding, is it not like that you, to whom they all have been beholding, shall, were ye in that case as I am now, be both at once

---

1 Often identified as Thomas Nashe (1567–1601), a writer of satirical pamphlets and plays such as *Piers Penniless His Supplication to the Devil* (1592), *The Unfortunate Traveller* (1594), and, with Ben Jonson, *The Isle of Dogs* (1597) (Jordan 75–76).

2 To which comedy Greene is referring here is unknown, but Nashe collaborated with Marlowe on *Dido Queen of Carthage* (date uncertain) and with Ben Jonson on *The Isle of Dogs* (1597).

3 Rail, declaim.

4 Often identified as George Peele (1556–96), an Elizabethan playwright, poet, and pageant writer. His biblical drama *David and Bathsheba* is one of the neglected jewels of Elizabethan drama (Jordan 75–76).

5 Patron saint of England. To swear by Saint George in Protestant Elizabethan England would be "idolatrous" because it would, according to Protestant theology, place the saint in the position of Christ as intercessor between the individual and God.

6 Support. Greene is referring to actors and playwrighting.

7 Actors.

8 Words, lines, rhetoric.

of them forsaken? Yes, trust them not, for there is an upstart crow,[1] beautified with our feathers, that with his "tiger's heart wrapped in a player's hide,"[2] supposes he is as well able to bombast out a blank verse[3] as the best of you, and being an absolute *Iohannes fac totum*[4] is in his own conceit the only Shake-scene in a country. Oh, that I might entreat your rare wits to be employed in more profitable courses and let those apes imitate your past excellence and never more acquaint them with your admired inventions. I know the best husband of you all will never prove a usurer, and the kindest of them all will never prove a kind nurse, yet, whilst you may, seek better masters, for it is a pity men of such rare wits should be subject to the pleasure of such rude grooms.

In this I might insert two more, that both have writ against these buckram[5] gentleman, but let their own works serve to witness against their own wickedness, if they persevere to maintain any more such peasants. For other newcomers, I leave them to the mercy of these painted monsters, who, I doubt not, will drive the best-minded to despise them. For the rest, it skills[6] not though they make a jest of them.

But now return I again to you three, knowing my misery is to you no news, and let me heartily entreat you to be warned by my harms. Delight not, as I have done, in irreligious oaths, for from the blasphemer's house a curse shall not depart. Despise drunkenness, which wasteth the wit and maketh men all equal unto beasts. Fly lust as the deathman of the soul, and defile not the temple of the Holy Ghost. Abhor those Epicures whose loose life hath made religion loathsome to your ears, and when they soothe you with terms of Mastership,[7] remember Robert Greene, whom they so often flattered, perishes now for want of comfort.

---

1 Shakespeare.
2 Echoing the captured York's denunciation of his captor Queen Margaret in Shakespeare's *3 Henry VI*: "O tiger's heart wrapped in a woman's hide!" (1.4.136).
3 Unrhymed iambic pentameter verse, popularized in dramatic verse by Christopher Marlowe's *Tamburlaine* plays (1587–88).
4 "Jack of all trades" (Latin).
5 "A kind of coarse linen or cloth stiffened with gum or paste. *men in buckram*: sometimes proverbially for non-existent persons" (*OED*, n., 2a). Figuratively, "buckram" suggests hollowness here: the "buckram gentleman," or actors, appear to be gentlemen because of their clothes but underneath are not.
6 Matters.
7 By calling you "master." Greene was Master of Arts at both Oxford and Cambridge.

Remember, gentlemen, your lives are like to many lighted tapers that are with care delivered to all of you to maintain. These with wind-puffed wrath may be extinguished, which drunkenness put out, which negligence let fall, for man's time is not of itself so short but it is more shortened by sin. The fire of my light is now at the last snuff, and, for want of wherewith to sustain it, there is no substance left for life to feed on. Trust not, then, I beseech ye, to such weak stays, for they are as changeable in mind as in many attires. Well, my hand is tired, and I am forced to leave where I would begin, for a whole book cannot contain their wrongs, which I am forced to knit up in some few lines of words.

> Desirous that you should live, though himself be dying,
> Robert Greene.

Now to all men I bid farewell in like sort, with this conceited fable of that old comedian Aesop.[1]

An ant and a grasshopper walking together on a green, the one carelessly skipping, the other carefully prying what winter's provision was scattered in the way, the grasshopper, scorning, as wantons will, this needless thrift (as he termed it), reproved him thus:

> The greedy miser thirsteth still for gain,
> His thrift is theft, his weal[2] works other's woe.
> That fool is fond which will in caves remain
> When 'mongst fair sweets he may at pleasure go.

To this the ant, perceiving the grasshopper's meaning, quickly replied:

> The thrifty husband spares what unthrift spends,
> His thrift no theft, for dangers to provide.
> Trust to thyself, small hope in want yield friends;
> A cave is better than the deserts wide.

In short time these two parted, the one to his pleasure, the other to his labour. Anon, harvest grew on and reft from the grasshopper his wonted moisture. Then, weakly skipped he to the meadow's brinks, where till fell winter he abode. But, storms

---

1 Classical Greek author (620–564 BCE) of beast fables, including "The Ant and the Grasshopper."
2 Benefit, wealth.

continually pouring, he went for succour to the ant his old
acquaintance, to whom he had scarce discovered his estate but
the waspish little worm made this reply:

> Pack hence, quoth he, thou lazy worm!
> My house doth harbor no unthrifty mates.
> Thou scorndst to toil, and now thou feelst the storm
> And starv'st for food while I am fed with cates.[1]
> Use no entreats. I will relentless rest,
> For toiling labour hates an idle guest.

The grasshopper, foodless, friendless, helpless, and strength-
less, got into the next brook and in the yielding sand dug for himself a pit, by which he likewise engraved this epitaph:

> When spring's green prime arrayed me with delight
> And every power, with youthful vigour filled,
> Gave strength to work whatever fancy willed,
> I never feared the force of winter's spite.
> Then too late I praised the emmet's[2] pain,
> That sought in spring a harbour 'gainst the heat
> And in the harvest gathered winter's meat,
> Preventing famine, frosts, and stormy rain.
>
> My wretched end may warn green, springing youth
> To use delights as toys that will deceive
> And scorn the world before the world them leave,
> For all world's trust is ruin without ruth.
> Then blessed are they that like the toiling ant
> Provide in time 'gainst winter's woeful want.

With this, the grasshopper, yielding to the weather's extremity,
died comfortless without remedy. Like him, myself; like me, shall
all that trust to friends or time's inconstancy. Now faint I of my
last infirmity, beseeching them that shall bury my body to publish
this last farewell written with my wretched hand.

Felicem fuisse infaustum.[3]

---

1 Delicacies.
2 Ant's.
3 "Sad it is once to have been happy" (Latin).

A letter written to his wife, found with this book after his death.

The remembrance of the many wrongs offered thee and thy unreproved virtues add greater sorrow to my miserable state than I can utter or thou conceive. Neither is it lessened by consideration of thy absence (though shame would hardly let me behold thy face) but exceedingly aggravated, for that I cannot, as I ought, to thy own self reconcile myself, that thou mightst witness my inward woe at this instant, that have made thee a woeful wife for so long a time. But equal heaven hath denied that comfort, giving at my last need like succour as I have sought all my life, being in this extremity as void of help as thou hast been of hope. Reason would that, after so long waste, I should not send thee a child to bring thee greater charge, but consider he is the fruit of thy womb, in whose face regard not the father's faults so much as thy own perfections. He is yet Greene and may grow straight if he be carefully tended; otherwise, apt enough, I fear me, to follow his father's folly. That I have offended thee highly I know; that you canst forget my injuries I hardly believe. Yet persuade I myself, if thou saw my wretched estate, thou couldst not but lament it. Nay, certainly I know thou wouldst. All my wrongs muster themselves before me, every evil at once plagues me. For my contempt of God, I am contemned of men. For my swearing and forswearing,[1] no man will believe me. For my gluttony, I suffer hunger. For my drunkenness, thirst. For my adultery, ulcerous sores.[2] Thus God hath cast me down, that I might be humbled, and punished me, for example of other sinners, and although He strangely suffers me in this world to perish without succour, yet trust I in the world to come to find mercy by the merits of my Saviour, to whom I commend thee and commit my soul.

Thy repentant husband for his disloyalty,
Robert Greene.

Felicem fuisse infaustum.

FINIS.

---

1 Oath-breaking.
2 Sexual diseases.

Appendix B: Atheism and Machiavellianism

1. From Innocent Gentillet, *A Discourse Upon the Means of Well Governing and Maintaining in Good Peace a Kingdom or Other Principality ... Against Nicholas Machiavel the Florentine.* Translated into English by Simon Patterick (1602)

[In 1513 Niccolò Machiavelli (1469–1527) wrote his notorious work on the art of government, *The Prince.* In 1576, Gentillet (d. c. 1595) published his work (written in French; Latin translation 1577), which came to be known popularly as the *Anti-Machiavell.* In the preface to his attack on Machiavelli's ideas, Gentillet argues that Machiavelli's ideas are the source of all the evil tearing France apart. The body of Gentillet's work is a point-by-point refutation of what Gentillet considers to be the key propositions or maxims of Machiavellianism. Each chapter begins by stating in italics (very appropriately) one of Machiavelli's maxims and then proceeds to refute it. At least in England, however, Gentillet's work had an ambiguous effect: as Gentillet's work was translated by 1602 at the latest and as Machiavelli's *Prince* wasn't translated into English until 1640, Gentillet's attack on Machiavelli was for some time the interested English reader's most readily accessible source of Machiavellian ideas. What follows are excerpts from Gentillet's work and a list of the maxims by which he attempts to summarize Machiavelli's thinking. Gentillet breaks the maxims into three categories: maxims of counsel, maxims of religion, and maxims of policy. The references in square brackets preceding the maxims are Gentillet's.]

a) Maxims of Religion:

1. [*Prince* 18] A prince above all things ought to wish and desire to be esteemed devout, though he be not so indeed.

2. [*Discourses* 1.12–14] A prince ought to sustain and confirm that which is false in religion if so be it turn to the favour thereof.

3. [*Discourses* 2.5] The paynim[1] religion holds and lifts up their hearts, and so makes them hardy to enterprise great things, but the Christian religion, persuading to humility, humbleth and too much weakeneth their minds, and so makes them more ready to be injured and preyed upon.

4. [*Discourses* 2] The great doctors of the Christian religion by a great ostentation[2] and stiffness have sought to abolish the remembrance of all good letters[3] and antiquity.

5. [*Discourses* 1.12] When men left the paynim religion they became altogether corrupted so that they neither believed in God nor the Devil.

6. The Roman Church[4] is cause of all the calamities in Italy.

7. Moses could never have caused his laws and ordinances to be observed if force and arms had wanted.

8. [*Discourses* 2.9] Moses usurped Judea[5] as the Goths usurped part of the Empire.

9. [*Discourses* 1.12] The religion of Numa[6] was the chief cause of Rome's felicity.

10. [*Prince* 25, *Discourses* 2.29] A man is happy so long as Fortune agreeth unto his nature and humour.

b) From Gentillet's refutation of Machiavelli's first maxim of religion, "A prince above all things ought to wish and desire to be esteemed devout, though he be not so indeed."

The World (saith Machiavelli) looketh but to the exterior and to that which is in appearance, and judges of all actions not by the causes but by the issue and end, so that it sufficeth, if that the prince seem outwardly religious and devout, although he be not

---

1 Pagan.
2 Show, display.
3 Literature.
4 The Roman Catholic Church.
5 Region in Palestine to which Moses led the Israelites.
6 Roman king (r. 717–673 BCE).

so at all. For let it be so, that some which most narrowly frequent his company do discover that feigned devotion, yet he or they dare not oppugne[1] the multitude, who believe the prince to be truly devout.

This maxim is a precept whereby this atheist Machiavelli teacheth the prince to be a true contemner[2] of God and of religion and only to make a show and fair countenance outwardly before the world to be esteemed religious and devout, although he be not. For divine punishment, for such hypocrisy and dissimulation, Machiavelli fears not because he believes not there is a God but thinks that the course of the sun, of the moon, of the stars, the distinction of the spring time, summer, autumn, and winter, the politic government of men, the production that the earth makes of fruits, plants, living creatures, that all this comes by encounter and adventure, following the doctrine of Epicurus[3] (the doctor of atheists and master of ignorance), who esteems that all things are done and come to pass by Fortune and the meeting and encountering of atoms. But if Machiavelli believed that those things came by the disposition and establishment of a sovereign cause (as common sense hath constrained Plato, Aristotle, Theophrastus,[4] and all the other philosophers which have had any knowledge, to confess it), he would believe there is one God, he would also believe that men ought to honour him as the sovereign governor and that he will not be mocked of his creatures.[5] And therefore will not he give such precepts, to make a show to be devout and not to be. For what is it to mock God, if that be not? But they that learn such lessons of atheism, and which put out their eyes that they may not see so clear a light, and which take pleasure to be ignorant of that which (as Cicero saith) even nature itself teacheth the most barbarous nations, "That there is a God which governeth all things,"[6] let them (I say) know that if they will not know God well, God will well know them and will make them well feel that such as spit against heaven shall spit against themselves. When they shall feel

---

1 Fight, oppose.
2 Despiser, scorner.
3 Greek philosopher Epicurus (341–270 BCE) was a materialist who argued that the universe consisted of nothing but particles of matter (atoms) and space. His ideas are preserved in Lucretius' *De rerum natura* ("Of the nature of things").
4 Aristotle's student.
5 "Be not deceived; God is not mocked: for whatsoever a man soweth, that shall he also reap" (Galatians 6:7).
6 See Cicero's *De natura deorum* ("On the nature of the gods").

how heavy his hand weigheth, then shall they know that there is a God, a revenger of them which reverence him not, but this knowledge shall be to their confusion and ruin. Many atheists have been seen which of a brutish boldness have made a mock of God, but it was never seen that they felt not the punishment and vengeance of their audaciousness and impiety, as hereafter we will show by examples. Yet we have cause greatly to deplore the misery and calamity of the time wherein we are, which is so infected with atheists, and contemners of God and all religion, that even they which have no religion are best esteemed and are called, in the court-language, "people of service," because being freighted[1] with all impiety and atheism, and having well studied their Machiavelli, which they know upon their fingers, they make no scruple nor conscience at anything. Command them to slay and massacre, they slay and massacre; command them to rob and spoil good Catholics, and clergymen, they rob and spoil all. They hold benefices[2] with soldier's garments and short clothes, yet exercise no religion nor cares but for the gain thereof. Command them to enterprise the betraying or empoisoning of this or that person, they make no scruple at it. Yea, they themselves excogitate[3] and devise all wickedness and impieties, as the invention of so many new imposts[4] upon the poor people, which they destroy and cause to die with hunger, without having any commiseration or compassion upon them, no more than upon brute beasts. Not many years ago, did not they invent the impost of processes and contentions of law in France? By the means of which impost, a poor man cannot seek by law to recover his own, unless beforehand he pay the said impost and that he showed his acquittance.[5] ... Have they not, and yet every day do they not, cause the value of money to be augmented for their own profit? For after that by the means of their banks, farms,[6] and other their dealings in the realm, they have gathered great heaps of money, they can at their pleasure enhance the value thereof, both in their hands and out of their hands. Yet none complains thereof. But in the end it will produce and bring forth some great disorder and confusion (as hath sometimes been seen for like actions) for the reasons well enough known to wise people. As for peace, these people never like of (for they fish always in a troubled

---

1 Loaded, full (of).
2 Church livings.
3 Think up, plan.
4 Fees, taxes.
5 Receipt.
6 Monopolies.

water), gathering riches and heaps of treasures of the realm, whilst it is in trouble and confusion. They always have in their mouths their goodly maxims of their Machiavelli to impeach[1] and hinder a good peace. A prince (say they) must cause himself to be feared rather than loved:[2] and this must be held as a resolved point. But if a peace be accorded to these rebels, such as they desire, then would it seem that the king were afraid of his subjects, whereas he should make himself to be feared. True it is, that if such a peace could be made with them as it might again procure another Saint Bartholomew's journey,[3] nothing were so good and pleasant as that. For that is another resolved point and maxim, That a prince ought not to hold any faith or promise but so far as concerns his profit,[4] and that he ought to know how to counterfeit the fox, to catch and entrap other beasts and, as soon as he hath them in his nets, to play the lion in slaying and devouring them.[5] We have set down unto us that goodly example of Caesar Borgia,[6] who in our country could so well counterfeit the said two beasts. Behold here the language and dealings of our Machiavelistes, which at this day men call "people of service," for that there is no wickedness in the world so strange and detestable but they will enterprise, invent, and put it into execution, if they can. From whence comes it that they be thus inclined to all wickedness? It is because they are atheists, contemners of God, neither believing there is a God which seeth what they do nor that ought to punish them. It is that goodly doctrine of Machiavelli, which amongst other things complains so much that men cannot be altogether wicked (as we shall touch in his place.) These good disciples (seeing that their master found this imperfection amongst men, that they could not

---

1 Attack.
2 See Gentillet's ninth Maxim of Policy.
3 1572 massacre of French Huguenots in Paris and other French cities on Saint Bartholomew's Day (24 August). Huguenot leaders had gathered in Paris in the summer of 1572 to celebrate the marriage of the Huguenot Henry king of Navarre (1553–1610) to Margaret Valois (1553–1615), sister of the Catholic king of France Charles IX (r. 1560–74), an event that ostensibly heralded the end of religious warfare in France. The wedding, however, was followed by the massacre, which Protestant writers argued had been planned by Charles, his mother Catherine Medici, and her favourite the Duke of Guise (Jouanna, *The St Bartholomew's Day Massacre*). Marlowe dramatizes these events in his play *The Massacre at Paris*.
4 See Gentillet's twentieth Maxim of Policy.
5 See Gentillet's twelfth Maxim of Policy.
6 See Gentillet's seventh Maxim of Policy.

show themselves altogether and in all things wicked) do seek by all means to attain a degree of perfect wickedness. And indeed they have so well studied and profited in their master's school, and can so well practice his maxims, that none can deny but that they are come unto the highest degree of wickedness. What need men then to be abashed,[1] if they see in the world, and especially in this poor kingdom of France, such famine, pestilence, civil wars, the father to band against his son, brother against his brother, they of the same religion one against another, with all hatred, envy, disloyalty, treasons, perfidies,[2] conspiracies,[3] empoisonments, and other great sins to reign? Is there any marvel if the people go to wrack, the clergy be impoverished, the nobility almost extinct? For it is the first judgement and vengeance of God, which he exerciseth against us: because some are filled with all impiety and atheism, which they have learned of Machiavelli; and others which should resist such impieties, lest they should take root, do suffer them to increase and augment. So that indeed all men are culpable[4] of atheism, impiety, of the despite of God and religion, which at this day reigneth. Therefore most righteously doth God punish us all. For atheism and impiety is so detestable and abominable before God that it never remaineth unpunished.

2. Thomas Kyd, Letters to Sir John Puckering about Christopher Marlowe (1593)

[Thomas Kyd (1558–94) was a scrivener (copyist), professional playwright, and for a while one of Christopher Marlowe's (1564–93) closest associates. His revenge tragedy *The Spanish Tragedy* (1587), which retained its popularity long after its author died in 1594, provided the model for subsequent early modern English revenge tragedies, and some critics have speculated that Kyd wrote an early version of *Hamlet*. Kyd also wrote *Soliman and Perseda* (1588) and translated the sixteenth-century French humanist playwright Robert Garnier's *Cornélie*. In 1593 he was arrested and tortured after his rooms were searched as part of an investigation into what has become known as the Dutch Church libel. Coming at the peak of an outbreak of popular xenophobia in London directed at resident aliens, a lengthy

---

1 Ashamed.
2 Treacheries, deceits.
3 Conspiracies.
4 Guilty.

doggerel poem attacking foreigners was posted on the wall of a Dutch Protestant church in London. The poem alludes to several of Marlowe's plays and is signed "Tamburlaine" (Kuriyama 123). Nothing implicating Kyd in the libel was found in the search, it seems. Part of an heretical treatise was, however, and it seems that this led the Elizabethan authorities to suspect Kyd of atheism, another of their worries at this time. Kyd was arrested on 12 May 1593. On 20 May, Marlowe was ordered to be prepared to appear before the Privy Council, but on 30 May he was killed. Kuriyama dates Kyd's letters to June 1593, after Kyd's release. Kyd addresses the letters to Queen Elizabeth's chancellor, Sir John Puckering (c. 1544–96), in an attempt to clear himself of the suspicion of atheism and to request Puckering's aid in regaining the favour of his erstwhile patron and patron of the acting company for which he wrote, Ferdinando Stanley, Lord Strange (c. 1559–94). The letters have been transcribed from digital images of British Library Harleian manuscripts 6849 f. 218 (first letter) and 6848 f. 154 (second letter).]

a) [First letter.] At my last being with your Lordship[1] to entreat some speeches from you in my favour to my Lord,[2] who (though I think he rest[3] not doubtful of mine innocence) hath yet in his descreeter judgement feared to offend in his retaining[4] me without your honour's former privity,[5] so it is now, Right Honourable, that the denial of that favour (to my thought reasonable) hath moved me to conjecture some suspicion that your Lordship holds me in concerning atheism, a deadly[6] thing which I was undeserved[ly] charged withal. And therefore have I thought it requisite,[7] as well in duty to your Lordship and the laws as also in the fear of God and freedom of my conscience, therein to satisfy the world and you.

The first and most (though insufficient surmise) that ever as therein might be raised of me, grew thus. When I was first suspected for that libel[8] that concerned the state,[9] amongst those

---

1 Sir John Puckering, Queen Elizabeth I's chancellor.
2 Ferdinando Stanley, Lord Strange.
3 Remain.
4 Employing.
5 Favour, privilege.
6 A capital crime.
7 Necessary.
8 The Dutch Church libel. See the headnote.
9 The Elizabethan government.

waste and idle papers (which I cared not for) and which unasked I did deliver up were found some fragments of a disputation[1] touching that opinion affirmed by Marlowe to be his and shuffled with some of mine (unknown to me) by some occasion of our writing in one chamber two years since. My first acquaintance with this Marlowe rose upon his bearing name to serve my Lord,[2] although his Lordship never knew his service but in writing for his players, for never could my Lord endure his name or sight when he had heard of his conditions, nor would indeed the form of divine prayer used daily in his Lordship's house have quadred[3] with such reprobates. That I should love or be familiar friend with one so irreligious were very rare, when Tully saith *Digni sunt amicitia quibus in ipsis inest causa cur diligantur*,[4] which neither was in him for person, qualities, or honesty. Besides, he was intemperate and of a cruel heart, the very contraries to which my greatest enemies will say by me. It is not numbered amongst the best conditions of men to tax or to upbraid the dead, *Quia mortui non mordent*,[5] but thus much have I with your Lordship's favour dared in the greatest cause, which is to clear myself of being thought an atheist, which some will swear he was. For more assurance that I was not of that vile opinion, let it but please your Lordship to enquire of such as he conversed withal, that is (as I am given to understand) with Harriot,[6] Warner,[7] Royden,[8] and some stationers[9] in Paul's churchyard,[10] whom in no sort can accuse nor will

---

1 Treatise, essay.
2 Lord Strange.
3 Squared, agreed.
4 "They are worthy of friendship who possess in themselves the cause why they are to be loved" (Cicero, *De amicitia* XXI).
5 "Since the dead do not bite" (Latin).
6 Thomas Harriot (c. 1560–1621), mathematician and scientist patronized by Sir Walter Ralegh (c. 1552–1618), a prominent Elizabethan courtier interrogated about his rumoured atheism by a royal commission in 1594 (Nicholl 297).
7 Walter Warner (c. 1558–1643), mathematician patronized by Henry Percy, ninth earl of Northumberland (1564–1632), whose intellectual adventurousness earned him a reputation for atheism and the epithet "the wizard earl" (*DNB*).
8 Matthew Royden (d. 1622), poet and part of Marlowe's and Kyd's literary circle.
9 Members of the Stationers' Company, to which printers, booksellers, and others belonged.
10 The churchyard of Saint Paul's cathedral, where many printers and booksellers had their shops.

excuse by reason of his company, of whose consent if I had been, no question but I also should have been of their consort,[1] for *ex minimo vestigio artifex agnoscit artificem.*[2] Of my religion and life I have already given some instance to the late commissioners and of my revered meaning to the state, although perhaps my pains and undeserved torture felt by some would have engendered more impatience when less by far hath driven so many *imo extra caulas,*[3] which it shall never do with me.

But whatsoever I have felt, Right honourable, this is my request, not for reward but in regard of my true innocence, that it would please your Lordships so to [use] the same and me, as I may still retain the favours of my Lord,[4] whom I have served almost these vi years now, in credit until now, and now am utterly undone without herein be somewhat done for my recovery. For I do know his Lordship holds your honours and the state in that due reverence as he would in no way move the least suspicion of his loves and cares both towards her sacred Majesty,[5] your Lordships, and the laws whereof, when time shall serve, I shall give greater instance which I have observed. As for the libel laid unto my charge, I am resolved with receiving of the sacrament to satisfy your Lordship and the world that I was neither agent nor consenting thereunto. Howbeit if some outcast Ishmael,[6] for want or of his own dispose[7] to lewdness,[8] have with pretext of duty or religion, or to reduce himself to that he was not born unto, by any way incensed your Lordships to suspect me, I shall beseech in all humility and in the fear of God that it will please your Lordships but to censure me as I shall prove myself, and to repute them as they are indeed. *Cum totius iniustitiae nulla capitalior sit quam eorum, qui tum cum maxime fallunt id agunt ut viri boni esse videantur.*[9] For doubtless even then your Lordships shall be sure to break [up] their lewd designs and see into the truth, when but

---

1 Company.
2 "From the smallest traces the craftsman knows his work" (Latin).
3 "Beyond the sheep-fold" (Latin).
4 Lord Strange.
5 Queen Elizabeth I.
6 Son of Abraham and Hagar, Abraham's wife's servant. Ishmael and Hagar were sent away when Abraham's wife Sarah observed Ishmael mocking her own son Isaac. See Genesis 21.
7 Disposition.
8 Wickedness.
9 "For there is no higher injustice than that of those who while being most deceptive act so that they appear to be good men" (Latin).

their lives that herein have accused me shall be examined and ripped up effectually, so may I chance with Paul to live and shake the viper of my hand into the fire for which the ignorant suspect me guilty of the former shipwreck.[1] And thus (for now I fear me I grow tedious) assuring your good Lordship that if I knew any whom I could justly accuse of that damnable offence to the awful Majesty of God or of that other mutinous sedition toward the state[2] I would as willingly reveal them as I would request your Lordship's better thoughts of me that never have offended you.

Your Lordship's most humble in all duties
Th. Kyd

b) [Second letter.] Pleaseth it your honourable Lordship[3] touching Marlowe's monstrous opinions: as I cannot but with an aggrieved conscience think on him or them, so can I but particularize few in the respect of them that kept him greater company. Howbeit in discharge of duty both towards God, your Lordships, and the world, thus much have I thought good briefly to discover in all humbleness.

First, it was his custom, when I knew him first and as I hear say he continued it in table talk or otherwise, to jest at the divine scriptures, gibe[4] at prayers, and strive in argument to frustrate and confute what hath been spoke or writ by prophets and such holy men.

1. He would report Saint John to be our saviour Christ's Alexis,[5] I cover it with reverence and trembling, that Christ did love him with an extraordinary love.

---

1 Shipwrecked on Melita, Paul builds a fire. While he is doing so, a snake crawls on him, and the local inhabitants conclude that he is a murderer and responsible for the shipwreck; when he shakes the snake into the fire unharmed, the inhabits conclude that he is a god. See Acts 28:3–6.
2 As Riggs points out, Elizabethans considered atheism politically as well as theologically dangerous: "Since atheists lacked any deep-seated loyalties to the Elizabethan establishment, they would have no moral inhibitions about turning upon it" (325).
3 Sir John Puckering.
4 Mock.
5 In classical Latin poet Virgil's *Eclogues* the young man Alexis is the object of the shepherd Corydon's passion. The relationship between these two fictional characters figured prominently in early modern discourse on male–male erotic love and friendship.

2. That for me to write a poem of Saint Paul's conversion[1] as I was determined, he said would be as if I should go write a book of fast and loose, esteeming Paul a juggler.[2]

3. That the prodigal child's[3] portion was but four nobles,[4] he held his purse so near the bottom in all pictures,[5] and that it either was a jest or else four nobles then was thought a great patrimony, not thinking it a parable.

4. That things esteemed to be done by divine power might have as well been done by observation of men, all which he would so suddenly take slight occasion to slip out as I and many others, in regard of his other rashness in attempting sudden privy injuries to men, did overslip[6] though often reprehend[7] him for it and for which, God is my witness, as well by my Lord's commandment as in hatred of his life and thoughts, I left and did refrain his company. He would persuade with men of quality to go unto the king of Scots[8] whether I hear Royden is gone and where if he had lived he told me when I saw him last he meant to be.

3. Richard Baines, "A note containing the opinion of Christopher Marlowe concerning his damnable judgment of religion and scorn of God's word" (1593)

[Richard Baines is a shadowy yet important figure in Christopher Marlowe's biography. Graduating from Cambridge several years before Marlowe, from 1578 to 1582 Baines was a double agent for the Elizabethan spymaster Sir Francis Walsingham (c. 1532–90)

---

1 The account of the apostle Paul's conversion to Christianity can be found in Acts 9.
2 Magician, con artist.
3 In Luke 15:11–32 Christ tells the story of the child who asks his father for his inheritance and then leaves home to seek his fortune. Having squandered his money and fallen on hard times, he returns home and is forgiven by his father. The parable was a popular subject in Renaissance art.
4 Gold coins.
5 Paintings, engravings, wood cuts, etc.
6 Overlook, let pass.
7 Rebuke, admonish.
8 James VI of Scotland (r. 1567–1625), later James I of England (r. 1603–25).

in the English Catholic seminary at Rheims (Nicholl 122–24). Gathering intelligence on the seminary's students, whom the Elizabethan government deemed to be embryonic conspirators against the queen, was not Baines's only intention, apparently. His cover was blown in 1582, and in a written confession he stated that his intention was to poison the entire seminary (Nicholl 124). In 1583 Baines was released from imprisonment and made his way back to England, possibly serving as a recruiter for Walsingham's spy network. This may be how Baines and Marlowe came to be in Flushing together in January 1592, where they were arrested for counterfeiting. Baines accused Marlowe of instigating the endeavour and of planning to convert to Catholicism (Nicholl 235–37). The two were deported back to England, and it is unclear what role, if any, Richard Baines might have had in Marlowe's death a year later. Charles Nicholl, however, contends that Marlowe was the victim of factional fighting between two of Elizabeth's most powerful courtiers, the Earl of Essex and Sir Walter Ralegh, the former attempting to blacken the latter by linking him with Marlowe, whose reputation for potentially seditious atheism could be magnified into threatening proportions through such documents as the Baines Note. Although nothing ultimately came of it, in 1594 a royal commission was established to investigate Ralegh's rumoured atheism (Nicholl 297). The Baines Note, which may or may not have been written by Baines himself, was submitted to Sir John Puckering, Queen Elizabeth's chancellor and the same person to whom Kyd wrote the two letters included in Appendix B2, four days before Marlowe's death on 30 May 1593. An edited version of the note was prepared for submission to the queen herself in June of the same year (Kuriyama 219–20). The text of the note has been transcribed from digital images of British Library Harleian manuscript 6848 ff. 185–86.]

That the Indians and many authors of antiquity have assuredly written of above sixteen thousand years ago whereas Adam is proved to have lived within six thousand years.

He affirmeth that Moses was but a juggler[1] and that one Harriot,[2] being Sir Walter Ralegh's man, can do more than he.

---

1 Magician, con artist.

2 Thomas Harriot (c. 1560–1621), mathematician and scientist patronized by Sir Walter Ralegh (c. 1552–1618), a prominent Elizabethan courtier interrogated about his rumoured atheism by a royal commission in 1594 (Nicholl 297).

That Moses made the Jews to travel eleven years in the wilderness (which journey might have been done in less than one year) ere[1] they came to the promised land, to the intent that those who were privy to most of his subtleties might perish and so an everlasting superstition remain in the hearts of the people.

That the first beginning of religion was only to keep men in awe.

That it was an easy matter for Moses, being brought up in all the arts of the Egyptians, to abuse the Jews, being a rude and gross[2] people.

That Christ was a bastard and his mother dishonest.

That he[3] was the son of a carpenter, and that if the Jews among whom he was born did crucify him, they best knew him and whence he came.

That Christ deserved better to die than Barabbas[4] and that the Jews made a good choice, though Barabbas were both a thief and a murderer.

That if there be any god or any good religion, then it is in the Papists[5] because the service of God is performed with more ceremonies, as elevation of the mass, organs, singing men, shaven crowns, et cetera. That all Protestants are hypocritical asses.

That if he were put to write a new religion, he would undertake both a more excellent and admirable method and that all the New Testament is filthily written.

That the woman of Samaria and her sister were whores and that Christ knew them dishonestly.[6]

---

1 Before.
2 Ignorant, uncultured.
3 Christ. '
4 Pilate offered the Jews a choice of whom to be crucified, Christ or a convict called Barabbas. The Jews chose Christ. See Matthew 27.
5 Catholics.
6 John 4:7–42 recounts Christ's conversion of a Samaritan prostitute and other Samaritans.

That Saint John the Evangelist was bedfellow to Christ and leaned always in his bosom, that he used him as the sinners of Sodoma.[1]

That all they that love not tobacco and boys were fools.

That all the apostles were fishermen and base fellows neither of wit nor worth, that Paul only had wit but he was a timorous fellow in bidding men to be subject to magistrates against his conscience.[2]

That he has as good right to coin[3] as the queen of England, and that he was acquainted with one Poole,[4] a prisoner in Newgate,[5] who hath great skill in mixture of metals, and having learned some things of him he meant through help of a cunning stamp maker to coin French crowns, pistolets, and English shillings.

That if Christ would have instituted the sacrament with more ceremonial reverence it would have been had in more admiration, that it would have been much better being administered in a tobacco pipe.

That the angel Gabriel was bawd[6] to the Holy Ghost, because he brought the salutation to Mary.

That one Richard Cholmley[7] hath confessed that he was persuaded by Marlowe's reasons to become an atheist.

These things, with many other, shall by good and honest witness be approved to be his opinions and common speeches, and that this Marlowe doth not only hold them himself, but almost

---

1 Genesis 18–19 recount God's destruction of Sodom and Gomorrah for their homosexual practices.
2 See Colossians 3:22 and Titus 3:1.
3 Mint coins.
4 John Poole, counterfeiter and Catholic (Kuriyama 84).
5 London prison.
6 Pimp.
7 Elizabethan spy and informer who, according to a 1593 government document, "believeth that one Marlowe is able to show more sound reasons for atheism than any divine in England is able to give to prove divinity" (Nicholl 267).

into every company he cometh he persuades men to atheism, willing them not to be afeared of bugbears and hobgoblins, and utterly scorning both God and his ministers, as Richard Baines will justify and approve both by mine oath and the testimony of many honest men, and almost all men with whom he hath conversed anytime will testify the same, and, as I think, all men in Christianity ought to endeavour that the mouth of so dangerous a member may be stopped. He saith likewise that he hath quoted a number of contrarieties[1] out of the Scripture which he hath given to some great men who in convenient time shall be named. When these things shall be called in question the witness shall be produced.

Richard Baines

4. From Francis Bacon, "Of Atheism," *The Essays or Counsels Civil and Moral*, Essay XVI (1625)

[Francis Bacon (1561–1626), known as the father of the empirical scientific method, was a prominent lawyer and the writer of several major works, including *The Advancement of Learning* (1605) and the *Novum Organum* (1620), both of which attempted to rectify earlier Aristotelian methods of acquiring and organising knowledge. Among his major literary achievements are the *Essays*. The first publication of this work was in 1597, and included ten entries, whose style carried some of the objective quality in Bacon's "philosophical" works. By 1625 (its last printing in Bacon's lifetime), the work had expanded to 58 essays. The essay excerpted here, "Of Atheism," is from the 1625 edition of the *Essays*. In 1621 Bacon, who had been Attorney-General and was currently Lord Chancellor under James I, was impeached by parliament for bribery. After his impeachment, a number of his contemporaries added to the cloud of ill-repute under which Bacon lived his final years by circulating rumours that Bacon had engaged in sodomitical relations with his male servants (Jardine and Stewart 464–66).]

---

1 Contradictions.

I had rather believe all the fables in the *Legend*[1] and the *Talmud*[2] and the *Alcoran*[3] than that this universal frame is without a mind. And therefore God never wrought a miracle to convince atheism because His ordinary works convince[4] it. It is true that a little philosophy inclineth man's mind to atheism, but depth in philosophy bringeth men's minds about to religion. For while the mind of man looketh upon second causes scattered, it may sometimes rest in them and go no further, but when it beholdeth the chain of them, confederate and linked together, it must needs fly to providence and deity.[5] Nay, even that school which is most accused of atheism doth most demonstrate religion, that is, the school of Leucippus and Democritus and Epicurus.[6] For it is a thousand times more credible that four mutable elements[7] and one immutable fifth essence, duly and eternally placed, need no God, than that an army of infinite small portions or seeds, unplaced, should have produced this order and beauty without a divine marshal. The Scripture saith, "The fool hath said in his heart, 'There is no God.'"[8] It is not said, "The fool hath thought in his heart." So as, he rather saith it by rote to himself, as that he would have, than that he can thoroughly believe it or be persuaded of it. For none deny there is a God. It appeareth in nothing more, that atheism is rather in the lip than in the heart of man, than by this: that atheists will ever be talking of that their opinion, as if they fainted in it within themselves and would be glad to be strengthened by the consent of others. Nay more, you shall have atheists strive to get disciples, as it fareth with other sects, and, which is most of all, you shall have of them, that will suffer for atheism and not recant, whereas, if they did truly think that were no such thing as God, why should they trouble themselves? Epicurus is charged that he did but dissemble, for his credit's sake, when he affirmed there were blessed natures, but such as enjoyed themselves without

1 Jacob Voragine's *The Golden Legend*, a medieval collection of saints' lives.
2 Book of Jewish religious law.
3 Qur'an.
4 Demonstrate it conclusively.
5 Providence and God are first causes.
6 Leucippus, Democritus, and Epicurus were all ancient Greek philosophers who propounded an atomistic materialism.
7 Water, earth, air, and fire.
8 Psalm 14:1.

having respect to the government of the world. Wherein they say, he did temporize, though in secret he thought there was no God. But certainly he is traduced, for his words are noble and divine: *non Deos vulgi negare profanum; sed vulgi opiniones diis applicare profanum.*[1] Plato could have said no more, and although he had the confidence to deny the administration, he had not the power to deny the nature. The Indians of the West have names for their particular gods, though they have no name for God, as if the heathens[2] should have had the names *Iupiter, Apollo, Mars,* etc., but not the word *Deus,* which shows that even those barbarous people have the notion, though they have not the latitude and extent of it. So that against atheists the very savages take part with the very subtlest philosophers. The contemplative atheist is rare: a Diagoras, a Bion, a Lucian[3] perhaps, and some others. And yet they seem to be more than they are, for that all that impugn a received religion or superstition are by the adverse part branded with the name of atheists. But the great atheists, indeed, are hypocrites, which are ever handling holy things, but without feeling, so as they must needs be cauterized in the end. The causes of atheism are divisions in religion, if they be many, for any one main division addeth zeal to both sides, but many divisions introduce atheism. Another is scandal of priests, when it is come to that which Saint Bernard saith: *non est iam dicere, ut populus, sic sacerdos, quia nec sic populus, ut sacerdos.*[4] A third is the custom of profane scoffing in holy matters, which doth by little and little deface the reverence of religion. And lastly, learned times, especially with peace and prosperity, for troubles and adversities do more bow men's minds to religion. They that deny a god destroy men's nobility, for, certainly, man is of kin to the beasts by his body, and if he be not of kin to God by his spirit he is a base and ignoble creature. It destroys likewise magnanimity and the raising of human nature, for take an example of a dog and mark what a generosity and courage he will put on when he finds himself maintained by a man who to him is instead of a God or *Melior Natura,*[5] which courage is manifestly

---

1 "It is not sacrilegious to deny the gods of the common people, but it is sacrilegious to apply to the gods the opinions of the common people" (Latin) (Diogenes Laertius X.123).
2 Here, ancient Greeks and Romans.
3 Ancient Greek writers reputed for their atheism.
4 "One can no longer say the priest is as [bad as] the people, for the people are not [so bad] as the priest" (Latin) (Vickers 736).
5 "Better nature" (Latin).

such as that creature without that confidence of a better nature than his own could never attain. So man, when he resteth and assureth himself upon divine protection and favour, gathereth a force and faith which human nature in itself could not obtain. Therefore, as atheism is in all respects hateful, so in this, that it depriveth human nature of the means to exalt itself above human frailty. As it is in particular persons, so it is in nations. Never was there such a state for magnanimity as Rome. Of this state hear what Cicero saith: *Quam volumus licet, patres conscripti, nos amemus, tamen nec numero Hispanos, nec robore Gallos, nec calliditate Poenos, nec artibus Graecos, nec denique hoc ipso huius gentis et terrae domestico natiuoque sensu Italos ipsos et Latinos, sed pietate ac religione atque hac una sapientia, quod deorum immortalium numine omnia regi gubernarique perspeximus, omnes gentes nationeque superauimus.*[1]

---

1 "However much we may love ourselves, Roman senators, we are not superior to the Spanish in number, the Gauls in strength, the Carthaginians in skills, the Greeks in arts, or the Italian and Latins in affection for their native people and land, but we are superior to all peoples and nations in piety and religion and because we perceive all things to be ruled and governed by the power of the immortal gods" (Latin) (*De haruspicum responsis* ix.19).

Appendix C: Early Modern English Representations of Islam

1. From George Whetstone, *The English Mirror* (1586)

[In Whetstone's *The English Mirror*, the Elizabethan reader would have encountered the following biographical sketch of Mahomet and account of the rise of Islam. The stereotypes that Whetstone (c. 1544–c. 1587) circulates in this excerpt are representative of Western European medieval and early modern perceptions of Islam, which register the similarities between Islam and Christianity even in their strenuous assertions of the differences between the two religions and their attempts to defame and degrade Islam.]

[Chapter 7. Of the envy of Sergius, a monk of Constantinople who, being banished for heresy, fled into Arabia unto Mahomet, by whose devilish policies ambitious Mahomet forced the people to hold him for a prophet, which damnable sect until this day hath been nourished with the blood of many thousands.] Lamentable and most lamentable are the bloody cruelties manifested in my former discourses, but this one act of envy broached the extremest venom of the devil. For although in my recited examples I have published open injuries both against God and man, yet were they executed on those persons whose glory the envious beheld or, in the worst degree, to bury the remembrance of their virtues, which they imagined would lessen their account. But this fact[1] of Sergius was drawn many degrees more extreme, who though he sufficiently betrayed the envy that he bore to his superiors' authority, being a monk in Constantinople, in that he raised damnable heresies to make himself famous, yet the sect of Mahomet, which his accursed head first planted in Arabia, hath left an impossibility to Beelzebub[2] to scatter in the world, a more blasphemy against God and injury towards men, whose opinions buried millions of souls in hell whose bodies were to form many

---

1 Deed.
2 The devil.

hundred years after his departure unto the devil. The actions of whom and original of Mahomet's sect ensueth.

Sundry are the opinions of what parentage and country this false prophet Mahomet was. Platinus[1] sayeth that he sprung from noble line. But Pomponius Letus,[2] a most diligent author, in the abridgement of the Roman history, affirmeth that he was of a race base, vile, and obscure, which may the rather be credited for that a man so evil, in whom was nothing worthy of memory but malice and iniquity, may hardly be the issue of noble blood. Some say he was a Persian, some other an Arabian, and both opinions not without reason, for that at that time the Persians governed Arabia. Touching his father, were he noble or villain, sure it is that he was a gentile and neither Jew nor Christian. By his mother's side, the better opinion is that he descended from Abraham, by the line of his son Ishmael, whom he had by his chambermaid Agar, and so, as a Jew, observed the law of the Jews. This Mahomet had a quick spirit and easily learned whatsoever he was taught, who in his youth was sold as a slave unto a rich merchant named Adimonople, who, regarding the towardness of the young man, entertained him as his son and in no point as his slave, who so well managed his master's affairs that in short time he returned Adimonople great riches, and by reason of his great traffic both with Christians and Jews he was well exercised in either of their laws. During this time, Mahomet's master died without issue and left Ladigua his wife very rich, who, having before proved the sufficiency of Mahomet, took him to husband and so, of a bondsman,[3] raised him unto the degree of a rich lord.

In the prime of Mahomet's advancement, the forenamed Sergius arrived in Arabia, who to be revenged of the clergy that banished him Constantinople or, more properly to show his malice, to despite God because he suffered him to prosper no better in his heresies, in every place he tormented the poor Christians with whose outward habit he was but lately attired. In the end he lighted in acquaintance with Mahomet, whom Sergius found in ability and power great, in wit quick and subtle, in mind proud and ambitious, of disposition froward and envious, a great practiser of magic and nigromancy,[4] and, to be short, that he was ignorant in no vice, neither was there any lewd attempt that he

---

1 John Platinus, Exarch of Ravenna 687–702.
2 Junius Pomponius Laetus (1425–98), Italian humanist.
3 Slave.
4 Black magic.

feared to enterprise. [Sergius,] taking his best opportunity, counselled Mahomet to take upon him the name of a prophet, and, to give him the greater credit by magic and other devilish practices, he illuded[1] the people with some false miracles, insomuch as his wife and most familiar friends began to admire Mahomet and to reverence him as a holy prophet.

But were it the vengeance of God sent to abase his pride or the malice of the devil by this plague to colour[2] his impious enterprise, Mahomet was many times stricken with the falling evil,[3] whose strange passions much amazed both his wife and household servants, which Mahomet thus excused, that the Angel of God oftentimes talked with him and, unable as a man to sustain his divine presence, he entered into this agony and alteration of spirit, and that by this visitation, he forelearned what was the almighty will and pleasure of God, whose express charge he followed.

By these subtle illusions and protestations, he not only seduced his familiar friends and allies, but, by his cunning and their false rumours, he was admired and reputed through the greater part of Arabia as the prophet of God. Mahomet growing to be thus popular and, after the death of his wife, sole possessed of a great mass of wealth, by the encouragement of Sergius he published abroad that he was sent from God into the world to give laws unto the people. And, for that he was by his industry learned in all laws, in the beginning till he had well rooted his damnable sect, to reave[4] himself of many dangerous enemies, in part he accorded with the Jews, in part with the Christians, and moreover in many things he agreed with the heretics which reigned in his time. He denied the Trinity with the Sabellicans, with the Macedonians he denied that the Holy Ghost was God, and approved the multitude of wives with the Nicolaites.[5] On the other part he confessed that our Saviour and Redeemer was a holy Prophet and that he had the spirit of God, with the Jews he received circumcision, and, to be short, being of no religion, he entertained the professors of every religion. But especially, his wicked law tolerated all carnal vices

---

1 Deceived.

2 Provide justification or support for.

3 Epilepsy.

4 *OED* gives two senses: "rob" and "split," both of which might make sense in this context.

5 The Sabellicans, Macedonians, and Nicolaites were all heretical sects within the early Christian church.

without controlment. Mahomet being by these means strong and puissant,[1] he made his law named the Alcoran,[2] and, for that he distrusted the goodness thereof, he generally forbade all men, upon the pain of death, not so much as to dispute of his law.

In the beginning of these matters, he was strengthened with the multitude and such as were seduced with his false persuasions. Also there joined with him all the vicious and carnal men which in those days abounded through the world, by whose aid he assaulted the confines of Arabia and subjected a great part thereof. His beginning was about the year of the Lord 620, in the time of the Emperor Heraclius,[3] who so soon as he had news of Mahomet's proceedings (as Platinus witnesseth) he prepared a remedy and performed the same in part, entertaining for this service with large promises the Scenites, a warlike people of Arabia, so that this new sect was in a manner stifled for a time. Notwithstanding, the Emperor greatly erred that he followed not his purpose until he had clean plucked up this wicked root which brought forth such dangerous and damnable seed, for in not continuing his enterprise he did much hurt in the beginning of the same, for because he kept not promise with the Scenites and paid them their accustomed wages, they in despite thereof joined with Mahomet, and, seeing that he was in great reputation and holden for the prophet of God, they chose him for their captain. Afterwards he and his people assailed the Empire of the Romans, and, entering into Syria, they conquered the noble city of Damascus, with all Egypt, Judea, and the adjoining countries. Mahomet then persuaded the Saracens, a people of Arabia, that the land of promise belonged unto them as the legitimate successors of Abraham, and, having thus fortunate success in his enterprises, he made war upon the Persians, by whom he was at the first vanquished, but in the end he had the upper hand.

To conclude, after that Mahomet had compassed great and horrible matters, he was poisoned in the 40th year of his age, and, as Sabellicus sayeth, in the year of our Lord 6[3]2. And for that Mahomet would often say that after his death he should ascend up into heaven, his disciples kept him above the ground until his body stunk as bad as his soul, which was then closed in iron and by his said disciples was carried into the city of Mecca in Persia,

---

1 Powerful.
2 Qur'an.
3 Holy Roman Emperor 610–41 CE.

where he is worshipped of all the people of the East, yea of the greater part of the world.

2. From Anonynous, *Sir Bevis of Hampton* (1585)

[From the eleventh-century *Song of Roland* to Edmund Spenser's *The Faerie Queene* (1590), a major narrative framework of medieval and early modern European romance is Christendom's war against the encroaching Arab and Turkish forces of Islam. Against the Saracens, Paynims, and Turkish "infidels," Christendom pitted its own military heroes, chivalric figures such as Roland and Saint George, whose crusading and amorous exploits constitute the subject of romance epic's song. Romance typically narrates the conflict between Islamic and Christian knights, ladies, and cultures in the simplistic, binary terms of good and evil, true and false. Yet complications do emerge. "Infidel" knights can be as heroic as their Christian opposites, and men and women do fall in love across romance's barbed and entrenched cultural and religious divides. The following excerpts are taken from *Sir Bevis of Hampton*, an anonymous popular romance frequently reprinted throughout the sixteenth century. The poem begins with treachery in England that culminates in Bevis's forced journey to Islamic territory, recounts Bevis's exploits there and his Islamic beloved's conversion to Christianity, and concludes with Bevis's son becoming the earl of Cornwall.]

a) How Bevis was sold unto the Paynims[1] and carried over the sea into Armeny,[2] and was presented unto King Ermine

> They found ships both more and less of Paynims and of
>   heathenness,
> They sold the child with much thought, and to the Paynims
>   Bevis they raught.[3]
> Bevis' heart waxed cold, for he was to Paynims sold,
> But yet him list[4] not to rage, over they made good voyage.

---

1 Pagans, non-Christians; used in medieval and early modern texts interchangeably with Saracens to refer to Muslims.
2 Armenia.
3 Literally: reached, grasped (*OED*).
4 Wished, cared.

Their sail they draw, the wind was good, they sailed forth as
     they were wood,[1]
Till they came to the river into the land of Armeny.
The King Ermine of that land, his wife was I understand.[2]
He had a daughter fair and bright, Josian that fair maid hight.[3]
Her visage was white as lily flower, therein ran the red colour,
With bright brows and eyes sheene,[4] with hair as gold were on
     the green,
With comely nose and lips sweet, with lovely mouth and fair
     feet,
With teeth white and even set, her hands were sweet as violet,
With gentle body withouten lack, well shapen both belly and
     back,
With small hands and fingers long, nothing of her was shapen
     wrong.
Wherefore should I her not deceive,[5] there was never one fairer
     on live.
The merchants are to the court gone, and presented the king
     with Bevis anon;
Therefore the king was fain[6] and blithe,[7] and thanked the mer-
     chants an hundred sith.[8]
"By Mahound,"[9] said the king, "I were gay, would the child
     forsake his lay,[10]
For by Mahound that sitteth on high, yet saw I never child with
     eye
That bare so much fairness, neither in length nor in broadness."
"Child," he said, "thy name tell me, where thou wert born and
     in what country."
"Sir," he said, "Bevis is my name, where I was born think I no
     shame.
In England my mother bore me, at Southampton-upon-the-Sea,
My father thereof was earl a while, my mother let slay him by a
     guile,

---

1 Mad.
2 A line seems to be missing here.
3 Was called.
4 Shining.
5 Misrepresent.
6 Glad.
7 Gentle.
8 Times.
9 Muhammad.
10 Faith, creed.

And hath me sold to the Paynims, a wickeder woman may none
  be, iwis.[1]
And I may live, certainly, I shall avenge my father, Sir Guy."
The King of Armeny said, "Full well of Guy of Hampton I have
  heard tell,
Many a Paynim and Saracen he hath slain with much pain."
"Bevis," he said, "I have no heir but a daughter that is fair.
And thou wilt thy Lord forsake and to Apollin[2] our God thee
  betake,
I shall give her to be thy wife, and all my land after my life."
"Sir," he said, "that will I nought, for all things that ever was
  wrought,
Neither for gift that may be, nor for thy daughter that is so free.
I did myself great dishonour if I should forsake my creator."

b) Having defeated King Bradmond and his knights, Bevis quarrels with Josian, who promises to convert to Christianity to gain
his love

When they had well eaten and on a bed together sit,
Josian that was so true thought she would her love renew.
She said, "Bevis, I vow to thee, above all things I so love thee.
And if thou love me not again, I shall be dead through woe and
  pain."
"Then," said Bevis, "be thou still, methinks thou speakest
  without skill.
Thou mayst have, all unliche,[3] the King Bradmond that is so
  rich.
In all the world is no man, neither king, duke, or sultan,
But they would have thee to their queen, and if they had thee
  once seen.
I am a knight of strange land and have no more than I in stand."
"Mercy Bevis," said Josian, "I had rather have thee for my
  leman,[4]
Thy body in thy shirt naked, than all the good that Mahound
  maked."

---

1 Truly, certainly.
2 Medieval and early modern writers often claimed that Muslims
  worshipped (at least) three gods: Mahound (Muhammad), Apollin
  (Apollo), and Termagant (Chew 389).
3 Literally: unlike.
4 Mate, lover.

"Bevis," she said, "tell me thy thought." Bevis sat still and said
    nought.
She fell down and wept sore, saying, "Thou said'st here before,
There is no king that me hath seen but that he would have me
    to queen.
And thou thinkst on me great spite, wend[1] thou out of my
    chamber right.
More comely it were thee like, for to hedge and make a dike,
Than now for to be dubbed a knight and to dwell among maid-
    ens bright.
Go, churl,[2] and evil mayst thou fare, Mahound give thee sorrow
    and care."
"Demoiselle," he said, "I am no churl, my father was both
    knight and earl.
To my country I will me hie,[3] never after thou shalt me see.
Thou gavest me horse, take him here. I keep not to be in
    danger."
Bevis went forth, he would not blin,[4] till he came into his inn,
Sore grieved as he were blamed, for Josian had him so ashamed.
The two knights that Bevis loved asked him who had him
    grieved.
Bevis said neither good nor ill, but sat him down and held him
    still.
When Bevis went Josian from, then did begin all the woe.
Then she called the chamberlain Boniface, and his help in that
    case.
To Bevis a message she him send, and said she would all things
    amend,
All that she did say truly, and pray him for to come to me.
Boniface his way is gone; to Bevis' chamber is he come,
And said that Josian had him send and that she would all amend,
And all that she had said, loud and still, so that you would come
    her till.
Bevis said, "Why should I do so? She bade me wend her cham-
    ber from."
A robe gave Bevis to the messenger, with other weeds[5] fair and
    clear,

---

1 Go.
2 Peasant, villain.
3 Go.
4 Stop.
5 Clothes.

Well furred, of great valour.[1] "Have this," he said, "for thy
    labour,
And greet well thy lady from me, and say I will her never see."
Boniface thanked him then, and to Josian went again.
He said, "My Lady, make good cheer, for Bevis will no more
    come here.
Certes, Madam, ye did unright, for to mis-say a noble knight.
For it was never a churl's deed to give a messenger such a
    weed."
"If Bevis will not come to me, I will not blin while[2] I him see.
Befall me therefore well or woe, unto his chamber will I go."
Josian would no longer blin, till she came to Bevis' inn;
When Bevis heard her without, as he should sleep he began to
    route.[3]
"Bevis," she said, "awhile awake, I am come peace to make."
"Fair demoiselle," then said he, "let me alone and go from me.
I am weary of fighting full sore, so will I for love no more."
"Mercy," she said, "my leman sweet." She fell down and began
    to weep.
"Forgive me that I have mis-said, I will that ye be well apaid.
My false gods I will forsake, and Christendom for thee to take."
"On that covenant," said Bevis then, "I will thee love, fair
    Josian."

c) How Bevis went on message to King Bradmond, and how he
fought in the city of Damascus against the Saracens that made
sacrifice to idols, and how he tore them down and cast them into
the dirt and afterward was taken and put in prison

When Bevis came the city within, great mirth and noise he saw
    begin.
The Saracens then should sacrifice to their maumets[4] in this
    wise.
And Bevis came near for to see, saying "What devil of hell do
    ye?
Why make you Mahound this present, and despise God
    Omnipotent?
I shall wit,[5] before I go, what Mahound can say or do."

---

1 Value.
2 Until.
3 Snore.
4 Idols.
5 Learn, know.

Bevis leapt unto Mahound, and took him right by the crown,
And cast him amidst the mire, and bade them take up their sire.
The Saracens that by Bevis stood, for ire and teen[1] they were
     near wood.
They swore all he should abye,[2] for he despised their maumetry.
There was no more for them to say, but all at once on him they
     lay.
Bevis saw that, his sword he drew, and all that would abide he
     slew.

d) Josian and the giant Ascapart, their page, are christened.

Bevis went into the land, and soon a friend there he found,
The bishop of the town Percas; to Sir Bevis sib[3] he was.
Bevis greet well the bishop bold, and what he was he him told.
The bishop then was well apaid, "My dear cousin, welcome," he
     said.
"To see you here I am full fain, my mind gave me you were
     slain."
"Whence," he said, "is thy Lady sheene?" Sir Bevis said, "In
     heathenness a queen.
For her I have suffered much pain, and she would become a
     Christian fain."
He said, "What is that bad visage?" "Sir," said Bevis, "He is my
     page.
He must be christened also, though he be both black and blue."
The bishop christened Josian, that was as white as any swan;
For Ascapart was made a fount, and when he should therein be
     put,
He leapt over the bench and said, "Churl, wilt thou me drench?
The devil of hell thy bane[4] be, I am too much to be christened
     of thee!"
The folk had good game and lough,[5] but the bishop was wroth[6]
     enough.

---

1 Hurt, pain.
2 Pay (for his attack on their idols).
3 Relative.
4 Harm, destruction.
5 Laughed.
6 Angry.

3. From Giles Fletcher, *The Policy of the Turkish Empire* (1597)

[Giles Fletcher (1548–1611) was an academic, parliamentarian, diplomat, translator, poet, and author of several ethnographical and historical works, such as *Of the Russe Common Wealth* (1591). In the address to the reader prefacing *The Policy of the Turkish Empire*, Fletcher remarks that "Many men do wonder at the great power and puissance of the Turks, and they think it strange how this nation, being a people most rude and barbarous, and their beginnings base and ignominious, could attain within the compass of so few years to excessive height of their present greatness" (sig. A3r). Fletcher's work is a response to that wonder. In the following excerpts, Fletcher provides a history of the Turks' religion, Islam, and a summary of its religious doctrines. Although he systematically denigrates Muhammad and Islam and makes considerable effort to distinguish Christianity as the true religion from its supposedly parodic counterpart Islam, Fletcher cannot help but register the success and virtues of Islam, which he attempts to use as a mirror with which to display Christianity's corruption. Like most early modern English works on Turkish history, Fletcher's work is based on earlier continental histories.]

a) Of the first beginning of the Turkish religion and of the establishment thereof amongst the Saracens by their prophet Mahomet

That the religion of the Turks was first forged and invented by their false prophet Mahomet, and that the Saracens and Arabians, his own people and countrymen, were the first to whom he published it, and that they, being seduced by his devilish doctrine and illusions, did first entertain the same and make profession of it, there is no man either of learning or judgement in matters of history that will in any sort make any question of it. Notwithstanding, touching the matter and time, how and when it began, and upon what occasion, and how the Turks, being a distinct nation from the Saracens, came to embrace and profess it, is not perhaps a thing so commonly known unto the world but that the discovery thereof may of some be accepted, and therefore it shall not be amiss briefly to lay it open.

In the year of our redemption 591 (Mauritius[1] then Emperor of the Romans, reigning in Constantinople) was Mahomet born in Arabia in a village called Itrarip. His parents were of diverse nations and different in religion. His father Abdallas was an Arabian, his mother Cadige a Jew both by birth and profession. His parentage, according to most histories, was so mean and base that both his birth and infancy remained obscure and of no reckoning till that his riper years, betraying in him a most subtle and crafty nature and disposition, did argue some likelihood that the sharpness and dexterity of his wit would in time abolish the obscurity and baseness of his birth. And soon did he make show and proof thereof, for being trained up a lad in the service of a most rich and wealthy merchant, by his great industry and diligence he so insinuated and wrought himself into the good favour and liking both of his master and mistress that when his master died and had left all his wealth and riches unto his wife, she made choice of her servant Mahomet for her husband, making him lord and master both of her person and of her substance. The man, being thus raised from base and low degree to great wealth and possessions and having a working and aspiring head, did from thenceforth plot and imagine how he might raise himself in honour and reputation, presuming that the greatness of his wealth would be a fit mean so to work his higher fortunes. Neither was he deceived in the expectation of his hope. For consorting himself with one Sergius, a fugitive monk, a notable heretic of the Arian[2] sect whom he had made bounden unto him by his great liberality, there grew so strict a league of amity and secret familiarity between them that they had many times private conference how and by what means Mahomet might make himself way to rise in honour and estimation. After much consulting and debating of the matter, the best course which they conceived to effect their purpose was to coin a new kind of doctrine and religion, under colour whereof (the times being then troublesome, the people full of simplicity and ignorance, religion also waxing cold and neglected) they thought it an easy matter to draw many followers unto them and by that means to grow great in the eye and opinion of the world. Hereupon these two hellhounds, one of them being an arch enemy to Christ and the truth of his religion, and the other seeming a mere

---

1 Roman Emperor Flavius Maricius Tiberius (r. 582–602).
2 In Fletcher's own words, the Arians "deny his [Christ's] divinity and the conjunction of his divine nature with his humanity" (see 3d ["On the nature of God"], p. 229).

atheist or profane person, neither perfect Jew nor perfect Christian, patched up a particular doctrine unto themselves out of the Old and New Testament, depraving the sense of either of them. And framing their opinions according to their own corrupt and wicked affections, they brought forth a monstrous and most devilish religion savouring partly of Judaism, partly of Christianity, and partly of Arianism.

This new doctrine, after they had digested and put it down into some rude and confused form, Mahomet began privately and in secret to set it abroach, making it known first unto his wife and some others that were his followers, and made them believe that the same was commanded and delivered unto him by divine revelation and that many times he had secret conference with the Angel Gabriel purposely sent unto him, as he pretended, from God himself out of heaven. With these and many other cunning sleights and illusions he abused the simplicity of diverse [people] and drew men to have him in great admiration, insomuch that albeit he durst not at the first openly publish his new devised religion for fear of the magistrate, yet within a while his followers, having caused the same underhand to be spread abroad more and more, and the common rumours which they gave out of many miraculous acts done by him, brought the barbarous Arabians, devoid of true knowledge and religion, into such a blind conceit of his holiness and worthiness that multitudes began to adhere unto his new religion. And the common people, seduced by his impostures and juggling devices, did not only repute and esteem him for a prophet, but they attributed unto him reverence more than human, with divine honours. The magistrates of Mecca, a chief city in Arabia, having intelligence of these practices of Mahomet and perceiving that the contagion of this wicked doctrine did so mightily increase that it was like to endanger both the public safety of their estate and the purity of the Christian religion, they thought to have surprised the ringleader and to have executed him according to his demerits. But he, having some advertisements of their intent and purpose, did not only very cunningly avoid their trains[1] laid to entrap him but, gathering together a great number of his followers and disciples, he armed them against the power of the magistrate. And, after some bickerings passed between them, he withdrew his company for a time into the deserts and by-places of Arabia, where he stood upon his guard, still enlarging his forces by the continual

---

1 Strategies, plans.

preaching and publishing of his new-found doctrine, by means whereof in process of time the most part of the Arabians seemed to cleave unto him and to embrace the profession of his damnable religion. And they were the rather induced so to do for that the time itself seemed to favour him in his proceedings by reason of the sundry troubles and tumults wherewith the Roman Empire was as then pitifully distracted and sore distressed. The which, having at the first animated and encouraged him to proceed in his seditious practices, did also minister unto him fit opportunity and occasion afterwards both to make himself great in credit and reputation, and to lay a most sure foundation for the establishment of his new doctrine, as shall appear by the discourse following.

Not long before that Mahomet did enter into his detestable and pernicious practices in setting abroach his superstitious and devilish traditions, it happened that the Empire of Rome was usurped by one Phocas, who, being a chief favourite and in principal authority under the Emperor Mauritius yet aspiring to the imperial crown and sceptre, most traitorously murdered his lord and master together with his children, and so took upon him the name and title of Emperor. Now, as it is commonly seen that one mischief draweth another and that mischances do seldom come unaccompanied, so the hateful and odious act of this usurper was the occasion of many commotions and tumults, and of many changes and alterations in diverse parts of the Empire. For the head and chief commander having encroached upon the estate by so notorious an example of disloyalty, treason, and murder, it seemed a small matter unto the members to participate in the like vices. For thereupon began all care of religion quite and clean to be abandoned, and ambition and avarice in all estates and persons so abounded, that the prelates of the Church, contemning Christian humility, aspired to temporal[1] government and, challenging the double sword, thirsted after regal authority insomuch that the desire of superiority swallowed up all regard of piety, and the covetousness of the clergy made them neglect their particular duty. Then grew the usurpation of supremacy in the Church of Rome, after which ignorance and superstition increased in the West, no less than Mahometism prevailed in the East. In like manner the laity, forgetting their allegiance and following particular profit, inclined to mutinies, sedition, and rebellion insomuch that sundry nations both in Europe and Asia began to decline and revolt from the imperial government. By means whereof the

---

1 Secular, worldly.

Roman Empire was mightily encumbered with many great and grievous wars and sore pressed on all sides with the armies both of rebels and foreign enemies. Thus that empire which Phocas had purchased with blood and treason, he held all his lifetime with continual trouble and vexation, and at his death he left the same to his successors full of tumult and confusion.

Heraclius the Emperor, who succeeded after him, being driven to great extremities by the multitude of his enemies, found himself most encumbered by the armies of the Persians, who, having before revolted from the Roman obeisance, had raised a strong and mighty kingdom in Persia. Against the fury and violence of this so puissant an enemy, he determined to serve himself with the forces and succours of the Saracens, who, inhabiting in Arabia Petrea, had the name of a town in the same country called Saraca, seated not far from Petra, which, being the chief and metropolitan city of that part of Arabia, gave the whole province the name of Petrea. These Saracens, being grown famous partly by reason of their great and populous numbers and partly by the course and manner of their life, for that they were accustomed to live by robbery, spoil, and pillage (a usage familiar to most of the Arabians), they had the name in that age to be a most stout and warlike kind of people. In regard whereof Heraclius resolved to use their aid against the Persians, and the rather for that their nation, having been lately seduced and perverted by the damnable doctrine of Mahomet, whose power and authority was then grown great amongst them, they seemed at that time to be seditiously addicted and were suspected to be inclining to a rebellion. To the intent therefore he might avoid the danger threatened to the empire on the one side by the wars and fury of the Persians and on the other side by the seditious disposition of these misbelieving Saracens, the Emperor thought it good policy to serve his turn of the one against the other and so to make each of them the mean of the other's ruin and destruction. According to this determination he hired diverse great and huge numbers of them to serve him in these wars, supposing that the country being thus purged from so pernicious and pestilent a people, and they exposed to the sword and fury of a stout and warlike enemy, the imminent dangers would soon cease and be avoided. But that counsel which seemed to the Emperor to be most sagely and politickly devised, turned afterwards by the covetousness and folly of his officers to be the utter ruin and confusion both of the Empire and of Christian religion. For after that the Saracens had for certain years served very valiantly against the Persians and had so harried and spoiled that kingdom that it was reduced under the subjection of the Roman Empire, they coming to demand their pay of the Emperor his treasurer, answer was made them that the Emperor had scarce money sufficient to pay the Greeks and Romans and the Christians his other soldiers, much less had he any for such a company of dogs as they were. The indignity of this injury and disgrace was taken so heinously of the Saracens and did so exasperate their courages who of themselves were always prone and ready enough to rebellion that presently they revolted from the Emperor, and, shaking off the yoke and obeisance of the Roman Empire, in their return homeward they spoiled and harried all the country, towns, and villages about Damascus in Syria. Which done, and knowing that Mahomet was then grown to be of great power and estimation by reason of his wealth and the opinion of his religion, which made him highly adored, both of the Arabians and the Egyptians, they were easily drawn to elect and choose him for their head and governor. And being thereunto solicited both by secret persuasions and by large and bountiful rewards, whereby he had wrought and won them, they both gave unto him the name and honour of a prophet and proclaimed him for their duke and prince, not only the Saracens but the rest also of the Arabians and a great part of the Egyptians acknowledging him for their lord and governor.

In this manner did Mahomet erect a new religion and kingdom amongst the Saracens in the year of grace 623. And making Syria the seat of his new empire, he lived the rest of his days in the confines of Damascus. During which time, it is said that he made the Alcoran,[1] a book wherein are written all the laws, ceremonies, and traditions of his religion, with an infinite multitude of fantastical tales and feigned miracles. Howbeit sundry times before his death he altered and changed, added, and detracted many of his precepts and institutions, according as the variety and vanity of his passions and lewd conceits[2] did induce and lead him. Notwithstanding, it is thought that that form of religion which is at this day prescribed and observed out of their Alcoran was for the most part reformed and perfected by his next successors, at what time they had made themselves lords of the most part of Asia. Howsoever it was, after Mahomet had reigned about nine or, as some say, ten years, he departed this life, being forty years of age and, as is reported, died of poison. For having oftentimes

---

1 Qur'an.
2 Thoughts.

boasted before his end that the third day after his death he would rise again, and having therefore given strait[1] commandment that his body should not be buried nor interred in the earth, one of his disciples, called Albunor, being desirous to prove and make trial of the truth of his doctrine and prophecies, did secretly cause poison to be conveyed into his drink. The which Mahomet having taken, his body presently in all parts began to swell extremely, and so he gave up the ghost most miserably. For twelve days did his body lie unburied, during all which time there appeared no likelihood of any resurrection, but his carcass yielded an intolerable and most filthy stench. In the end Albunor, coming to see him, found his body torn in pieces and devoured by dogs, whereupon, gathering together the bones that remained and putting them into a coffin, he caused him to be buried. This was the end of this monster of mankind, who, having filled the world with idolatry and infidelity by his blasphemous traditions and damnable forgeries, seemed to have been born for the utter overthrow and desolation of many kingdoms, estates, and provinces, and for the ruin and confusion of many millions of souls.

b) Of the Turkish Alcoran, and of the great reverence which the Turks bear unto it

Hitherto have we delivered the invention and first beginning of the Turkish religion with the continuance and establishment thereof, both under the Saracen and Turkish Empire, whose original also and increase hath in part been touched. Now are we to consider of the substance of their religion, wherein first we will speak somewhat of their Alcoran, in which their law and traditions are contained and delivered, and then will we proceed to the grounds and principles of their religion. The whole sum and substance of the Turkish religion, laws and ceremonies, together with the manner and form of their prayers, sacrifices and alms, and whatsoever else they do hold needful and necessary to the salvation of their souls is derived and drawn out of a certain book, which in their language they call "Musaph." This book is divided into 30 parts or tomes.[2] The Arabians call the same "Curaam," which is as much to say as, "The beginning and end of the Turks' law." And it seemeth to be the very same

---

1 Strict.
2 The Qur'an is divided into 114 suras.

word which is usual amongst other nations, although with some difference; it is most commonly called by the name of "Alcoran."

Upon this book, as upon the very groundwork and chief foundation, doth the whole religion and law of the Turks seem to rely and depend. And it is a common and general tradition constantly held and affirmed by all Turks whatsoever that the Archangel Gabriel and their prophet Mahomet did by the singular grace and favour of God first publish and disperse this book throughout all parts of the world and that Mahomet together with his disciples did frame and put the same in writing in the same manner and form as it is now received amongst them. But howsoever the Turks do dream of the first writing and invention of this their Alcoran and attribute the same to their prophet Mahomet, yet it is more than probable by many conjectures even out of their own books and writings that neither the religion now professed by the Turks nor that Alcoran out of which they do now derive their superstitions and ceremonies is not the same that was first invented and written by Mahomet. Besides it is apparent, by the testimony of many, and those most approved histories, that at such time as the Saracen empire, being risen to some strength and perfection, was first established under their Caliph in Babylon and that the Turks came to be united and incorporated into the society and religion of the Saracens, there was a new draft made by the authority of their chief governors and with the advice and consent of their priests, who secretly amongst themselves caused another book to be devised and written of such traditions, rites, and ceremonies as were thought requisite and needful to be used and observed amongst them. And because that form of religion which had been at first conceived and invented by Mahomet and his disciples was found in many things greatly repugnant in itself and full of contrarieties and absurdities, it was in most points either altered or abrogated and new traditions and ordinances inserted in their places. The which, for that it was done in secret and without the notice and knowledge of the common sort, from whom it was purposely concealed, all those that are of the Mahometan sect and religion have ever been and are yet still persuaded (their priests and governors still nourishing and feeding that conceit in them) that it was the same which was first supposed to be written by their great prophet Mahomet and that there was no change nor innovation made of any of their ancient traditions, laws, or ceremonies but that all things did continue and remain entire and unaltered in their Alcoran according to the first prescript and invention of them. Which opinion, although it be current amongst them, yet it is thought, that not only the Saracens (as it hath been already touched) in the time of their empire did in many points alter their religion and frame a new Alcoran, but that the Turks also (even since their monarchy began to rise to that flourishing estate wherein we now see it under the house of Ottoman) have in some sort done the like. And it is not to be doubted but that their religion as well as their empire is drawn and reduced into another manner and form both of order and perfection than it was at the first beginning. For it was written of Mahomet the Second[1] (he that took and conquered the city and empire of Constantinople and was the first of the line and house of Ottoman that took upon him the name and title of Emperor of the Turks) that he also did in many things alter and change the laws and religion of the Turks, abrogating and abolishing many of their old and ancient traditions and instituting and ordaining new in their place.

But howsoever it be, whether that this Alcoran were written at first by Mahomet himself or by some others his successors, this is one thing most assured and certain: that the Turks generally in outward show and appearance do hold and esteem this their Musaph or Alcoran in no less honour and reverence than the ancient Jews did their books of the Old Testament written by Moses and the prophets or the Christians do the whole Bible and sacred books of Holy Scriptures, written by the spirit of God himself and by the pen of his prophets and apostles. This may we manifestly perceive by their outward gesture and usage when they come either to the handling or reading of any part of this book. For, first, there is none of them whosoever that dareth to touch or handle it unless he be first either clean washed with fresh water from the top of the head to the sole of the feet or that he do wrap and cover his hands all over in some clean and fine piece of linen before he adventure to lay hands upon it. Besides, as often as they repair to the temple to hear any part of this book publicly read unto them, the same being done with a loud and clear voice, all of them do most attentively hearken and give ear thereunto with a singular and notable show and devotion. And they do hold it a very devout and religious part a little to move and incline their bodies whilst they do intend to the reading of the same. The manner and fashion of him that readeth it is to hold the book aloft between both his hands, and he deemeth it a most sinful matter and an act of great impiety to hold the book at any time beneath

---

1 Mehmed II (r. 1444–46, 1451–81).

his waist. Whilst he is reading it unto the people, he standeth as a man ravished in spirit and besides himself, seeming to have his mind wholly bent and fixed upon those things which he readeth and pronounceth unto them. When he hath signified and made an end of his reading, he kisseth the book with great reverence, and, casting his eyes down upon the same in a most sober and devout manner, he afterwards layeth it up with great solemnity in an high place purposely provided for the keeping of the same, as being a most sacred and holy relic and of far greater account and reckoning than all the residue of their books any way appertaining to their law and religion. Thus we see that the curiosity of these misbelieving Turks is greater in their idolatry and superstition, covering their inward deformities with outward appearances of holiness and pretended shows of devotion, than the reverence used by many Christians in the right worshipping of God and the observation of true religion.

c) Of the principles and grounds of the Turks' religion and of the eight commandments prescribed in their Alcoran

Amongst infinite matters contained in the Turkish Alcoran, though there be many things delivered touching their faith and doctrine, yet is it for the most part full stuffed and replenished with vain and fantastical conceits of feigned dreams, apparitions, visions, and revelations, and it aboundeth throughout all the volumes thereof with a number of fond tales and fables which are everywhere intermingled with the delivery of their superstitions. All which do tend rather to make some colourable show and pretence of truth in their religion and to give a grace and countenance of their sect than to prescribe directly any matter of doctrine or to deliver the sum and substance of their traditions. And it seemeth that that book was purposely invented to induce and draw all men that shall read or hear the same (by the strange revelations and forgeries therein contained) unto an opinion and belief that all things therein prescribed are enjoined unto them by a kind of divine ordinance and institution and that their prophet Mahomet, the supposed author of their Alcoran, was a most holy and singular devout man and one whom God highly favoured and loved. Now touching the sum and substance of their religion and the chiefest matters of doctrine delivered in their Alcoran, they do depend upon certain grounds and principles, and they may be reduced to three special points. Of which the first is: that they observe diligently and devoutly certain laws and commandments prescribed unto them. The second, that they shun and avoid certain notable vices which they term deadly sins and which they are commanded likewise by their law to have in special hatred and detestation. And thirdly, that they do precisely conform themselves to the observation of all such rites and ceremonies as are either taught in their law or received amongst them by tradition. Of each of these we will discourse severally and in order, beginning first with their precepts or commandments prescribed in their Alcoran. For as the Jews had a particular law given unto them and published by God himself in Mount Sinai, the which, being written in two tables and containing ten commandments, is received also by all Christians as a most sacred and holy law and is held to be a certain rule of justice and piety, whereunto all their actions are to be conformed and directed, teaching them what is to be done or left undone, so have the Turks, in imitation of the same, certain laws and precepts or commandments laid down in their Alcoran, the observation whereof is so necessarily required in their lives and conversations that whosoever shall transgress or violate any of them is held by their law to be a most sinful and wicked person. And they repute it very hard and difficult for such a man to be saved. Contrawise, they do believe that who so doth observe and keep those commandments and escheweth those sins which they esteem to be mortal, he shall be sure to be saved, be he either Turk or Christian. Which argueth that their confidence and hope of salvation consisteth chiefly in the piety and merit of their virtuous life and good deeds and that they do not much differ in that point from the opinion of some Christians, who do attribute their salvation unto their merits. But of this we shall have occasion to speak hereafter in the particular discovery of their opinions. For being now to show what those precepts are which be commanded in their law, we will here set them down in such order as they are reported out of their Alcoran.

1. The commandments of the Turks' law are eight in number. The first of which in their language is thus written: "La Illa Eillala Mehemmet Resullala." That is to say: "There is but one God alone and Mahomet is his prophet."

2. Their second commandment is "Honour thy father and thy mother with all possible love, reverence, and fidelity, and attempt not anything against the good will and liking of thy parents."

3. Their third commandment is "That which thou wouldst not should be done unto thee, do not thou to any other."

4. Their fourth commandment willeth "That every man at the same time limited and appointed thereunto do repair unto their mosque or temple to public prayers."

5. Their fifth commandment is "That each man do within the compass of every year orderly consecrate and spend one month in abstinence and fasting."

6. The sixth commandment exacteth "That every man according to his estate and calling do give alms liberally out of his goods and substance."

7. The seventh commandment requireth "That each man do embrace and frame himself to marriage and that he do diligently observe all such solemnities, rites, and ceremonies as are ordained and required in the solemnizing thereof which are hereafter expressed in the exposition of this commandment."

8. The eighth commandment chargeth "That no man kill another in any case by no means whatsoever but upon violent compulsion or by order of law and public justice."

d) On the nature of God

Touching the Godhead, they acknowledge both with the Jews and Christians that there is one only God, wherein they differ from the gentiles, who had their multiplicity of Gods. And they hold that God alone is to be worshipped, and all adoration to saints, idols, images they abhor and condemn, as being an honour proper and peculiar to God alone, contrary to the traditions of some Christians. Howbeit this their knowledge of the Godhead is but in a general, confused and gross manner, and only, as it were, by conceit and imagination. For what God should be, and what is the nature and essence of the Deity, they know not. Neither do they acknowledge any distinction of persons in the Godhead, either of Trinity in Unity or of Unity in Trinity, as do the Christians, albeit they do acknowledge that there is a Holy Ghost, and they do confess that the spirit of God doth inspire good motions into the heart of man and incite us to good and holy deeds. And yet do they not acknowledge it to be a distinct person in the Godhead, but they do by a gross conceit imagine it to be only a bare power and virtue in God working by a secret kind of inspiration. Likewise touching Christ, although they do hold him for a great and holy prophet (as shall be elsewhere declared) yet with the Jews they deny him to be the Son of God and the Messiah and Saviour of the world, for they say that God hath no sons, and with the Arians they deny his divinity and the conjunction of his divine nature with his humanity. Notwithstanding, they do in a sort acknowledge the power, wisdom, and justice of God, as also his goodness, his mercy, and his providence. For they believe that he made the heavens and the earth, that he created all things, and that by his providence he ruleth and governeth all things, that he hath ordained a heaven or Paradise for the reward of those that live well and godly and a hell for the wicked and ungodly. All this they do constantly confess and believe, yet so as they seem to conceive of them by a gross, carnal, and outward consideration and by contemplating of the Godhead only in the external workmanship of his creatures. And measuring the divine bounty and goodness only by the multitude of his corporal blessings and benefits bestowed upon mankind and not by his spiritual graces, they do honour, serve, and praise him only for his providence in providing for their earthly bodies. And therefore, as they do hold it notable impiety any way to doubt of the grace and favour of God, so doth their faith altogether rest and depend upon this confidence and opinion: that God hath appointed unto every man the manner, means, and certainty of his living and sustentation forty years before his birth and, because man is made after the image and similitude of God, that therefore God hath made certain and sure provision for him. For this cause they do teach that God is to be honoured and worshipped in a decent and comely manner with praise and thanksgiving.

e) Moses, Christ, and Mahomet

Let us now examine the other part of their belief and see what the Turks do think of their prophet Mahomet, whom, as they have blasphemously joined and associated with God himself in this commandment, so do they attribute unto him no less than divine and holy worship, by reason that from him they derive their law and religion, as they think that he had it from God by special grace and revelation. Notwithstanding, though the Turks do hold that their law prescribed and written in their Alcoran is now the only true law of God, wherein his will is revealed and according to the which they are bound to serve and worship him, yet they do not deny but that God did heretofore give a law unto the Jews by Moses, after the which he commanded himself then to be served, and that all the Jews that lived according to the same shall be saved by the observation of that law. And they acknowledge also that that law continued in force until the time that Christ came into the world, whom they confess likewise to be the son of the Virgin Mary and to have been sent from God as a most holy prophet with a new law for the reformation of the world, and that from thenceforth men were bound to observe the doctrine, gospel, and commandments of Christ till such time as it pleased God afterwards to send his prophet Mahomet, by whom, they say, God last of all made known his will and pleasure how and in what sort he would be worshipped, and that all other laws should from thenceforth be abolished, and that the law taught and written by Mahomet should only be received and observed, which, as they pretend, is the same law and no other than such as God gave of alone unto Abraham, from whom Mahomet, being descended directly of the line and seed of Ishmael, he was appointed by God himself to revive and to restore the same. And therefore having it revealed unto him by special grace and favour from God, he was commanded to publish and to re-establish it in the world. And for this cause they call Mahomet in their language "Acurzaman Penegaber," that is to say, "The last prophet sent from God." Hereupon it is a common opinion and tradition amongst the Turks that Moses, Christ, and Mahomet are three of the greatest prophets and of principal account and reckoning above all others, that they were each of them sent from God and were most excellent, holy, and good men, all of them highly favoured and beloved of God. They affirm also that both Moses, Christ, and Mahomet are of equal and like account and estimate in the sight of God, not one of them having pre-eminence above another. And therefore if anyone do happen to blaspheme either Christ or his mother the Virgin Mary, he is by their law to sustain the like punishment as is inflicted upon them that blaspheme the name of Mahomet. Especially if it be a Jew, he is sure to be burned. Besides they will not admit any Jew to become Turk unless he be first professed a Christian and do eat swine's flesh, notwithstanding that it be forbidden both to Jews and Turks by either law, as well of Moses as of Mahomet. For they affirm that the law of the Christians is far better and to be preferred before that of the Jews, which argueth that they do attribute much unto Christ and to his religion. Howbeit, in regard of their own law, which they do think to be most excellent both for goodness and profit, they do utterly disallow, condemn, and hate it. And notwithstanding the equality which they acknowledge in these three prophets, yet they do hold that Mahomet is to be loved, honoured, and reverenced in the highest and chiefest place next to God himself because he is the last prophet that God will send into the world and because the law which God hath revealed by him is now only in force and so ought to continue and to be observed unto the end of the world.

f) Heaven and hell

As soon as the souls have heard their judgement pronounced by the divine sentence, they say that then the angels shall appear on all sides in a most glorious and beautiful habit, distributed and divided into several troops and companies, each of them having his place assigned unto him, the Cherubim on the one side and the Seraphim on the other, some of them playing upon instruments of music and some singing of psalms and hymns, and that many of them shall attend, singing and rejoicing, at the gates of Paradise to welcome the blessed souls of such as have observed the divine commandments. And they affirm that there shall be no difference between Turks and Christians, Jews and Moors, neither shall one be known from another, but all such as have lived well and have done good deeds in the sight of God shall be of equal beauty and blessedness. Howbeit, that amongst the wicked and reprobate there will be evident and apparent difference and that each shall be discerned from other. Moreover, they dream that God will appoint a large and spacious place in heaven for those souls that shall be admitted into Paradise where, according to their merits and deserts, everyone shall have a perpetual habitation and a goodly mansion place of a most glorious and beautiful brightness, and that they shall have many sunbeams appointed for them, upon which they may at their pleasure ride up and down about Heaven to take a view of those delights and precious things which God hath there made and created. Besides all this, they do dream of other pleasures in Paradise both of venery[1] and also for the belly. For they imagine that they shall have there certain apples and fruits of a most heavenly

1 Sex, love.

taste and that as soon as they have eaten one of those apples, God will immediately cause others to grow in stead thereof. Likewise, for the quenching of their thirst, that they shall have certain rivers in Paradise, clear as the crystal and sweet as sugar, of the which after that they shall have tasted, both their sight and their understanding shall be so quickened and enlarged that they shall be able to see from one pole to the other, and that both the meat and drink which they take shall consume within their bodies only by a fine and subtle kind of sweat distilling from them. Moreover, they do imagine that they shall have there delicate and choice wives, which they call "Uri", that is, "Women shining bright and beautiful as the sun." For you must note that the Turks do hold that none of the women living in this world shall enter into Paradise but that such as have lived well shall have a place without the gates of Paradise, where they shall ever remain in great joy and blessedness.... It is written in the Alcoran that all those who are damned by the justice of God for their sinful and wicked lives are particularly known and discerned by their names, for that they carry them written upon their foreheads, and every one of them hath a pack or satchel laid upon his shoulders containing both the greatness and number of the sins which he hath committed. Being this laden with the burden of their sins, they are led between two great mountains through a straight and narrow passage, and that from both those mountains there leadeth a bridge of thirty miles in length, which being made arch-wise, one part thereof is mounting upwards, in the middest it is smooth and plain and at the farther end thereof it hath a great downfall. This bridge, they say, was made, by God's appointment, of keen and sharp iron cut out and indented with many short pricks and points in it. They call it "Sera Cuplissi," that is, "The Bridge of Justice," upon the which all the sinful souls are to pass with the weighty burden of their sins upon their shoulders. And that on the one side of this bridge shall tumble down headlong into hell all those which have been drowned in sin and wickedness in this world, where, being consumed with extreme torments in flames of fire, they shall be revived again to the same pains and torments anew, and so shall they continue everlastingly without end. On the other side of this bridge, all those who have not been altogether given over to sin and wickedness shall fall down not into Hell but into a certain purgatory, out of which they shall be at length freed and delivered sooner or later according to the quantity and quality of their sins, and from thence they shall be taken up and received into the joys of

Paradise. Moreover, they believe that there is in the middest of Hell a certain tree growing which they call "Zoacum Agacci," that is, "The Tree of Bitterness," which, though it grow in the midst of the fiery flames of Hell, yet (such is the will of God) that it is always green and flourishing, with great abundance of apples continually growing on it, which apples, they say, are like to the heads of devils, and that of these apples the damned souls shall eat, hoping to cool themselves and to find some refreshing of their burning heat, but what with the bitterness and poisoned taste of the fruit and with infernal pains which they endure, the anguish of their tortures shall rather increase and be augmented more and more, and their torments shall be most grievous and unspeakable. The devils also shall bind them with fiery chains and so drag them up and down Hell for their greater plague and torment. Howbeit, they affirm that all those souls which in the midst and extremity of their torments do call upon the name of God and crave aid and help from his Majesty, afterwards they shall be released and received up into Paradise. And that none shall rest or remain forever in Hell without hope of redemption but only such as do utterly despair of salvation and do continue hopeless of God's favour and mercy.

g) Conclusion

[H]owsoever their religion be erroneous and abominable, and though God himself have it in hatred and detestation as being opposite to his truth and derogating from the majesty of his Deity, yet hath God suffered these reprobates to prevail against the Christians because they have not walked in the right way and truth of his religion nor with that sincerity, reverence, and due obedience as becometh the professors of Christian piety. For the cry of their sins, having pierced the heavens, hath brought down upon them a most heavy vengeance and hath drawn the sword of these miscreants[1] against them and against the places of their habitation as a just plague for all their unthankfulness, security,[2] and negligence. Whereof we have at this day too too lamentable a proof and experience by the prosperous success which that people hath had in their conquests gotten upon many great kingdoms, nations, and provinces of Christendom.

---

1 Misbelievers.
2 Complacency.

Works Cited and Further Reading

Early Modern Editions of *Selimus*

The First Part of the Tragical Reign of Selimus, Sometime Emperor of the Turks. Thomas Creede, 1594.

T.G. *The Tragedy of Selimus Emperor of the Turks.* John Crooke and Richard Serger, 1638.

Modern Editions of *Selimus*

Greg, W.W., and W. Bang, editors. *The Tragical Reign of Selimus.* Malone Society Reprints. Chiswick Press, 1909.

Grosart, Alexander, editor. *Selimus.* Vol. 14 of *Life and Complete Works in Prose and Verse of Robert Greene,* 14 vols., Hazell, Watson and Viney, 1883.

——, editor. *Selimus.* Dent, 1898.

Hopkinson, A.F., editor. *The Tragical Reign of Selimus.* Sims, 1916.

Raid, Nadia Mohamed. "A Critical Old-Spelling Edition of 'The Tragicall Raigne of Selimus.'" *Dissertation Abstracts International,* vol. 56, no. 4, Queen's University (Ontario). ProQuest, Oct. 1995, p. 1372A.

Vitkus, Daniel, editor. *Three Turk Plays from Early Modern England.* Columbia UP, 2000.

Early Modern Texts

Allott, Robert, editor. *England's Parnassus.* London, 1600.

Ascham, Roger. *The Schoolmaster.* London, 1570.

Ashton, Peter. *A Short Treatise Upon the Turk's Chronicles.* London, 1546.

Bacon, Francis. *The Essays or Counsels, Civil and Moral, of Francis Lord Verulam, Viscount St. Alban.* London, 1625.

Blundeville, Thomas. *His Exercises, Containing Eight Treatises.* London, 1597.

The Compost of Phtolomeus Prince of Astronomye. London, n.d.

Fletcher, Giles. *The Policy of the Turkish Empire.* London, 1597.

Garnier, Robert. *Cornelia.* Translated by Thomas Kyd, London, 1594.

Gentillet, Innocent. *A Discourse Upon the Means of Well Governing and Maintaining in Good Peace a Kingdom or Other Principality ... Against Nicholas Machiavel the Florentine.* Translated by Simon Patrick, London, 1602.

Greene, Robert. *The Comical History of Alphonsus King of Aragon.* London, 1599.

——. *Greene's Groatsworth of Wit, Bought with a Million of Repentance.* London, 1592.

——. *The History of Orlando Furioso, One of the Twelve Peers of France.* London, n.d.

——. *The Honourable History of Friar Bacon and Friar Bungay.* London, 1594.

——. *Menaphon: Camilla's Alarum to Slumbering Euphues in His Melancholy Cell at Silexedra.* London, 1589.

——. *A Notable Discovery of Cosenage Now Daily Practiced by Sundry Lewd Persons Called Cony-Catchers and Cross-Biters.* London, 1591.

——. *Perimedes the Blacksmith.* London, 1588.

——. *A Pleasant Conceited Comedy of George a Green, the Pinner of Wakefield.* London, 1599.

——. *The Scottish History of James the Fourth, Slain at Flodden.* London, 1592.

Greene, Robert, and Thomas Lodge. *A Looking Glass for London and England.* London, 1594.

Knolles, Richard. *The General History of the Turks from the First Beginning of that Nation to the Rising of the Ottoman Family.* London, 1603.

La Primaudaye, Peter de. *The French Academy.* London, 1586.

Mela, Pomponius. *The Cosmographer.* Translated by Arthur Golding, London, 1585.

Newton, Thomas. *Notable History of the Saracens.* London, 1575.

Ortelius, Abraham. *The Theatre of the Whole World.* London, 1606.

Pliny. *The History of the World, Commonly called The Natural History, of C. Plinius Secundus.* Translated by Philemon Holland, 2 vols., London, 1603.

Plutarch. *The Lives of the Noble Grecians and Romans.* Translated by Thomas North, London, 1579.

Record, Robert. *The Castle of Knowledge.* London, 1556.

Sir Bevis of Hampton. London, n.d.

Whetstone, George. *The English Mirror.* London, 1586.

[W.S.] *Locrine.* London, 1595.

Modern Editions of Classical, Medieval, and Early Modern Texts

Apollodorus. *The Library of Greek Mythology*. Translated by Robin Hard, Oxford UP, 1997.

Beard, Thomas. *Theatre of God's Judgements*. *The Jew of Malta*, by Christopher Marlowe, edited by Mathew R. Martin, Broadview Press, 2012, pp. 276–78.

The Bible: Authorized King James Version with Apocrypha. Introduction by Robert Carroll and Stephen Prickett, Oxford UP, 1997.

Boccaccio, Giovanni. *Genealogia Deorum Gentilium*. Edited and translated by Vittorio Zaccaria, vols. 7–8 of *Tutte Le Opere di Giovanni Boccaccio*, edited by Vittore Branca, 10 vols., Arnoldo Mondadori, 1998.

Cicero, Marcus Tullius. *De Haruspicum Responsis*. *Cicero: Orations*. Translated by N.H. Watts, Harvard UP, 1923.

———. *De senectute, de amicitia, de divinatione*. Translated by William Armistead Falconer, Harvard UP, 1923.

———. *The Nature of the Gods*. Translated by Horace C.P. McGregor, Penguin, 1972.

———. *Tusculan Disputations*. Translated by John Edward King, Harvard UP, 1927.

Diogène Laërce. *Vie, doctrines et sentences des philosophes illustres*. Translated by Robert Genaille, 2 vols., GF Flammarion, 1965.

Ford, John. *'Tis Pity She's a Whore*. Edited by N.W. Bawcutt, U of Nebraska P, 1966.

Hesiod. *Theogony*. *Hesiod and Theognis: Theogony / Works and Days and Elegies*, translated by Dorothea Wender, Penguin, 1973.

Homer. *The Iliad*. Translated by A.T. Murray, Harvard UP, 1978.

Kyd, Thomas. *The Spanish Tragedy*. Edited by J.R. Mulryne, rev. ed. A & C Black, 2009.

Lanquet, Hugh. *Vindiciae contra Tyrannos: A Defence of Liberty against Tyrants*. *Edward the Second*, by Christopher Marlowe, edited Mathew R. Martin, Broadview Press, 2010, pp. 231–37.

Lucretius. *On the Nature of the Universe*. Translated by R.E. Latham, Penguin, 1951.

Machiavelli, Niccolò. *The Prince and The Discourses*. Random House, 1940.

Marlowe, Christopher. *Dido, Queen of Carthage. The Complete Plays*, edited by J.B. Steane, Penguin, 1969.

———. *Doctor Faustus: The B Text.* Edited by Mathew R. Martin, Broadview Press, 2013.

———. *Edward the Second.* Edited by Mathew R. Martin, Broadview Press, 2010.

———. *The Jew of Malta.* Edited by Mathew R. Martin, Broadview Press, 2012.

———. *Massacre at Paris.* Edited by Mathew R. Martin, Manchester UP, 2021.

———. *Tamburlaine the Great Part One and Part Two.* Edited by Mathew R. Martin, Broadview Press, 2014.

Martin, Mathew R., editor. *The Famous Victories of Henry V*, Queen's Men Editions, 2016, https://qme.uvic.ca/edition/FV/index.html.

More, Thomas. *Utopia.* Translated by Paul Turner, Penguin, 2003.

Ovid, Publius Naso. *Metamorphoses.* 1567. Translated by Arthur Golding, edited by John Frederick Nims, Paul Dry Books, 2000.

Pausanius. *Description of Greece.* Translated by W.H.S. Jones and H.A. Ormerod, 3 vols., Harvard UP, 1955.

Peele, George. *David and Bathsheba.* Edited by Mathew R. Martin, Manchester UP, 2018.

Plato. *The Republic.* Translated by Desmond Lee, 2nd ed., Penguin, 1985.

Seneca, Lucius Annaeus. *The Sixth Tragedy of the Most Grave and Prudent Author Lucius Annaeus Seneca, Entitled Troas.* Translated by Jasper Heywood. 1559. *Seneca's Tragedies*, edited by Eric C. Baade, Macmillan, 1969, pp. 43–94.

Shakespeare, William. *The Norton Shakespeare.* Edited by Stephen Greenblatt et al., 2nd ed., W.W. Norton, 2008.

Siculus, Diodorus. *The Library of History.* Translated by C.H. Oldfather, 10 vols., Harvard UP, 1933.

Spenser, Edmund. *The Faerie Queene.* Edited by Thomas P. Roche, Penguin, 1978.

Suetonius. *Lives of the Caesars.* Translated by J.C. Rolfe, vol. 1, Harvard UP, 1914.

Thomas, Vivian, and William Tydeman, editors. *Christopher Marlowe: The Plays and Their Sources.* Routledge, 1994.

Tourneur, Cyril. *The Atheist's Tragedy.* Edited by Brian Morris and Roma Gill, A & C Black, 1976.

Vickers, Brian, editor. *Francis Bacon: The Major Works*. Oxford UP, 1996.

Virgil. *The Aeneid*. Translated by Jasper Griffin, Oxford UP, 1986.

——. *Aeneid*. Edited by T.E. Page, Macmillan, 1962.

Whitney, Geffrey. *A Choice of Emblemes (1586)*. Edited by Peter M. Daly and Anthony Raspa, vol. 1 of *The English Emblem Tradition*, U of Toronto P, 1988, pp. 79–337.

Wyatt, Thomas. *The Complete Poems*. Edited by R.A. Rebholz, Penguin, 1978.

Secondary Literature

Allen, D.C. *Doubt's Boundless Sea: Skepticism and Faith in the Renaissance*. Johns Hopkins UP, 1964.

Barbour, Richmond. *Before Orientalism: London's Theatre of the East, 1576–1626*. Cambridge UP, 2003.

Bartels, Emily C. *Spectacles of Strangeness: Imperialism, Alienation, and Marlowe*. U of Pennsylvania P, 1993.

Berek, Peter. "'Tamburlaine's Weak Sons: Imitation as Interpretation before 1593." *Renaissance Drama*, vol. 13, 1982, pp. 55–82.

Berman, David. *A History of Atheism in Britain from Hobbes to Russell*. Routledge, 1988.

Braddick, Michael J. *State Formation in Early Modern England c. 1550–1700*. Cambridge UP, 2000.

Buckley, George. *Atheism in the English Renaissance*. Chicago UP, 1932.

Buckley, Michael. *At the Origins of Modern Atheism*. Yale UP, 1987.

Burton, Jonathan. *Traffic and Turning: Islam and English Drama, 1579–1624*. U of Delaware P, 2005.

Bushnell, Rebecca W. *Tragedies of Tyrants: Political Thought and Theater in the English Renaissance*. Cornell UP, 1990.

Chew, Samuel C. *The Crescent and the Rose: Islam and England during the Renaissance*. 1937. Octagon Books, 1965.

Clot, André. *Suleiman the Magnificent*. Translated by Matthew J. Reisz, Saqi Books, 2005.

Cunliffe, John William. *The Influence of Seneca on Elizabethan Tragedy*. Macmillan, 1893.

Curatola, Giovanni. *Turkish Art and Architecture: From the Seljuks to the Ottomans*. Translated by Jo-ann Titmarsh, Abbeville Press, 2010.

Davidson, Nicholas. "Christopher Marlowe and Atheism." *Christopher Marlowe and English Renaissance Culture.* Edited by Darryl Grantly and Peter Roberts, Scolar, 1996, pp. 129–47.

Dessen, Alan C., and Leslie Thomson. *A Dictionary of Stage Directions in English Drama, 1580–1642.* Cambridge UP, 1999.

Dimmock, Matthew. *New Turkes: Dramatizing Islam and the Ottomans in Early Modern England.* Ashgate, 2005.

Fallon, Samuel. "Robert Greene's Ghosts." *Modern Language Quarterly: A Journal of Literary History,* vol. 77, no. 2, June 2016, pp. 193–217.

Fennell, Charles August Maude, editor. *The Stanford Dictionary of Anglicised Words and Phrases.* Cambridge UP, 1892.

Finkel, Caroline. *Osman's Dream: The Story of the Ottoman Empire, 1300–1923.* Basic Books, 2006.

Freebury-Jones, Darren. "Determining Robert Greene's Dramatic Canon." *Style,* vol. 54, no. 4, 2020, pp. 377–98.

Freud, Sigmund. *Totem and Taboo.* Translated by A.A. Brill, Vintage, 1918.

Gilbert, Hugo. *Robert Greene's Selimus: Eine Litterarhistorische Untersuchung.* Druck von H. Fiencke, 1899.

Goffman, Daniel. *The Ottoman Empire and Early Modern Europe.* Cambridge UP, 2002.

Greenblatt, Stephen. *Shakespearean Negotiations: The Circulation of Social Energy in Renaissance England.* U of California P, 1988.

——. *The Swerve: How the World Became Modern.* W.W. Norton, 2011.

Grimal, Pierre. *The Dictionary of Classical Mythology.* Translated by A.R. Maxwell-Hyslop, Blackwell, 1986.

Gurr, Andrew. *Playgoing in Shakespeare's London.* 2nd ed., Cambridge UP, 1996.

——. *The Shakespearean Stage 1574–1642.* 3rd ed., Cambridge UP, 2001.

——. *Shakespeare's Opposites: The Admiral's Company 1594–1625.* Cambridge UP, 2009.

Gurr, Andrew, and Mariko Ichikawa. *Staging in Shakespeare's Theatre.* Oxford UP, 2000.

Harris, John Wesley. *Medieval Theatre in Context: An Introduction.* Routledge, 1992.

Hourani, Albert. *A History of the Arab Peoples.* Harvard UP, 1991.

Hunter, Michael. "The Problem of 'Atheism' in Early Modern England." *Transactions of the Royal Historical Society*, vol. 35, 1985, pp. 135–57.

Hutchings, Mark. "The 'Turk Phenomenon' and the Repertory of the Late Elizabethan Playhouse." *Early Modern Literary Studies*, vol. 13, no. 2, October 2007.

Ichikawa, Mariko. *The Shakespearean Stage Space*. Cambridge UP, 2013.

Imber, Colin. *The Ottoman Empire*. 2nd ed., Palgrave Macmillan, 2009.

Jacquot, Jacques. "Ralegh's 'Hellish Verses' and 'The Tragicall Raigne of Selimus.'" *Modern Language Review*, vol. 48, no. 1, 1953, pp. 1–9.

Jardine, Lisa, and Alan Stewart. *Hostage to Fortune: The Troubled Life of Francis Bacon*. Hill and Wang, 1998.

Jordan, John Clark. *Robert Greene*. Octagon Books, 1965.

Jouanna, Arlette. *The St Bartholomew's Day Massacre*. Translated by Joseph Bergin, Manchester UP, 2013.

Keenan, Siobhan. *Travelling Players in Shakespeare's England*. Palgrave Macmillan, 2002.

Kuriyama, Constance Brown. *Christopher Marlowe: A Renaissance Life*. Cornell UP, 2002.

Locke, John. *A Letter Concerning Toleration. John Locke on Politics and Education*. 1689. Introduction by Howard R. Penniman, Walter Black, 1947, pp. 17–68.

Long, A.A. *Hellenistic Philosophy: Stoics, Epicureans, Sceptics*. 2nd ed., U of California P, 1986.

Matar, Nabal. *Islam in Britain 1558–1685*. Cambridge UP, 1998.

McJannet, Linda. *The Sultan Speaks: Dialogue in English Plays and Histories about the Ottoman Turks*. Palgrave MacMillan, 2006.

McMillin, Scott. "The Queen's Men in 1594: A Study of 'Good' and 'Bad' Quartos." *English Literary Renaissance*, vol. 14, no. 1, Winter 1984, pp. 55–69.

McMillin, Scott, and Sally-Beth MacLean. *The Queen's Men and their Plays*. Cambridge UP, 1998.

Melnikoff, Kirk, and Edward Gieskes. *Writing Robert Greene: Essays on England's First Notorious Professional Writer*. Routledge, 2008.

Mikhail, Alan. *God's Shadow: Sultan Selim, His Ottoman Empire, and the Making of the Modern World*. W.W. Norton, 2020.

Murphy, Donna M. "*Locrine, Selimus,* Robert Greene, and Thomas Lodge." *Notes and Queries,* vol. 56 [254], no. 4, December 2009, pp. 559–63.

Nicholl, Charles. *The Reckoning: The Murder of Christopher Marlowe.* Picador, 1993.

Norbrook, David, et al., editors. *Lucretius and the Early Modern.* Oxford UP, 2015.

Oxford Dictionary of the Bible. By W.R.F. Browning, 2nd ed., Oxford UP, 2009.

Oxford Dictionary of Philosophy. By Simon Blackburn, Oxford UP, 1996.

Oxford English Dictionary Online. Oxford UP, 2013, http://www.oed.com.

Popkin, Richard. *The History of Scepticism from Erasmus to Spinoza.* U of California P, 1979.

Ribner, Irving. "Greene's Attack on Marlowe: Some Light on *Alphonsus* and *Selimus.*" *Studies in Philology,* vol. 52, 1955, pp. 162–71.

Riggs, David. *The World of Christopher Marlowe.* Henry Holt, 2004.

Riley-Smith, Jonathan. *The Crusades: A History.* 2nd ed., Yale UP, 2005.

Ronan, Clifford J. "*Selimus* and the Blinding of Gloucester." *Notes and Queries,* vol. 33 [231], no. 3, September 1986, pp. 360–62.

Rozett, Martha Tuck. *The Doctrine of Election and the Emergence of Elizabethan Tragedy.* Princeton UP, 1984.

Ryrie, Alec. "Atheism." *The Cambridge Guide to the Worlds of Shakespeare.* Edited by Bruce R. Smith and Katherine Rowe, Cambridge UP, 2016, pp. 726–31.

Sager, Jenny. *The Aesthetics of Spectacle in Early Modern Drama and Modern Cinema: Robert Greene Theatre of Attractions.* Palgrave Macmillan, 2013.

Saintsbury, George. *History of Elizabethan Literature,* Macmillan, 1887.

Scott, Margaret. "Machiavelli and the Machiavel." *Renaissance Drama,* vol. 15, 1984, pp. 147–74.

Shaw, Stanford. *History of the Ottoman Empire and Modern Turkey.* 2 vols., Cambridge UP, 1976–77.

Shepard, Alan. *Marlowe's Soldiers: Rhetorics of Masculinity in the Age of the Armada.* Ashgate, 2002.

Sheppard, Kenneth. "Atheism, Apostasy, and the Afterlives of Francis Spira in Early Modern England." *The Seventeenth Century*, vol. 27, no. 4, Winter 2012, pp. 410–34.

Sugden, Edward Holdsworth. *A Topographical Dictionary to the Works of Shakespeare and His Fellow Dramatists*. 1925. Georg Olms, 1969.

Thomas, Keith. *Religion and the Decline of Magic*. Penguin, 1973.

Thomson, Leslie. "Beds on the Early Modern Stage." *Early Theatre*, vol. 19, no. 2, 2016, pp. 31–57.

Tilley, Morris Palmer. *A Dictionary of the Proverbs in England in the Sixteenth and Seventeenth Centuries: A Collection of the Proverbs Found in English Literature and the Dictionaries of the Period*. U of Michigan P, 1950.

Uyar, Mesut, and Edward J. Erickson. *A Military History of the Ottomans: From Osman to Atatürk*. Praeger Security International / ABC-CLIO, 2009.

Vitkus, Daniel. *Turning Turk: English Theater and the Multicultural Mediterranean, 1570–1630*. Palgrave Macmillan, 2003.

Wallace, Charles William. *The Evolution of the English Drama up to Shakespeare, with a History of the First Blackfriars Theatre*. George Reimer, 1912.

Walsh, Brian. *Shakespeare, the Queen's Men, and the Elizabethan Performance of History*. Cambridge UP, 2009.

Walsham, Alexandra. *Charitable Hatred: Tolerance and Intolerance in England, 1500–1700*. Manchester UP, 2006.

Wickham, Glynne. *The Medieval Theatre*. 3rd ed., Cambridge UP, 1987.

Williams, Carolyn. "'This Effeminate Brat': Tamburlaine's Unmanly Son." *Medieval and Renaissance Drama in England*, vol. 9, 1997, pp. 56–80.

Wooton, David, and Michael Hunter. *Atheism from the Reformation to the Enlightenment*. Clarendon, 1992.

Further Reading

Belle, Marie-Alice. "The Many Lives of *Raleigh's Ghost*: Reframing Atheism and the Afterlife in Early Stuart Britain." *Canadian Review of Comparative Literature*, vol. 46, no. 2, June 2019, pp. 295–317.

Berek, Peter. "*Locrine* Revised, *Selimus*, and Early Responses to *Tamburlaine*." *Research Opportunities in Renaissance Drama*, vol. 23, 1980, pp. 33–54.

Copenhaver, Brian, and Charles B. Schmitt. *Renaissance Philosophy*. Oxford UP, 1992.

Dixon, Leif. "William Perkins, 'Atheisme,' and the Crises of England's Long Reformation." *Journal of British Studies*, vol. 50, no. 4, October 2011, pp. 790–812.

Ekeblad, Inga-Stina. "*King Lear* and *Selimus*." *Notes and Queries*, vol. 4, 1957, pp. 193–94.

Lepage, John. *The Revival of Antique Philosophy in the Renaissance*. Palgrave Macmillan, 2012.

Mallin, Eric. *Godless Shakespeare*. Continuum, 2007.

Matar, Nabal. *Turks, Moors, and Englishmen in the Age of Discovery*. Columbia, 1999.

Meserve, Margaret. *Empires of Islam in Renaissance Historical Thought*. Harvard UP, 2008.

Pocock, J.G.A. *The Machiavellian Moment: Florentine Political Thought and the Atlantic Republican Tradition*. Princeton UP, 1975.

Raab, Felix. *The English Face of Machiavelli*. Routledge, 1964.

Werth, Tiffany Jo. "Atheist, Adulterer, Sodomite, Thief, Murderer, Lyer, Perjurer, Witch, Conjuror or Brute Beast? Discovering the Ungodly in Shakespeare's England." *Literature Compass*, vol. 10, no. 2, February 2013, pp. 175–88.

From the Publisher

A name never says it all, but the word "Broadview" expresses a good deal of the philosophy behind our company. We are open to a broad range of academic approaches and political viewpoints. We pay attention to the broad impact book publishing and book printing has in the wider world; for some years now we have used 100% recycled paper for most titles. Our publishing program is internationally oriented and broad-ranging. Our individual titles often appeal to a broad readership too; many are of interest as much to general readers as to academics and students.

Founded in 1985, Broadview remains a fully independent company owned by its shareholders—not an imprint or subsidiary of a larger multinational.

To order our books or obtain up-to-date information, please visit broadviewpress.com.

broadview press
www.broadviewpress.com

This book is made of paper from well-managed FSC® - certified forests, recycled materials, and other controlled sources.